Exclusive Theology

Exclusive Theology

The Slave Master's Religion

Stephen Augusta Redmond

Foreword by Taharka Adé

WIPF & STOCK · Eugene, Oregon

EXCLUSIVE THEOLOGY
The Slave Master's Religion

Copyright © 2025 Stephen Augusta Redmond. All rights reserved. Except for brief quotations in critical publications or reviews, no part of this book may be reproduced in any manner without prior written permission from the publisher. Write: Permissions, Wipf and Stock Publishers, 199 W. 8th Ave., Suite 3, Eugene, OR 97401.

Wipf & Stock
An Imprint of Wipf and Stock Publishers
199 W. 8th Ave., Suite 3
Eugene, OR 97401

www.wipfandstock.com

PAPERBACK ISBN: 979-8-3852-6066-9
HARDCOVER ISBN: 979-8-3852-6067-6
EBOOK ISBN: 979-8-3852-6068-3

VERSION NUMBER 11/10/25

Scripture quotations are taken from New Revised Standard Version Bible, copyright © 1989 National Council of the Churches of Christ in the United States of America. Used by permission. All rights reserved worldwide. www.friendshippress.org

This book is dedicated to my late mother, Rev. Linnie Juanita Booker

Contents

Foreword by Taharka Adé | ix
Preface: North Georgia Methodists: The Birth of a Nation | xiii
Acknowledgments | xix
Introduction | xxiii

1. Memoirs of My Doctoral Ministry Program | 1
2. Culture Shapes Behavior | 13
3. Better a Christian Slave Than a Freed Negro | 29
4. John Wesley and the Early Methodists in Georgia | 45
5. From Plantation Missions to the Rise of the Central Jurisdiction | 67
6. The Lost Cause in North Georgia | 96
7. Obama and Multiculturalism in North Georgia | 117
8. Conclusion | 135

Appendix | 137
About the Author | 193
Bibliography | 197
Index | 205

Foreword

It has been over fifteen years since I first met Dr. Stephen Redmond, a man widely known on the campus of Alabama State University as "Minister Redmond." Over time, as our conversations deepened and our bond grew, I came to refer to him simply as "Brother Redmond." At the time, he was a recent graduate of Emory University's Candler School of Theology, having earned his master of divinity degree, and had just been installed as the director of Alabama State University's Wesley Foundation.

Our meeting in the fall of 2009 was, in many ways, a chance encounter—one that ultimately set me on a course of intellectual and personal growth. Redmond had recently moved three doors down from me in the same apartment complex, and our first conversation was eye-opening. I had questions about history, faith, and the role of religion in the lives of people of African descent, and he engaged me in a way that was both challenging and encouraging. He pushed me to think more critically, introducing me to thinkers and perspectives I had never encountered before. That night, he handed me a documentary on the life and work of John Henrik Clarke, and from that moment, my intellectual world began to expand in ways I hadn't anticipated.

Redmond also encouraged me to read *The Education of the Negro Prior to 1861* by Carter G. Woodson, a work that examined the influence of churches—particularly the Methodists—on the education, miseducation, and cultural dislocation of African Americans. Through both Clarke's analysis of African and African American history and Woodson's examination of how religious institutions shaped Black education, I began to understand the deep entanglement of faith, power, and identity in ways I had never considered before.

During his tenure as director of the Wesley Foundation, Redmond's teaching method was unlike anything I had ever encountered. He did not simply lecture from behind a podium or assign readings from the Bible or standard theological texts. Instead, he took us out into the field, guiding us through the history that lived in the very walls of churches, in the pews where generations had gathered, and in the archives of dusty church libraries where rare books and forgotten documents held the keys to understanding how African Americans have navigated faith, oppression, and resistance.

I recall the many trips we took to churches across the South; each visit was an opportunity to explore, not only the theological frameworks of these institutions but also their role in shaping the social and political realities of African American communities. These were not just academic exercises; they were immersive experiences, opportunities to stand in spaces where history had unfolded and to engage with the living traditions that continue to inform contemporary faith and activism. In these churches, we discovered the resilience of enslaved people who found solace in the Bible's more humanizing passages, even as it was simultaneously being wielded as a tool for their subjugation. Redmond guided our research into historical examples of how African American religious communities became incubators for social change, birthing movements that would challenge the very structures of American inequality.

This guidance is what Redmond has always done—he does not simply provide answers; he equips his students, mentees, and readers with the tools to ask the right questions. He does not dictate conclusions; he sparks journeys.

That same spirit of inquiry and historical reckoning permeates *Exclusive Theology*. This book is not just an academic study—it is a bold critique of how theology has been weaponized to reinforce racial and social hierarchies. Redmond takes us on a historical journey, tracing the evolution of exclusive theology from its colonial roots through the rise of Methodism, the establishment of the Methodist Episcopal Church South, and its continued influence on contemporary religious and political movements.

Redmond argues that what he terms "exclusive theology" was embedded into American Protestantism from its inception. He highlights how early British Methodists, particularly John Wesley and the missionaries who accompanied General James Oglethorpe to the Colony of Georgia, laid the groundwork for a theology that justified racial hierarchy and White supremacy. He presents a compelling case that exclusive theology shaped the very foundation of American Christianity, reinforcing systems of oppression through religious doctrine. Rather than being an aberration, racialized theology was a central component of early Methodism, particularly in the South, where it became deeply intertwined with plantation missions and the justification of slavery.

The book explores how exclusive theology persisted long after the abolition of slavery, morphing into different forms to support segregation, discrimination, and modern right-wing religious movements. Redmond examines how the United Methodist Church, particularly in North Georgia, maintained these theological frameworks even as it publicly professed inclusivity. He connects the legacy of exclusive theology to contemporary issues, showing how its influence continues to shape religious and political discourse, from opposition to civil rights movements to the rise of conservative evangelical support for figures like Donald Trump.

The most powerful aspect of this work is its connection to the present, drawing on history. Redmond does not simply analyze past theological debates—he exposes how their legacies persist today in the political landscape, in the racial divisions of religious institutions, and in the very ways people justify social exclusion under the guise of faith. He forces us to ask: How has theology been shaped by power? How has it been used to subjugate rather than liberate? And most importantly, how do we move forward?

Reading this book, I was reminded of the countless hours we spent in church libraries, poring over historical records and primary documents that revealed the unspoken and often uncomfortable truths about religious history. I was reminded of the deep conversations we had about faith, justice, and the moral responsibility of religious scholars to speak truth, even when it is unpopular. I was reminded, most of all, of the passion with which Redmond approaches his work—passion not just for history but for the people whose lives have been shaped by that history.

For those of us who had the privilege of learning from Redmond in person, this book will feel like an extension of his teachings—an opportunity to sit at his table, engage with his thoughts, and be challenged to think deeper. For those encountering his work for the first time, prepare yourself for a journey. This is not a book to be read passively; it is a text to be wrestled with, questioned, and, ultimately, acted upon.

I am honored to write this foreword, just as I was honored to be mentored by Redmond. His work is a call to action, a challenge to confront the uncomfortable truths of our history and faith. *Exclusive Theology* is more

Foreword

than a book—it is a mirror held up to the past, demanding that we see its reflection in the present. May we have the courage to face it.

Taharka Adé, PhD
Assistant Professor of Africana Studies at San Diego State University
San Diego, CA
February 1, 2025

Preface

North Georgia Methodists: The Birth of a Nation

Exclusive Theology: The Slave Master's Religion originated in 2016 and is a successor to my doctoral project, which focused on the use of short-term missions as a means of increasing the cross-cultural intelligence of youth who were members of small rural churches within the North Georgia Conference of the United Methodist Church. The original research study was conducted at Union Hill United Methodist Church in Canton, Georgia (Cherokee County), spanning three consecutive years. The youth, as well as many adult members of the congregation, participated in a cultural-intelligence research study (the research study was conducted through the use of David Livermore's Self-Assessment of Cultural Intelligence using pre- and posttests), which included weekly discussion sessions, individual journal reflections, quarterly immersion journeys, and short-term mission/outreach engagements designed to evaluate and increase the participants' cross-cultural competency.

According to the 2010 US Census Bureau report, Canton, Georgia's population was steadily increasing and becoming more diverse. Furthermore, the US Census Bureau's demographic study also showed that the Hispanic and Latino American population had grown to 22.5 percent and the African American population to 8.9 percent in Cherokee County, Georgia, over the past decade.[1] While Cherokee County still consisted largely of White middle-class people, the county was quickly becoming more ethnically and racially multicultural. However, the religious-social values and

---

1. US Census Bureau, "Race and Ethnicity."

Preface

beliefs of conservative White United Methodists inhabiting North Georgia had been primarily based on racial reasoning stemming from ideologies of White superiority and non-White inferiority persisting from the antebellum period and beyond.

On April 21, 1732, the British Crown granted a charter to the Georgia Trustees for the establishment of the Colony of Georgia. Then, in November of 1732, General James Oglethorpe, the newly appointed deputy-governor of the Royal African Company (RAC) and a member of the Georgia Trustees, set sail on the frigates *Anne* and *Simmonds* to what would become the British Colony of Georgia.[2] From 1672 until 1731, the Royal African Company (the world's largest slave transporting company) shipped 187,697 enslaved Africans to British colonies in the Americas (653 voyages), and 38,497 died en route.[3]

In December 1730, General Oglethorpe purchased stock in the Royal African Company; however, his financial relationship with the RAC ended on December 21, 1732, one month after he set sail for the Colony of Georgia. On February 1, 1733, General Oglethorpe landed at Yamacraw Bluff, and there he would establish the Savannah settlement.[4] General Oglethorpe envisioned a British colony as an asylum for the materially poor and persecuted Protestants, a debtor's prison for the unemployed British underclass.

While General Oglethorpe was initially a ship captain transporting enslaved Africans during the transatlantic slave trade and used slave labor for the cultivation of land in the Colony of Georgia,[5] he refused to transport enslaved Africans into the Savannah settlement because of the potential for slave revolts as well as fear that enslaved Africans would join Native American rebellions against the young Georgia colony or escape to the Spanish colony of Florida. The Spanish military offered enslaved people freedom if they would join the Spanish military and fight against the British.[6]

General Oglethorpe, as well as John Wesley, were beneficiaries of slave labor and relied on it throughout their tenure in the colonies of Georgia. While slavery was legally prohibited in the colony of Georgia, the Savannah settlement was never free of enslaved people of African descent, starting from the initial birth of the small frontier settlement. In the 1730s,

2. Sublette and Sublette, *American Slave Coast*, 177.
3. See the data at SlaveVoyages, "Voyages."
4. Thurmond, *James Oglethorpe*, 196.
5. Jackson, "James Oglethorpe."
6. Sublette and Sublette, *American Slave Coast*, 176–78.

PREFACE

the Savannah settlement had not yet grown into a fully functioning slave society, as was Charles Town, South Carolina, where enslaved people outnumbered Whites settlers.

In Savannah, when enslaved people were not cultivating the land or building the wharf along the Atlantic Coastline of the Savannah settlement, they were primarily kept on the periphery of the settlement, serving as boatmen (Black sailors) and merchandise and supply handlers—transporting goods from Charles Town and Beaufort via the waterways of the Savannah River to the Savannah settlement.[7] In addition to transporting merchandise and supplies to the settlement, the enslaved boatmen's labor was used to transport Savannah settlers (including John Wesley's journeys to Charles Town) to and from Charles Town and Beaufort. According to historian Michael L. Thurmond (chief executive officer of DeKalb County, Georgia), the need for slave labor was fueled by "colonists not possessing the work ethic, physical stamina, or skills needed to support themselves and their families."[8]

While Oglethorpe and Wesley depended upon slave labor in their daily functions in the Savannah settlement, their public rejection of the institution of chattel slavery on socioreligious grounds as well as from a military standpoint in the colony of Georgia would futuristically cast these Englishmen as humanitarians and anti-slavery advocates.

The establishment of the Colony of Georgia would also help protect northern British colonies from Spanish and French naval intruders, who patrolled the Caribbean Islands and British American colonies in search of new lands to add to their empires.[9] In 1735, John Wesley was appointed by the Church of England to accompany General Oglethorpe on his second journey to the Colony of Georgia. Wesley's commission was to serve as a foreign missionary to the Creek Indians. Wesley's appointment as a foreign missionary to the Creek Indians would be vital to Britain's import and foreign trade because the Creek–English relationship was centered on the exchange of enslaved Native Americans and deerskins, which were important for the foreign production of textiles and kettles. In addition to the port of Charleston, South Carolina, Savannah, Georgia, would become a leading port in exporting animal skins to England. By the 1750s, more than sixty

---

7. Pressly, *Southern Underground Railroad*, 10–16.
8. Thurmond, *James Oglethorpe*, 39.
9. Sublette and Sublette, *American Slave Coast*, 141–90.

PREFACE

thousand animal skins would be bound for English factories yearly, where the skins were cut into breeches and book covers and sewn into gloves.[10]

John Wesley's younger brother, Charles, also received an appointment to travel to the Colony of Georgia and act as Oglethorpe's personal secretary.[11] What John Wesley eventually introduced into the British colonies would be an exclusive theology grounded in Protestant White supremacy, which gave rise to the "Birth of a Nation," called Methodism, which continues today in the North Georgia Conference of the United Methodist Church and globally.

For nearly three centuries, Protestant White supremacy became a worldwide pandemic, providing the blueprint for conservative, White, North Georgia United Methodists and alt-right political movements such as the Tea Party and Birther movements.

These racially-motivated movements embodied divisive politics and provided platforms for Donald Trump's rise to power. The present-day religious beliefs and conservative, right-wing politics of conservative, White, North Georgia United Methodists were rooted in Anglican and Methodist church value systems historically constructed through Christian instructions, promoting Protestant White supremacy and non-White cultural inferiority.

A geographic overview will provide the reader with an understanding of the social and political power of the North Georgia Conference of the United Methodist Church. During the time I wrote this book, the North Georgia Conference was the largest United Methodist Conference in the United States, comprising nearly eight hundred churches, over 1,300 clergy members, and approximately 340,000 lay members, spread across eight districts that encompassed seventy counties out of the state's total of 159 counties. On July 1, 2024, after the 2024 annual conference adopted the new district structure, the North Georgia Conference was reduced from eight districts to five districts (see the geographical map of the North Georgia Conference United Methodist Churches in the appendix, and the names of the North Georgia Conference of the United Methodist Churches, which are also in the appendix).[12]

In 2024, the North Georgia Conference, a regional body of the United Methodist Church, was headquartered in Atlanta, Georgia. Throughout the

10. Saunt, "Creek Indians."
11. Smith, *John Wesley and Slavery*, 35–54.
12. Setili, "Redistricting in North Georgia."

Preface

state of Georgia, there are nine United Methodist Church–affiliated colleges and universities (Andrew College, Clark Atlanta University, Emory University, LaGrange College, Oxford College, Paine College, Reinhardt University, Wesleyan College, and Young Harris College) and two theological schools (Candler School of Theology and Gammon Theological Seminary).

In addition to the local churches and affiliated educational institutions, the North Georgia Conference of the United Methodist Church is a major stakeholder in numerous public and private corporations and government agencies in Georgia, such as Georgia Methodist Credit Union, the Coca-Cola Company, the Center for Disease Control and Prevention, and Emory University Hospital.

The 2022 Conference Apportionment Budget Report showed that the North Georgia Conference budget for 2022 was $17,099,834—a decrease of $899,688 from 2021. The decrease in apportionments was primarily due to an estimated four hundred local church closings over a ten-year period and the impact of the COVID-19 pandemic. According to the report, the 2022 budget was the lowest conference apportionment in over twenty years.[13] The 2022 Conference Apportionment Budget Report provides an overview of the geographical and economic landscape of the North Georgia Conference, as well as insight into the conference's social and political influence in Georgia.

---

13. North Georgia Conference, "North Georgia Annual Conference."

Acknowledgments

I WANT TO THANK many people for their insight, encouragement, and dedication throughout the various phases of this project. The staff at Pitts Theological Library, Candler School of Theology, Woodruff Library (Emory University, Atlanta, Georgia), Bridwell Library, Perkins School of Theology (Southern Methodist University, Dallas, Texas), Leontyne Price Library (Rust College, Holly Springs, Mississippi) and Robert W. Woodruff Library, Gammon Theological Seminary, and Clark Atlanta University (Atlanta, Georgia) were all indispensable in helping to develop this project.

I owe special appreciation to the academic scholars who served as mentors and motivated me throughout my scholarly journey to be able to research and author this project: Dr. Gemma Beckley, Dr. David Beckly, Dr. Teresa Fry Brown, Dr. Erskin Noel, Ms. Lilly McNeal, Rev. Dr. Warren G. Booker Jr., Bishop Woodie White, Dr. Robert Franklin, Dr. Rex Matthews, Dr. Robert Hunt, Dr. Harold Recinos, Dr. Taharka Adé, Dr. Jacquelyn Grant, Dr. Alfred Stovall, Dr. Elizabeth Williams, Dr. Hilda Williams, Dr. Charles Williams, Dr. Rodney Redmond, Dr. Ted Cambell, Dr. Vivian W. DeShields, and Rev. John Brooks.

In addition to these professors and scholars, I render thanks to Epworth United Methodist Church (Lexington, Mississippi), Gulfside Assembly Retreat Center (Waveland, Mississippi), Central United Methodist Church (Atlanta, Georgia), Hoosier Memorial United Methodist Church (Atlanta, Georgia), Rust College (Holly Springs, Mississippi), Clark Atlanta University (Atlanta, Georgia), Candler School of Theology, Emory University (Atlanta, Georgia), Perkins School of Theology, (Dallas, Texas), Gammon School of Theology, (Atlanta, Georgia), and the North Georgia Conference of the United Methodist Church for nurturing, usage of resources, and inspiring me throughout my spiritual journey.

Acknowledgments

This project would not have been possible without the early teachings and guidance of family and friends. Firstly, I acknowledge and give thanks to my late mother, Rev. Linnie Juanita Booker, for being my greatest inspiration and cornerstone during both the good and the troublesome times. This project would not have been possible without my mother's wisdom and continuous support—she transitioned on July 7, 2022.

As an illustration of her strength, in 1972 she was employed as the first Black female police officer for the Atlanta City Police Department and later became the first Black female police officer in her hometown of Lexington, Mississippi. In addition to her service as a police officer, she attended Candler School of Theology (Emory University) and later became a licensed local pastor serving in the Greenwood, Mississippi district. I would also give special thanks to my grandfather Rev. Warren G. Booker Sr. (deceased), grandmother Mrs. Zeporah Elizabeth Gilley-Booker (deceased), great-grandfather Elder Robert Booker (deceased), Mrs. Frances "Louise" Parks Smith Sahling (deceased), Wayne Allen Gilley, Frances Alexia Hodges, and Dorothy Booker for helping to sow the seeds that nurtured my spiritual growth and provided me with passion and maturity to fight against social injustice and human inequality. Moreover, I would like to express my gratitude to my siblings, Beverly D. Anderson, Warren A. Hallmon, and Charles G. Williams, for their lifetime of love and support. My mother and grandfather were both alumni of the Course of Study Program at Candler School of Theology, Emory University, and their attendance at Candler motivated me to attend seminary.

Furthermore, it was my grandmother's response to a question that I posed to her that inspired me to apply to Candler and served as the foundational inquiry for this project. I asked, "Grandma, how did we become Methodists?" And she replied, "I don't know—why don't you go find out?"

In addition to my mother, grandparents, great-grandfather, aunts, uncles, and siblings (Beverly Hallmon-Anderson, Warren A. Hallmon, and Charles G. Williams), I also thank my extended families, the Bookers, Gilleys, and Redmonds, for their continued support and love. Furthermore, I would like to thank my best friends, Akil Mensah, Eric Hodge, Alprentice "Bunchy" Rawls, and Charles Farmer (deceased), for listening to me rant about this project for over fifteen years.

Finally, I am deeply appreciative of the patience, endurance, and support of my spouse, Aliya Bisa McCullough-Redmond and our four wonderful children, Brittany, Stephen (Samari), Aaron, and Elijah, throughout

Acknowledgments

this long and tedious journey. Aliya served as my grammatical proofreader in seminary and during my doctoral studies; I would not have been able to complete this project without her love and support. Furthermore, I would like to thank my in-laws, Harry and Joyce McCullough, for babysitting while Aliya and I were traveling. For the numerous others whom I failed to mention, thank you for your love, prayers, and support.

Introduction

It is the twin evils of discrimination and segregation that the Church has failed to lament. It has, by its practices, sanctified the racial prejudice which is rampant in the world today . . . but it cannot say a convincing word to society unless and until it eliminates these cancerous evils from its own Christian Community.
—Bishop Robert N. Brook

Photo by Warren (Ghost) Hallmon, January 2021. Dr. S. Redmond Photo Collection

Introduction

THE ABOVE PHOTO IS from the Chattahoochee Hills Cemetery of Campbellton United Methodist Church (8650 Campbellton-Fairburn Road, Fairburn, GA 30213), affectionately known as "The Little White Church with the Red Door." The Atlanta–College Park, Georgia district superintendent conducted Campbellton United Methodist Church's final worship service on June 2, 2019.

From 1830 until 2019, Campbellton United Methodist Church served as a beacon of hope for the surrounding Fulton County, Georgia, communities, helping to provide a regional identity for Methodists in the North Georgia Conference of the United Methodist Church for 189 years. Campbellton United Methodist Church's cemetery is racially divided, with White laity members who include Confederate soldiers' graves atop the hill neatly encased by a concrete wall. Outside the cemented burial walls are forty-three nameless grave sites identified by small, white wooden crosses to indicate where the enslaved members lay scattered on the back side of the embankment, hidden within the tree line. The photo is an honest depiction of the regional and racial traditions and divisive reality that lie beneath the surface of earlier Methodists and present-day United Methodists in the North Georgia Conference.

In 1866, from the beginning, White North Georgia Methodists adhered to racial reasoning and outwardly practiced an "exclusive theology" that was rooted in ideologies of White supremacy, good society, and Southern heritage from which Eurocentric notions of Protestant White supremacy and racial segregation sprouted.

"Exclusive theology" is an interpretation of biblical Scripture that maintains that God desires to exalt one supreme racial group, including their cultural beliefs and values, over all of humanity. On the other hand, the "inclusive theology" interpretation of biblical Scripture argues that God loves all of humanity irrespective of their race or cultural background.

The practice of exclusive theology has been a crucial component in the identity of the North Georgia Conference of the United Methodist Church and the standard lexicon of its institutional identity, which developed over five centuries of Westernized notions of racial imperialism and religious piety. Furthermore, exclusive theology not only seeks to develop within society the norms of racial hierarchy with Anglo-Saxons as superior humans, but it also seeks to divide people based on other social factors such as gender, economic class, sexuality, age, disability, and other areas. The goal of exclusive theology is to suppress the cultural values and beliefs

Introduction

of non-Whites through ongoing means of acculturation, assimilation, and violence.

While the North Georgia Conference of the United Methodist Church continues to emphasize the importance of "social inclusivity" within its social creed, the fact remains that the North Georgia Conference has been committed to its historical legacy of socio-theological exclusion and acculturation practices, which have been passed down from one generation to the next. With each passing generation, the traditional White Protestant values and belief systems are reinforced and handed down, shaping these cultural systems by adopting the behaviors of the so-called dominant group toward all marginalized groups.

In conjunction with the opinion of Methodist founder John Wesley, historically White Georgia Methodists considered Native American tribes affiliated with the Cherokee Nation to be racially inferior and corrupted.[1] As far as enslaved Black people, they were considered the source of most of the difficulties in Georgia and throughout the Americas due to the continuous threat of slave revolts.[2]

The racial makeup and Southern heritage of the White North Georgia Methodists provided them with an embellished cultural identity, which shaped their racialized core values and beliefs, and, in so doing, gave birth to a region that embraced oppression, segregation, and physical violence against diverse/marginalized communities while simultaneously arguing for social-moral improvement, cultural refinement, and spiritual maturity. In short, White North Georgia Methodists have historically been insincere in adhering to their social principle—"We affirm all persons as equally valuable in the sight of God"—which *The Book of Discipline of The United Methodist Church* advocates.[3]

---

1. Heitzenrater, *Wesley and the People*, 67.
2. Raboteau, *Slave Religion*, 289–317.
3. *Book of Discipline*, 119.

Chapter 1

Memoirs of My Doctoral Ministry Program

WHILE WAITING FOR AN interview to be the youth pastor in the welcoming area of Union Hill United Methodist Church, I glanced around at the framed pictures lining the walls and looked in the sanctuary. The old black-and-white pictures hanging on the walls were mostly group pictures of the congregation; everyone was White. As an African American, I felt somewhat uneasy, but I continued to focus on the task at hand: the interview.

As a doctoral candidate at the Perkins School of Theology at Southern Methodist University (Dallas, Texas), I was required to complete twenty-seven hours of coursework, develop a qualitative research project, and defend my research in front of a doctoral committee. Additionally, the doctoral program required all doctoral candidates to commit to serving in a ministry setting for three consecutive years, during which they were to identify, develop, and implement a ministry that was needed within that setting.

While applying to the Perkins School of Theology Doctor of Ministry Program, I was simultaneously searching for a youth director position in the North Georgia Conference. After months of searching, I finally received a call for an interview from Union Hill United Methodist Church. Union Hill United Methodist Church is situated in a small rural community in Canton, Georgia, approximately thirty miles north of Atlanta, in the foothills of the Blue Ridge Mountains.

On the drive to Union Hill United Methodist Church for the initial interview, I was highly attentive to the geographical surroundings in Canton, Georgia. I quickly noticed the beautiful rolling hills and the diversity of small and large homes along the roadsides. The number of expensive ranch homes caught my attention because they illustrated the wealth in the area surrounding Union Hill United Methodist Church. At first glance, I assumed that the beautiful horse ranches belonged to the congregational members of the church, but after being employed as the youth minister, I learned that none of the owners of the surrounding ranches were members of the church.

In addition to noticing the physical makeup of the homes, I was also attentive to the natural beauty of the Blue Ridge Mountains and the narrowness of the roadways. The mountainous terrain and the narrowness of the roadways provided a natural boundary between Canton's suburban conservative communities and Atlanta's multicultural urban communities.

With the Global Positioning System (GPS) as my guide, I drove along the narrow hillside until I reached AJ Land Road, a narrow dirt road cutting through several horse ranches and small privately owned farms. Once on AJ Land Road, I thought that I might be lost. However, I kept driving and taking in the natural beauty of the terrain while reflecting on my upcoming interview. After driving for about 1.5 miles, I noticed two old, white wooden buildings on the right side of the road. The first building was the Union Hill Community Center, and directly behind the community center, the next wooden structure was Union Hill United Methodist Church (United Method Church) on the corner of AJ Land Road and Union Hill Road. Located near the church was a burial ground. I later learned that was where many present members of the congregation had loved ones who were laid to rest.

The physical construction of Union Hill United Methodist Church reminded me of several old wooden churches in Douglasville, Georgia, that were constructed before the Civil War. As I was exiting my vehicle, I noticed the general features of the church and its surroundings, such as the bell enclosed in the steeple, the stained-glass windows, and the make of cars in the parking lot. When I walked into the church, I was immediately greeted and directed to wait in the welcoming area until someone came to get me for the interview.

After a short waiting period, a teenager asked me to follow her to the fellowship hall for my interview to be the youth minister. The members of the Staff Parish Relations Committee (SPRC) were all White and included one youth member, also White. Throughout the interview, I noticed that the youth remained quiet and allowed the adults to ask all the questions. The interview questions seemed relevant to the youth minister's position and in accordance with The United Methodist Church's *Book of Discipline*. The initial interview lasted about an hour.

Directly following the interview, the SPRC chair informed me that he wanted me to have a second interview with him and the pastor. So, we agreed on a date and time for a second interview. The second interview took place a week later, in the back of the church, near the pastor's office. As I entered the pastor's office, the pastor had his legs crossed, leaning back in his chair, which gave him a relaxed and highly confident appearance. The pastor's posture appeared intimidating, indicating that he was the senior authority figure in the room.

Throughout the interview, the pastor did most of the talking while the SPRC quietly listened to my responses to the pastor's questions.

The pastor began the interview by asking me to provide an overview of my career and educational background. Initially, I considered his line of questioning to be normal for an interview. However, when I mentioned I attended seminary at Candler School of Theology, he began to ask me several questions about my opinion on gay persons serving as ordained clergy in the United Methodist Church.

I replied, "The United Methodist Church believes in providing a safe space for all persons. However, acting in accordance with the *Book of Discipline*, gay persons are not allowed to serve as ordained clergy." Throughout the interview, the pastor continued to use an undertone that led me to believe that he opposed homosexuality and that the Candler School of Theology's open support of the LGBTQ+ community was against the church's doctrine and in opposition to biblical Scripture.

Beyond his questions concerning homosexuality, his only other question was about teenagers engaging in drug activities. I quickly deemed the pastor's questions and the overall second interview to be somewhat unethical, immoral, and lacking the professionalism that is generally associated with the United Methodist Church. The pastor's perceived opposition to the LGBTQ+ community would be expressed explicitly to the entire congregation later that year during Sunday worship service.

I later would regard my second interview with the pastor and the SPRC chairperson as my initial encounter with exclusive theology at Union Hill United Methodist Church. A few days passed before I received a call from the SPRC chairperson, offering me the job as youth director at Union Hill United Methodist Church. I was excited to be offered the position of youth director. However, I felt that their motivation to hire me was an attempt at becoming a more racially diverse church and having one black person (a token) on staff would satisfy the quota. The practice of hiring one non-White person became customary for many White conservative congregations in North Georgia during this period, partly due to President Obama's (the first Black president) presence in the Oval Office.

The following Sunday, after being employed as the youth minister, the pastor introduced me and my family, including my wife, Aliya, and our children, Aaron, Brittany, and Elijah, to the congregation during morning worship. Although I was excited about having the job and serving in a cross-cultural congregation, I felt uncomfortable being surrounded by so many individuals whom I perceived to be rural conservative Whites. In addition, I felt that Aliya and the children were equally uneasy. After church, on our drive home to Douglasville, Aliya and Brittany stated that everyone was staring at them, which made them feel awkward.

When I glanced at the faces of the congregational members, each person looked back at me with a welcoming smile. However, I was nervous that I wouldn't be able to perform the role of youth minister due to our racial and cultural differences. In addition to being nervous, I worried about how Aliya and the children would interact with the congregation.

From the beginning, I did not interpret the congregation's or the pastor's physical interaction with us following worship as genuine, but rather as highly guarded. Both Aliya and I greeted each person who welcomed us with a smile and handshake that said, "You're not the liberal White folks we are accustomed to that reside in Metropolitan Atlanta." And those members who dared to greet us seemed dumbfounded regarding our presence at their church. However, we all tried to ignore our obvious racial differences for the time being and be cordial.

My first Sunday teaching the youth Sunday school class felt like the greeting we received from the adults during the previous Sunday at our welcoming, superficial event. The youth sat in their seats and only spoke when asked a direct question; throughout the class, I doubted whether any of them made direct eye contact with me. I did not perceive the youth's interaction as abnormal because I was new, and this was our first time interacting.

On the other hand, I was nervous and unsure about whether I would ever be able to reach them due to our cultural and racial differences. I had never worked within a rural, southern, White, conservative congregation before. While I continued to be nervous about our obvious cultural and racial differences, I was motivated to go outside my comfort zone to make a connection with the youth and the congregation. To make a connection with the youth, I felt that the first Sunday school lesson had to illustrate my core theology, which is "love God and love neighbor," as a way of showing the youth that "love" is the foundational theme of our relationship with God and with each other.

Matthew 22:37–40, the "Greatest Commandment," served as the scriptural foundation that I would carry forward throughout my three-year tenure as youth director at Union Hill United Methodist Church. Matthew 22:37–40 states, "'You shall love the Lord your God with all your heart and with all your soul and with all your mind.' This is the greatest and first commandment. And a second is like it: 'You shall love your neighbor as yourself.' On these two commandments hang all the Law and the Prophets."

Matthew 22: 37–40, serving as the youth group's core theology, opened the door for future discussions involving social justice, cultural diversity, and community outreach/missions. At that juncture in my ministerial career, I did not fully comprehend that my seminary interpretation of Matt 22:37–40, regarding "loving your neighbor," was considered by Christian conservatives to be a liberal theological understanding of Scripture, which Union Hill United Methodist Church culturally, politically, and theologically opposed.

THE WORLDVIEW FROM UNION HILL

Union Hill United Methodist Church, along with many rural White Methodist congregations throughout North Georgia, combines its conservative, racialized theology and social politics to formulate its worldview and, by doing so, promotes its theological interpretation of the ideology of White Christian Nationalism.

While Union Hill's surrounding communities are quickly becoming more racially, ethnically, and culturally diverse, the congregation has been slow to embrace these changes, and in many respects, they interpret the demographic changes as threatening and in opposition to their idea of a "good society." This phobia of others is rooted in Southern civil traditions stemming from previous eras in history: the Jim Crow era, the pre–Civil War era, and dating as far back as their Anglican church traditions. It was common for North Georgia Methodists to proudly honor their Southern civil traditions by wearing Confederate garb and to embrace Confederate relics simply as normalized universal history.

However, White Southern civil traditions are interpreted differently by local non-Whites and ethnic groups migrating into rural North Georgia communities. For many new non-White residents (African Americans, Jews, Latinos, Muslims, and South Koreans) relocating to North Georgia, these Southern Civil War traditions and their relics (Confederate battle flag, Confederate officers' statues, and Tea Party flags) were representative of the Civil War and White supremacy.

The non-Whites and ethnic groups understood them to be offensive and threatening and associated with a history of racial segregation and violence. In comparison, many White North Georgia Methodists have attempted to distance themselves publicly from being associated with traditions and symbols that represent the Confederate Army and White supremacy; in many respects, they cannot because the core values and beliefs that they ascribe to stem from their Southern civil-religious traditions, which they have subconsciously internalized and have become fundamental to their behavior. These Southern socioreligious traditions continue to be passed down from one generation to the next, understood internally as being theologically, politically, and socially correct, and need to be protected from any outside threat.

Historical scholars representing diverse ethnic groups argue that the racist traditional values and beliefs that were the basis for Southern Methodists during the Civil War and Jim Crow eras are now foundational for White North Georgia Methodists today. These racial values and beliefs are evident within rural White United Methodist churches, shaping the sociopolitical landscape in the North Georgia Conference.

Moreover, ethnically diverse groups also see the Tea Party's current flag, which carries the slogan "Don't Tread on Me," as connoting the White supremacy spirit of the Confederate battle flag. The Tea Party has a strong presence in North Georgia and within the United Methodist Church. Additionally, many Tea Partiers claimed that the Tea Party movement was reminiscent of the Boston Tea Party of 1773, whereby the British Parliament imposed harsh taxation on the American colonies for the import of tea from China, while denying colonials representation in Parliament. The Tea Baggers argued that the US Government had grown too powerful and was unjustly embarking on state and individual rights. The Tea Party's political connection to the Boston Tea Party of 1773 was merely that of nationalism, racism, and capitalism. For many non-White people, there is an outward perception that Tea Baggers are another representation of White nationalist groups such as the KKK and Proud Boys, which have morphed into the Trump party.

While many Tea Party members affiliated with the church argue that racial supremacy is not a core value or belief of their sociopolitical agenda, most non-White Georgians would strongly disagree. Diverse ethnic groups believe that much of the language used by Tea Baggers to describe minority groups is derogatory and that the legislation Tea Baggers support is discriminatory and has long-term negative impacts on minority groups. Such legislation encompasses issues of immigration, law and order, religious rights, and other related matters.

During a luncheon conversation with Union Hills' SPRC chairperson (who was an affiliate of the Tea Party), he stated that some of the sociopolitical values and beliefs supported by Tea Baggers overlap with those of the Ku Klux Klan and the Old Confederate South. Furthermore, he explained that slavery in the Americas lasted for only eighty-nine years (1776–1865) and that states' rights should supersede federal law.

In my opinion, the chairperson was aware that the first import of enslaved Africans on North American soil occurred in 1619 and that slavery was abolished in 1865, so his statement was an attempt to minimize the long-term harmful impact that slavery has had on African Americans. He offered a scheme that revised the time frame of the institution of slavery to reflect the date when America gained its independence from England in 1776 until the abolishment of slavery in 1865. The SPRC chairperson realized that the Southern states' political fights with the Northern states over slavery stemmed from Southern lawmakers and plantation owners' desire to maintain the socioeconomic system of the South that depended on free slave labor and state autonomy.

The SPRC chairperson mistakenly failed or did not care to understand how his comments could be taken as offensive and upsetting to African Americans. I believed the SPRC chairperson's comments were meant to offend me because, like him, most of the Tea Baggers whom I interviewed felt that White conservative Americans had become too socially correct and afraid to express their views publicly for fear of being labeled racist.

For the SPRC to state its position openly would be considered a breaking of the silence and a display of bravery. In addition to the SPRC chairperson, I believe that many of Union Hill's members adhered to the values and beliefs of the Tea Party and felt that their Southern White conservative values and beliefs were theologically and socially connected and key to maintaining a "good society." Union Hill's pastor routinely attempted to link these White Southern, conservative sociopolitical values and beliefs to biblical Scripture during Sunday worship services. For example, regarding same-sex relationships, the pastor would quote Lev 18:22—"You shall not lie with a male as with a woman; it is an abomination"—in his sermons to illustrate his opposition to homosexuality and the growing campaign to ordain openly gay persons in the United Methodist Church.

According to the SPRC, the pastor had conducted a five-week sermon series illustrating the sinfulness of homosexuality. His statement was not surprising because the pastor routinely preached from a sociopolitical viewpoint based on White Christian Nationalism that has historically rejected marginalized groups such as LGBTQ+, immigrants, African Americans, and Muslim Americans, who he feels function counterclockwise to the traditional cultural norms of North Georgia Methodists.

Most White ordained clergy persons throughout the North Georgia Conference also shared the pastor's anti-gay theology and social opposition concerning the LGBTQ+ community. Most of the ordained clergy stated that they would vote against the ordination of gay persons and would not preside over gay marriages in the 2016 General Conference.

During a conversation with the district superintendent of the Atlanta–College Park district of the North Georgia Conference, she stated that the elders and deacons were attempting to prevent the LGBTQ+ petition from being voted on at the conference level, so that the issue would not be presented later at the General Conference.[1] The desire to exclude gay persons from ever becoming ordained in the United Methodist Church was shared by many Black Methodists and White Methodists within the North Georgia Conference.

According to Anne Wimberly (professor emerita of Christian education) of the Interdenominational Theological Center, Black Methodists historically understood homosexuality as sinful and incompatible with Scripture. Moreover, she stated that "Black Methodists were once more inclusive of marginalized groups under the leadership of the Central Jurisdiction, but since the end of the Central Jurisdiction, they have lost their prophetic voice. And, today's Black Methodists have a desire for political power and money, so a lot of Black Methodists are being called out of the

1. Personal conversation with author, Jun. 2019.

United Methodist Church due to the church's racism and exclusive practices." Wimberly went on to say, "The United Methodist Church should die to be reborn."[2] The Central Jurisdiction was a racially segregated ecclesiastical unit within the Methodist Church, formed for all African American members of the denomination following the Methodist unification in 1939.[3]

Like so many other laity members in the United Methodist Church, she believed that many local pastors and ordained clergy, such as the pastor of Union Hill and the Atlanta–College Park district superintendent, promoted a theology of social exclusion to advance their agendas. To think that Union Hill's pastor and other clergy members who embrace an exclusive worldview comprise only a minority group that developed over the recent years in the North Georgia Annual Conference is gravely mistaken.

The spirit of Southern Christian conservatism emerged from the exclusivity of the British Empire's economic and military rise, as well as the foreign mission of the Anglican Church.[4] It could be argued that the practice of social exclusion in the Southern socioreligious tradition is historical; it was already present during the periods of American colonization, the First and Second Great Awakenings, the Civil War and Jim Crow areas, and it continues in modern times with the church disaffiliation. The present-day practice of exclusive theology provides the core values and beliefs for North Georgia Methodists and many of the ordained clergy members appointed in the North Georgia Conference.

THE DEVELOPMENT OF EXCLUSIVE THEOLOGY IN GEORGIA METHODISM

The father of Black history, world-renowned scholar Carter G. Woodson, illustrated in his book *The Education of the Negro* that George Whitfield (an associate of John Wesley and missionary to the Colony of Georgia) commissioned slavery in the Colony of Georgia with the intent of converting the enslaved to Christianity as a means of creating docile enslaved people for his personal ownership. According to Woodson, Whitfield "was regarded by the Negro race as its enemy for having favored the introduction of slavery."[5]

2. Anne Wimberly, personal conversation with author, Jun. 2019.
3. Culver, *Negro Segregation*, 79.
4. Heitzenrater, *People We Call Methodists*, 316–17.
5. Woodson, *Education of the Negro*, 29–30.

Exclusive Theology

In the fall of 1735, John and Charles Wesley accompanied General James Oglethorpe (founder of the Colony of Georgia in 1733) to Georgia; the crew traveled from Gravesend in Kent, England, to Savannah, Georgia, to continue with the mission to settle the British colony of Georgia, which was originally designated for England's poorest citizens and to establish debtor's prisons.[6] In the Colony of Georgia, John, along with his brother Charles Wesley, served as scribes to General Oglethorpe, and they were responsible for evangelizing poor White settlers, enslaved Africans, and Indigenous peoples.[7]

While Methodist historians and scholars credit John Wesley as having an abolitionist spirit concerning African enslavement, John Wesley's missionary activities in the colonies of Georgia and South Carolina illustrate that while he may have opposed the brutal nature of chattel slavery, he shared the idea that slavery was a "necessary evil" for which slave labor was needed to establish the "New World" under British authority. Moreover, Wesley shared with other English gentlemen the secular and religious pseudo-scientific notions common among Western Europeans regarding racial hierarchy. These ideas were that the intellectual and cultural traditions developed in England would be beneficial to both the African and Indigenous people who lacked enlightenment and culture.

John Wesley had words of endearment and alliance with the Moravian missionaries, for which "his heart was strangely warm" after attending a Moravian worship service on Aldersgate Street in London. Wesley's endearing words and association with Moravian missionaries further illuminate his core beliefs and values regarding racial and cultural superiority. Moravian missionaries, such as Christian Georg Andreas Oldendorp, constructed mission societies on slave plantations throughout the Caribbean and British Islands. The Moravian missionaries taught a social gospel highlighting a racial and cultural hierarchy that was reinforced by violent slave codes, which were adopted by all inhabitants—White plantation owners and enslaved Africans.[8]

The social gospel that Wesley embraced and that the Moravian missionaries had constructed throughout the Caribbean and British Islands established the foundation for the moral and ethical atmosphere that proved economically and socially beneficial for the plantocracy and was adopted

6. Sublette and Sublette, *American Slave*, 176–90.
7. Smith, *John Wesley and Slavery*, 35–54.
8. Donoghue, *Black Breeding Machines*, 23–25.

by the Anglican clerics (newly forming Methodists) in the thirteen colonies, particularly in the southern states of America where slave societies flourished.

Slave revolts in the Caribbean and British Islands continuously threatened the overall economic welfare of plantocracies in America. To manage these threats and maintain the religious morals that helped to constitute a racialized society based on obedience from both the freed Negro and the enslaved, Methodist missionaries were given access to slave plantations. With access to the plantation, Methodist missionaries were now awarded the opportunity to proselytize the enslaved concerning religious morals to create more docile enslaved people who would no longer question their earthly social status but rather look to the sky above for their heavenly salvation.

Moreover, missionaries hoped that the enslaved would accept their lowly social status as divinely ordained and seek liberation and peace in the afterlife. Meanwhile, their earthly owners would enjoy the fruits of the enslaved free labor here on earth and in heaven. As a means of helping to reinforce the unequal relationship between master and slave for profit, the missionaries would use biblical Scriptures such as Eph 6:7–8, which states, "Render service with enthusiasm, as to the Lord and not to men and women, knowing that whatever good we do, we will receive the same again from the Lord, whether we are slaves or free." For the plantocracy, Scriptures such as Eph 6:7–8 removed all blame of an unjust society from the enslaved person's master by illustrating that slavery and White supremacy were divinely sanctioned.

In general, both enslaved people and enslavers alike held this belief. This idea of White racial supremacy and non-White inferiority taught by Methodist missionaries laid the foundation for the worldview of Protestants in North Georgia in pre- and post–Civil War eras.

While the majority of North Georgia United Methodists—Whites and non-Whites alike—would argue that times have changed for the better in North Georgia Conference from the days of slavery and Jim Crow, with which I agree, due to the absence of the physical chains, the old Southern cultural values and beliefs persist beneath the surface. For example, in 2014 I attended the annual meeting of youth ministers held at Orange United Methodist Church in Canton, Georgia. The youth ministers were discussing their motivation to engage youth in international missions with cross-cultural communities. One youth minister, who had taken several youth mission teams internationally, explained that his motivation was to "get them before they get us." My understanding was that he interpreted the purpose of cross-cultural missions to be a means of continued Western colonization and White supremacy rather than empathy and love of neighbor. Many White North Georgia Methodists would claim that this youth minister's motivation to engage in cross-cultural missions was misguided and an isolated personal worldview. However, from what I have observed throughout my experience serving in the United Methodist Church, particularly in the South, his motivation was not unique among White conservatives.

While the youth minister's public expression of hatred is not normally heard during youth meetings, numerous case studies illustrate that the primary issue cross-cultural communities have when hosting short-term mission groups is their bigoted perceptions of Indigenous persons and their cultural beliefs and practices. It could be argued that the youth minister's worldview is very common throughout White conservative churches nationally due to America's history of racism, segregation, and violence against diverse people of color (POC).

Chapter 2

Culture Shapes Behavior

John Wesley's theory of human behavior is that whatever is in the mind will manifest itself in the affections and from there, determine human behavior.

—Scott J. Jones

THE NORTH GEORGIA CONFERENCE of the United Methodist Church's ongoing struggle with racism and other forms of human exclusion is a behavior learned and adopted from the cultural traditions of the Methodist Episcopal Church, South (MECS) and the Anglican Church (predecessors of the United Methodist Church), which over three centuries expanded to include Indigenous people throughout the world.

Moreover, North Georgia Methodists' manners regarding racism and other social "isms" that excluded people different from Whites stemmed from its predecessor and were taught to Indigenous peoples through Protestant missionary zeal. In most cases, the Indigenous persons who were catechized and later converted were introduced to a Protestant Christianity that demanded their piety, loyalty, and docility.[1]

In Georgia and throughout the Southeastern jurisdiction of the United Methodist Church, "Methodism" is as Southern as the magnolia tree, cotton plantations, and Negro spirituals—its old Southern traditions. Throughout America's Southern history, racism and bigotry continued to be a factor undergirding all aspects of society, and Georgia Methodists were at the forefront of constructing and maintaining systems of racial separation,

1. Gerbner, *Christian Slavery*, 1–12.

Exclusive Theology

especially within the church and government. For Georgia Methodists, the Methodist Church was a restricted institution teaching an exclusive theology geared to validate the divinity and superiority of Southern White people.

My first encounter with White Georgia Methodists happened over thirty years ago, not in church, but as a Marine Corps recruit stationed at Marine Corps Recruit Training Depot, Paris Island, South Carolina/Burford, Georgia. During my platoon's first introduction to the drill instructors, we (recruits) were asked about our religious affiliation.

I responded: "United Methodist."

Staff Sergeant Merunka, a junior drill instructor, quickly confronted me and stated, "Blacks could not be United Methodists, but we could be Baptists." So, he ordered "Baptist" to be engraved on my identification tags, also known as dog tags.

At that moment, I felt that Staff Sergeant Merunka's comment and action to place "Baptist" on my dog tags were motivated by racism, but I felt powerless as a recruit to challenge his authority. However, upon completing basic training, I immediately had my dog tags changed to read "United Methodist." I kept the original dog tags as collectibles, not knowing that thirty years later, I would write about that incident.

My earlier thoughts regarding Staff Sergeant Merunka's racial remark were that it was the opinion of a single individual and not a part of a large cultural norm. However, three decades later, during an interview, church historian Anderson Wright of Rust Chapel United Methodist Church (Oxford, Georgia) revealed to me that Staff Sergeant Merunka's comment and action were part of a much larger belief and value system that encompassed both Methodism and Southern racial identity.

Wright stated that "people of color, prior to the emancipation of enslaved people [January 1, 1863], who accompanied their slave masters to church for Sunday worship could not be official members of the Methodist Episcopal Church, South, but rather, they were listed only as attendees."[2] I am unsure whether Staff Sergeant Merunka understood the depth of his comment or if he was familiar with the Methodist Church history that Wright shared. However, due to the history and geographical location of Paris Island (Buford, Georgia) and the interwoven traditions of the Marine Corps, MECS, and the Confederate Army that were embraced and shared by White Georgians throughout the state, I am prone to believe that he

---

2. Anderson Wright, personal interview with author, Apr. 2018.

was knowledgeable about the racially divisive history of both the United Methodist Church and that of the US Marine Corps.

In December 1775, a writer of the *Pennsylvania Journal* claimed that a drum of the newly created Marine Corps displayed a rattlesnake alongside the motto "Don't tread on me."[3] The slogan "Don't tread on me" became symbolic among White conservative United Methodists (and White conservatives in general) during the rise of Trumpism and the Tea Party movement. The slogan "Don't tread on me" will be discussed in greater detail in chapter 6. In 2020, after the murder of George Floyd that led to global protests, the Marine Corps finally announced that it was officially banning Confederate symbols from all its military installations.

In the spring of 2019, a fellow alumnus of the Paris Island Recruit Training Depot and I visited the training base for the first time since we graduated. Our return to Paris Island evoked a range of emotions and memories. As we were leaving Paris Island, a billboard near the exit gate reported that one Marine recruit had been killed earlier that year in a training accident.

The killed Marine recruit was twenty-year-old Raheel Siddiqui. Recruit Siddiqui had fallen forty feet to his death while running away from his drill instructor who violently targeted him and other Muslim recruits throughout their training.[4] Recruit Siddiqui's death was an indication to us that the Marine Corps still practiced high levels of racial-ethnic-religious discrimination, although in some cases the perpetrators of discrimination and violence were themselves of an ethnic/non-White background. In the Marine Corps, as in the United Methodist Church, minority individuals commonly adopt the values, beliefs, and behaviors of the White mainstream as a means of social acceptance, job security, and upward mobility.

Steve Walsh of National Public Radio (NPR) conducted a radio interview with Lieutenant Colonel Cameron McCoy (African American) on March 31, 2020, entitled "Marine Corps Aims to Tackle Evolving Face of White Supremacy." Walsh's interview was in response to the commandant of the Marine Corps, General David Berger, and his order to ban all Confederate symbols from Marine Corps bases around the globe. This directive came when the Marine Corps was trying to become more inclusive, but during a period under the Trump administration when the number of White supremacy groups was on the rise within the general society and in

3. Volle, "Gadsen Flag."
4. Lamothe, "Democracy Dies in Darkness."

the military. Moreover, General Berger's decision also came as a response to the Marine Corps' long history of internalized racism and xenophobia.

During Lieutenant Colonel McCoy's radio interview with Walsh, he stated that within his eighteen years of service, he had seen the Confederate battle flag pop up on Marine bases in the South, including being painted on the hood of a Marine's pickup truck.

In addition, Lieutenant Colonel McCoy added that the Marine Corps was slower than the other military branches to integrate African Americans and did not formally allow African Americans into its ranks until 1942. Moreover, Lieutenant Colonel McCoy said, "The Marine Corps still is the Whitest and most male of the service branches with the fewest number of African American officers."[5]

Walsh's interview with Lieutenant Colonel McCoy highlighted the historical interconnectedness between Marine Corps bases in the South, White Southern Protestant value systems, and White supremacy. He mentioned Confederate Army and Tea Party symbols that were also common within the military supply stores in Oceanside, California, and at Camp Pendleton. While in the Marine Corps, I encountered racism and de facto segregation during Desert Shield/Desert Storm at Paris Island, Camp Lejeune, and Camp Pendleton. In the Marine Corps, racism was just as common as our dress blue uniforms—it was a part of the internal cultural value system.

RAISED BLACK UNITED METHODIST IN THE MISSISSIPPI DELTA

While the unpleasant event between me and Staff Sergeant Merunka was memorable and disappointing, it was not my first encounter with bigotry, systemic racism, and institutional oppression—things that were the norm for Black folks growing up in the Deep South. As a Black boy growing up in the United Methodist Church during the 1970s and 1980s in the Mississippi Delta at a period when the Civil Rights Movement was very operational, bigotry and racism in local churches throughout the Mississippi Conferences was the standard for the social behavior at all organizational levels of the Southeastern Jurisdiction of the United Methodist Church—local church, district, and at the Annual Conference.

5. Walsh, "Marine Corps Aims."

Culture Shapes Behavior

According to my grandfather, Warren G. Booker Sr. (community organizer for the Mississippi Freedom Democratic Party and appointed elder of the Upper Mississippi Conference of the United Methodist Church), the Upper Mississippi Annual Conference and the United Methodist Church were long-standing supporters of racial segregation and perpetrators of racial violence against POC across the South.

Elder Warren Gammilia Booker Sr. Photo, S. Redmond Collection

Exclusive Theology

Elder Warren G. Booker Sr.'s ordination certificate. Photo, S. Redmond Collection

In general, the White United Methodists, who supported the activities of the civil rights workers in the Mississippi Delta, did so anonymously and feared the possibility of a violent backlash from their fellow White churchgoers and neighbors. For example, below is a letter written to my grandfather by an anonymous White supporter of civil rights workers. Former Mississippi senator David Jordan (Greenwood, Mississippi) later dated and signed the letter upon my request for authentication.

> Dear Brother Booker:
>
> I read where you all are going to march again today 1968 Senator Dowd Jr.
>
> I know this is the only way you all will ever get justic and your rights.
>
> You and David Jordan of Greenwood is two of the most important workers that the black have. There are some who talk before the public but dont ever get out for they are afraid of what they might suffer. There are still too many young Uncle Tom's around afraid of being kown that they are interested in rights for all people. There has been a lot accomplished but still more to be accomplished if you are able to keep it before the eyes of the people justic can still come around.
>
> If you recall the 40 chapter of Isaiah reminds us of the same conditions when the prophecy of the birth of Christ was announced. The people were in bondage and were just beginning to get set free. There is no better time to be put in jail then now to help bring peace on earth and good will to man. I gave to your fund that the church was raising this month and I heard there was a good offering . This shows that people are behind you and that you will be supported by gifts when some white folks can not be identified for we will lose our homes for we do not have a recourse like blacks do. White friend.

An anonymous letter was written to Rev. Warren G. Booker Sr. Photo, S. Redmond Collection

My earliest memory of racial discrimination occurred when I was merely five years old. At the age of five, my grandfather (leader of the protest) took me with him to participate in a civil rights protest, which took place around the town square of Lexington, Mississippi—my hometown. During the march, the chief of police of the city of Lexington stopped my grandfather and informed him that the protest was an illegal assembly. The chief of police ordered my grandfather to be placed under arrest and to leave me on the street corner. My grandfather adamantly refused to release my hand and boldly stated that he would not leave me alone on the street; he instructed the arresting officers to place me in custody along with him. The arresting officers, as instructed, handcuffed my grandfather and placed us both in the back seat of his squad car. I was extremely scared but comforted by my grandfather's touch.

A few moments later, my mother (a member of the Lexington police department) appeared on the scene, and I was released into her care. I watched as my grandfather was transported off to jail, which would not be the last civil rights protest I participated in with my grandfather. The experience of participating in the Civil Rights Movement at such a young age allowed me opportunities to witness firsthand the destructive nature of racism and the power of racial resistance. In addition, it also provided me with a level of cultural awareness whereby I was able to recognize systematic racism and develop the willingness to protest it.

However, on the flip side and as a result of these traumatic experiences, I was also left with many mental scars of resentment toward White people, police officers, and the United Methodist Church. These experiences as a child of racial conflict and resistance acquired within the cultural context of the Mississippi Delta influenced my behavior as a teenager and young adult. Culture shapes behavior.

HOMOPHOBIA AND RACISM IN THE UNITED METHODIST CHURCH

Over the past forty years, racial and ethnic progress have continued to improve slowly throughout the South. Since the 1970s and 1980s, however, many Southern Christians of diverse racial backgrounds still adhere to religious-cultural values and beliefs that endorse the practice of exclusive theology. The reality of the practice of exclusive theology was evident in the history and the present life of the North Georgia Conference of the United Methodist Church. *The Book of Discipline of the United Methodist Church* unambiguously denounces racism, deeming it to be a "sin," and affirms the ultimate and temporal worth of all persons.[6]

While the United Methodist Church is engaged in ongoing ministries through the General Commission on Religion and Race (GCORR) that

---

6. *Book of Discipline*, 133–34.

support racial justice and inclusivity, it remains evident that individual bigotry and institutional racism continue to be commonly practiced throughout the denomination, particularly in the Southeastern Jurisdiction.[7] In addition to the church's historical struggle to curtail racism within the denomination, the United Methodist Church continued to uphold its position that homosexuality was incompatible with scripture until the church changed its incompatibility stance on May 2, 2024 at its General Conference held in Charlotte, N.C.[8]

In the July/August 2019 edition of *By Faith Magazine*, Junius B. Dotson (general secretary, discipleship ministries) illustrated in his article, "The One Church Plan," that Black people were among the first people to become Methodist. However, slavery divided the church along racial lines. In the article, Dotson also stated that Black people founded several Methodist denominations, such as the African Methodist Episcopal Church (AME), African Methodist Episcopal Zion Church (AMEZ), and Colored Methodist Episcopal Church (CME), due in large part to the racial exclusion they encountered while attending White Methodist churches. Furthermore, Dotson added that as recent as the 1960s, Black Methodists were still being excluded from White Methodist churches, and in 1972, the year the Civil Rights Movement ended, the United Methodist Church officially included intolerant language into its *Book of Discipline* designed to subjugate the civil rights of gay persons within the denomination.[9]

In addition to Dotson's article, a second article was in the July/August 2019 edition of *By Faith Magazine* by an anonymous author entitled "Other Voices." This article illustrated that many Black denominations in America do not support the ordination of gay persons but have found ways to embrace gay persons within the Black church without ordaining them. This anonymous author also claimed that Black preachers have historically been progressive in acting against oppression as a marginalized people. However, regarding ordaining gay persons, their first responsibility is to proclaim biblical Scripture as the basis for their actions.[10] In short, Black preachers across denominational lines claimed that homosexuality was in contradiction to God's word.

7. See GCORR's website at gcorr.org.

8. Heather Hahn. Church ends 52-year-old-anti gay stance. UM News. May 2, 2024. www.unnews.org

9. Dotson, "One Church Plan," 5.

10. Dotson, "One Church Plan," 7.

In general, the Black United Methodist clergy in the North Georgia Conference shared the exclusive theological beliefs and values of their White United Methodist conservative counterparts concerning the incompatibility of Scripture and homosexuality and opposition to the ordination of LGBTQ+ persons. It should not be considered foreign for Black United Methodists to share similar exclusive theological values and beliefs as White United Methodist conservatives, primarily due to the MECS's history of enslavement and racial segregation.

Many White Southern Methodists who were enslavers and segregationists adhered to the Wesleyan social holiness doctrine, which provided the basis for the social morality and ethical principles that slaveowners and the enslaved observed. On Steve Manskar's blog post "No Holiness but Social Holiness," he states that John Wesley's doctrine on social holiness teaches that "social holiness is the practice of obeying Jesus' commandments to love God with all your heart, soul, and mind, loving . . . one another (fellow member of your congregation) as Christ loves."[11]

While Manskar offers a more modern understanding of John Wesley's thoughts on social holiness, which appears to emphasize human equality, racial and ethnic inclusion, and social justice, this was not the reasoning of Southern Methodist plantation owners during the 1700s and 1800s. For Southern Methodist plantation owners, the Wesleyan doctrine on social holiness was not intended to be an addendum to slavery or an appeal for human equality, racial and ethnic inclusion, or social justice. Instead, it was a practical-social theology that encouraged Christians (masters and enslaved) to love one another for heavenly salvation and community while simultaneously obeying the Southern sociopolitical norms that encouraged the ideology of White superiority and non-White inferiority.

A SEPARATE DENOMINATION FOR BLACK METHODISTS

On December 16, 1870, the General Conference of the MECS was convened in Jackson, Tennessee. During the General Conference, a vote was passed to transfer all remaining Black Methodists to the newly developed racially segregated denomination, the Colored Methodist Episcopal Church (CME).

In addition, the MECS, also made provisions for the transfer of church properties and the conferment of ordinations upon the Colored Methodist

---

11. Manskar, "No Holiness."

Episcopal Church. Early in the establishment of the denomination, the members of the Colored Methodist Episcopal Church (also referred to as Black Methodists) generally maintained cordial and warm relationships with the White members of the MECS.[12]

Although the Black Methodists now had their separate denomination, they continued to adhere to the values and belief traditions established and practiced within the MECS. The Black Methodists not only embraced the paternalism of the White Southern Methodists and the desire for racial separation, but they went as far as disputing political reconstruction as the legacy of their White Methodist brethren. From the Black Methodists' viewpoints during this period of Reconstruction, the MECS was also their Methodist tradition.

As a means of pacifying White fear, Black Methodists continued to affirm to White Methodists that their churches would not be used for political purposes or assemblages. In 1882, at their General Conference, Southern Methodists authorized the appointment of a joint commission with the Colored Methodist Episcopal Church to explore the establishment of a college for the education of Black teachers and preachers.

Led by Bishop George F. Pierce on November 1, 1882, at St. John Church in August, Georgia, the Joint Commission members were selected. The members representing the MECS were W. P. Pattillo, W. H. LaPrade, W. A. Candler (president of Emory College), and James E. Evans (commissioner of education). The CME representatives were J. S. Harper, R. A. Maxey, and Bishop L. H. Holsey. (Note: Bishop Lucius Henry Holsey had been a biracial enslaved person in Georgia and was married to Harriett Turner, one of Bishop George F. Peirce's former slaves.)

White Methodists of the North Georgia Conference continued to influence and oversee the religious and sociopolitical standards of Black Methodists in North Georgia through their joint establishment of Paine College in August, Georgia. The college was named after Bishop Robert Paine (a supporter of the Confederate Army), one of the bishops who presided at the establishment of the CME, along with his close colleague Bishop William Capers (enslaver and Confederate Army supporter). Bishop Warren A. Candler (Emory College president) was given the charge of establishing the school, and Morgan Callaway, vice president of Emory College, would serve as Paine College's first president.

---

12. Sheets, *Methodism in North Georgia*, 78–79.

Exclusive Theology

Bishop Isaac Lane of the CME had previously established a high school for African Americans in Jackson, Tennessee; however, he was not considered for the position to oversee Paine College. Paine College was the first Black college founded by the MECS and CME joint commission in the South. Bishops Robert Paine, William Capers, and Atticus Haygood, all former Confederate Army loyalists, strongly supported the establishment of Paine College through their leadership and financial support. Their motivations for supporting Paine College were to establish segregated educational systems for Blacks and to maintain control over the newly forming Black educated class in North Georgia, in particular the Mulattos, who they feared could gain sympathy among certain Whites.

By 1874, Black membership was approximately seventy-five thousand, and although the CME had added two bishops and ordained 607 traveling preachers, they still adhered to the segregating social and political values and beliefs of the MECS, officially begun in the Jim Crow Era.[13]

In other social justice issues beyond that of racism, *The Book of Discipline of The United Methodist Church*, under the section entitled "Social Principles," states that "we affirm that no identity or culture has more legitimacy than any other."[14] Moreover, the mission statement of the Candler School of Theology, Emory University (a United Methodist Church–affiliated seminary) illustrates that the "School of Theology is grounded in the Christian faith and shaped by the Wesleyan tradition of evangelical piety, ecumenical openness, and social concern. The school's mission was to educate faithful and creative leaders for the church's ministries throughout the world."[15] Candler seminarians are taught that the primary focus of the message of Christ and the United Methodist Church is to "love God and love neighbor" without prejudice.

However, many United Methodist clergy members serving in the North Georgia Conference and other conferences across the Southern Jurisdiction of the United Methodist Church continued to embrace religious doctrine that excluded gay persons from becoming ordained and fully accepted within the denomination.

On January 3, 2020, *The New York Times* reported that "United Methodists Announce Plan to Split over Same-Sex Marriage." *The New York Times* article stated that the United Methodist Church consists of thirteen

---

13. Sheets, *Methodism in North Georgia*, 115–18.
14. *Book of Discipline*, 110.
15. Candler School of Theology, "Mission, Vision, and Values."

million members worldwide and is the second largest denomination in the United States, and that they announced a plan to split over the concept of same-sex marriage. In addition to the church splitting, the article stated that a new "Traditionalist Methodist" denomination would be created and continue to ban same-sex marriage and the ordination of gay persons.[16]

Following this announcement, I interviewed Fredrick Fresh, a longtime lay member and finance committee member of Hoosier Memorial United Methodist Church, and a former member of the Gammon Theological Seminary Board of Trustees (Atlanta–College Park District of the North Georgia Conference). During the interview, I asked, "Which side (Progressive or Traditional Methodist) of the church split do you believe the Black Methodist Churches and affiliated Historical Black Methodist Colleges and Universities would support?"

Fresh stated, "In general, Black Methodist Churches historically have not supported ordaining gay persons. Plus, the Historical Black Methodist Colleges and Universities will most likely side with the Traditional Methodist Plan due to our (Black Methodist) theological traditions and needed financial support."[17]

In another interview, this time with Bishop James King, resident bishop of Gammon Theological Seminary and lifelong Black Methodist, Bishop King did not forecast which side of the church split Black Methodists would support. However, he did illustrate that the root of the church split was not solely due to LGBTQ issues alone, but also due to non-Whites making up a large percentage of United Methodist Bishops to whose authority conservative White United Methodists do not want to adhere.[18]

On June 3–5, 2021, during the North Georgia 155th Annual Conference presided over by Bishop Sue Haupert-Johnson, entitled "Love Is Making Room," an official vote was cast and approved, giving United Methodist Churches in the North Georgia Conference in good standing, the right to separate from the United Methodist Church. With the North Georgia Conference of The United Methodist Church being the largest of all Annual Conferences in America, the idea is that the rest of the Annual Conferences would follow the example of the North Georgia Conference and vote to separate as well prior to the 2022 General Conference.

---

16. Robertson and Dias, "United Methodists Announce Plan."
17. Fresh, interview with author, Nov. 2019.
18. King, interview with author, Nov. 2019.

Exclusive Theology

On March 20, 2022, Bishop Haupert-Johnson hosted the Central West District Lay Delegate lessoning session (in preparation for the North Georgia Annual Conference, 2022) at Marietta First United Methodist Church, Marietta, Georgia. Approximately four Blacks and over sixty White lay delegates attended the Central West District lessoning session. In response to several questions regarding the North Georgia Conference's position on same-sex marriage, Bishop Haupert-Johnson stated, "Several ordained clergy members have participated in gay weddings, which is not a problem. However, acting in accordance with the church's *Book of Discipline*, ordained clergy are not allowed to perform the wedding vows or sign off on marriage certificates for same-sex couples."[19]

In addition to being asked about the church's position on ordained clergy performing same-sex marriages, Bishop Haupert-Johnson was also asked, "What strategies are being developed to increase diversity and inclusion within churches located in the Central West District?" Bishop Haupert-Johnson did not reply to the question; however, the Central West district superintendent replied that the "Central West District has the most inclusive and diverse church in all of the North Georgia Conference."[20]

Moreover, when the Central West district superintendent was asked what the total number of diverse churches in the Central West District was and what the criteria for which a church can be classified as a diverse church was, the Central West District Superintendent replied that she did not know the number of diverse churches in her district, and that the term "diverse church" is not easily defined.

Furthermore, she explained that "eighty-four churches are in the Central West District." It is customary in the United Methodist Church for an ordained clergy member of color to be appointed to an all-white congregation (this is considered a cross-racial appointment) as either pastor or associate pastor, and the congregation is then considered a diverse church. In most cases, the clergy of color are appointed to the associate pastor position and given menial responsibilities for which lay members commonly understand their presence as a token appointment. Many non-White clergy have reported that cross-racial appointments are highly stressful and racially degrading.

---

19. Haupert-Johnson, presentation remarks at Central West District Lay Delegate Lessoning session, Marietta, GA, Mar. 20, 2022.

20. District superintendent, presentation remarks at Central West District Lay Delegate Lessoning session, Marietta, GA, Mar. 20, 2022.

Culture Shapes Behavior

In addition to the harsh realities appointed non-White clergy experience serving in cross-racial appointments, conservative, White, North Georgia United Methodists under the new Traditional Methodist Church Plan were looking to limit the number of years that an individual could serve as bishop, curtailing the authority and power of elected bishops, primarily non-White bishops.

While *The New York Times* report illustrated that LGBTQ+ issues were the primary cause of the division, ethnicity and racism were also factors in Church disaffiliations. The United Methodist Church's longstanding values and beliefs were constructed and progressed by way of British colonialism through the missional means of the Anglican Church, the Southern Confederacy, and the Jim Crow era—all of which illustrated the need for ethnic, racial, and gender repression and highlighted White and Eurocentric supremacy.

The historical racialized behavior of White United Methodist parishioners serving in the North Georgia Annual Conference not only continued to inspire their political-religious social actions throughout Barack Obama's presidency, but their political and religious motivations were already grounded in racial reasoning that illustrated a revitalization of a "Birth of a Nation," which overflowed with violence, exclusion, and racial hatred.[21]

The formation of this "New Birth of a Nation Movement," introduced in response to President Obama's multicultural social agenda, such alt-right White extremist groups and ideologies as the Tea Party Movement, Alt-Right Movement, and Trumpism. These realized groups were unfiltered in their disdain for multiculturalism.

They presented "alternative facts" to show that a more ethnic and culturally diverse America was a threat to traditional Protestant White American values and beliefs and nationalism. And, if Obama's multicultural agenda were allowed to flourish and become normalized, it would eventually bring about the end of the White race and America as they knew it. America and the North Georgia Annual Conference of the United Methodist Church entered a new era of political, religious, and social exclusionary practices that, at face value, appeared to be socially inclusive, aligning with the church's social principles.

---

21. Dixon, *Clansman*. *The Birth of a Nation* is a 1915 American silent epic drama film directed by D. W. Griffith. The film is adapted from Thomas Dixon Jr.'s 1905 novel *The Clansman*. *The Birth of a Nation* depicts African Americans as unintelligent and sexually violent toward White women and upholds White supremacy ideologies.

However, the mere racial makeup of the United Methodist Church clergy (90 percent White) highlights the underlying reality of the church and its struggle with attracting non-Whites to join the denomination. However, many studies indicate that church membership across various religious denominations is in steady decline.[22] In the author's observation, the United Methodist Church's history of racism and homophobia are two of the primary causes of the denomination's inability to attract diverse groups of people.

During a brief discussion with Gregory Williams, pastor of Golden Memorial United Methodist Church in Douglasville, Georgia, he explained that the percentage of Whites in the United Methodist Church had increased from 93 percent in 2000 to 96 percent in 2010.[23] While racism is understood to be a "sin," according to the United Methodist Church's social principles, racism continues to be a widespread practice throughout the denomination worldwide.

---

22. Pew Research Center, *In U.S., Decline.*
23. Williams, interview with author, Oct. 2018.

Chapter 3

Better a Christian Slave Than a Freed Negro

IN GENERAL, NORTH GEORGIA United Methodists' practice of exclusive theology is rooted in notions of a racial hierarchy based on historical inequalities and racial stereotypes, which became normalized within the United Methodist Church and in American society. These flawed notions of racial inferiority and superiority were long-established in the Church of England and the British Empire's reputation as a civilized society in a barbarous world—a world needing to be evangelized and culturally transformed into a European likeness.

A much earlier pronouncement of a racial hierarchy theory in European history can be traced to the Greek philosopher Aristotle. Politically, Aristotle (384–322 BCE) argued that "from the hour of their birth, some men are marked out for subjection, others for rule" as part of the divine order.[1] Moreover, Aristotle labeled Africans "burnt face"—the original meaning in Greek of "Ethiopian." In Aristotle's hypothesis of racial hierarchy, known as "Climate Theory," he argued that extreme natural climates, either "too cold or too hot," determined people's intelligence, physicality, morality, and ability to self-govern.[2]

As would be expected, Aristotle positioned Greece as having a climate suitable for a master race and Africa as having an improper climate befitting that of a lower race. Climate theory was a justification for the Greeks

---

1. Smith, *John Wesley and Slavery*, 13–14.
2. Kendi, *Stamped from the Beginning*, 17.

to normalize the enslavement of Africans and to rule over the Western Mediterranean.[3]

Aristotle's climate theory became acceptable in Rome among first-century Christians and later throughout Arabia, providing Muslims with a theological justification for the enslavement of African peoples during the lucrative sub-Saharan slave trade. In the first century, St. Paul (Christian apostle) introduced a three-tiered hierarchy of slave relations—heavenly master (top), earthly master (middle), and enslaved (bottom).[4] This racial prejudice against African peoples became entrenched in Eastern European belief, and the Islamic philosopher Ibn Khaldun (1332–1406), a proponent of climate theory, lent validation to the flawed theory during his educational and political career in North Africa and Arabia.[5]

Both Aristotle and Ibn Khaldun embraced climate theory as scientific and theological proof to justify racial prejudice, which rationalized the enslavement of African people in Greece and the Arabian Peninsula. Aristotle's climate theory isn't commonly known or mentioned in modern theological circles when discussing the essence of racial reasoning or systemic racism in the United Methodist Church. However, the rootedness of the climate theory has remained in the subconscious of Western society and has helped to shape the racialized belief and value systems of modern churchgoers and has motivated conscious acts of racial violence against POC around the world for over two millenniums.

SLAVES OBEY YOUR EARTHLY MASTERS

Historically, the United Methodist Church's racial belief and value system ("Wesleyanism") partly shares in Aristotle's climate theory. However, there's an additional theoretical aspect to the development of modern Wesleyan thought regarding racial hierarchy, which can be traced to the Anglican and Puritan religious traditions of the mid-1600s. The Puritan clergymen who settled in the New England colonies were the first to introduce a systematic racial hierarchy into what would later become North America.

Puritans rejected the climate theory as being the primary cause of inferior Blackness. Instead, Puritans argued that people of African origin

---

3. Kendi, *Stamped from the Beginning*, 17.
4. Kendi, *Stamped from the Beginning*, 17.
5. Kendi, *Stamped from the Beginning*, 20.

were divinely cursed and that the inferiority of African peoples was the divine will of God.

The Puritans' exegetical interpretation of biblical Scripture animalized African people. Such Scripture as Gen 9:20–27 validated their racial belief that African people were the descendants of Ham (the father of Canaanite people), a people divinely cursed by Noah to a lifetime of enslavement and suffrage under the bondage of Shem and Japheth (Ham's brothers) for all of eternity. The Anglicans later lumped the multiethnic Native Americans into the same cursed racial grouping as African people.

Early American Puritan preachers such as John Cotton and Richard Mather of Massachusetts espoused a racial theological doctrine based on this cursed theory for establishing the social order between the enslaver and the slave in their earthly lives, which would continue in the afterlife—heaven.[6] This system masked the exploitative master/slave relationship as a loving family relationship—the acculturation and assimilation of their slaves was the goal of Cotton's and Mather's plantation theology. Their theological belief and value systems supported the human subjugation of the enslaved and the racial superiority of the master for their personal safety and economic profit.

A social gospel of "slaves obey your earthly masters, as you would God" served as the basis for assimilationist slaveholders in the social ordering on slaveholding plantations and in society.[7] The philosophy of English theorists and assimilationist theologian William Perkins influenced both Cotton and Mather. Perkins's theological argument for the equality of the African soul and the inferiority of the African body was adequate for the sociopolitical desires of Cotton and Mather as they hoped to justify slavery in the New England colonies.[8]

According to Ibram X. Kendi, Mather, who had begun his ministry not far from the Port of Liverpool, which would become the central destination for the British slave trade, argued that slavery was the economic boost that England needed to compete with the Dutch, French, Portuguese, and Spanish empires.[9] Cotton Mather (maternal grandson of both John Cotton and Richard Mather) was so inspired by his grandfathers' endearment with London's Royal Society, the primary publisher of English scientific race

---

6. Kendi, *Stamped from the Beginning*, 33.
7. Raboteau, *Slave Religion*, 294.
8. Kendi, *Stamped from the Beginning*, 22–46.
9. Kendi, *Stamped from the Beginning*, 33.

theories in England and the New England colonies, that he modeled the Boston Philosophical Society in its likeness.

According to Kendi, William Pretty, an economist for the Royal Society, drafted a hierarchical "scale" of humanity in which Pretty wrote that the "Guinea Negroes" were at the bottom. Middle Europeans, he wrote, differed from Africans "in their natural manners and the internal qualities of their minds." Cotton Mather's hatred for Africans was second to his dislike of Native Americans as a young teenager; Cotton Mather (a student at Harvard College) separated the jaw of Metacomet (Native American leader of King Philip's War) from his skull after his fellow Puritans dismantled his body and displayed his remains in Plymouth.[10]

The Puritans' racialized ideas became a cornerstone of how the Anglicans would develop their racial theories and engage in plantation ownership throughout the Caribbean Islands and British colonies in the New World.

The racialized ideas that motivated notions of racial superiority and divine destiny in modern United Methodism stemmed from core socioreligious belief and value systems of both the Anglican Church and Puritan Church traditions. The Eurocentric notions of European intellectual and cultural exceptionalism were deeply ingrained in the Anglo-Saxon consciousness, motivating their worldwide exploration and expansion through commerce, foreign missions, slave trading, and global war. Anglo-Saxons believed that the creation of a superior civilization was a result of bio-cultural preeminence, whereby a "superior society" was tied directly to race, culture, and the natural environment.

Moreover, civilization was a genuine reflection of human abilities and intellectual and industrial progress, whereas Europeans understood themselves to be at the pinnacle of the racial scale. With racial consciousness being central to Europeans' racialized idea of a "good society" and White Protestant supremacy, British slavers understood themselves to be the stewards of all the world. It was their divine right and missional responsibility to reveal to all of God's subhuman creatures (Africans and Native Americans) the holiness of Christianity and the greatness of Western civilization.

Britain had already asserted majority control of the trading of enslaved Africans bound for the Americas and British West Indian Islands in the early 1700s, prior to John and Charles Wesley's (both Anglican priests) journey from England upon the *Simmonds* (accompanied by sister ship the *London Merchant*) en route to the British Colony of Georgia. The *Simmonds*

---

10. Kendi, *Stamped from the Beginning*, 53.

laid anchor off the shore of Cockspur Island at Fort Cockspur—present-day Fort Pulaski—on February 4, 1736.[11] However, by the 1750s the Colony of Georgia had become a slave state, and the British merchants inflated the Atlantic slave trade, surpassing the Portuguese and Spanish slave traders.

Monument commemorating the location where John Wesley first camped on Peeper Island. Photo, S. Redmond Collection

11. Smith, *John Wesley and Slavery*, 38.

> From
> THE JOURNAL OF JOHN WESLEY
>
> "FRI, 6, - ABOUT EIGHT IN THE MORNING I FIRST SET MY FOOT ON AMERICAN GROUND. IT WAS A SMALL UNINHABITED ISLAND,...OVER AGAINST TYBEE, CALLED BY THE ENGLISH PEEPER ISLAND. MR. OGLETHORPE LED US THROUGH THE MOORISH LAND ON THE SHORE TO A RISING GROUND,...WE CHOSE AN OPEN PLACE SURROUNDED WITH MYRTLES, BAYS, AND CEDARS, WHICH SHELTERED US BOTH FROM THE SUN AND WIND, AND CALLED OUR LITTLE FLOCK TOGETHER TO PRAYERS."

John Wesley's journal entry upon his arrival in the Colony of Georgia. Photo, S. Redmond Collection

THE PROPAGATION OF THE GOSPEL

In addition to inflating the transatlantic slave trade, the British elites, through their military might, had continued the Portuguese and Spanish murderous traditions of systematically annihilating the Chickasaw, Creek, Cherokee, Guale, Yamacraw, and Yamasee who lived in the territories along the Georgia Atlantic coastline and the British West Indian Islands.[12] In 1452, 249 years before the creation of The Society for the Propagation of the Gospel in Foreign Parts (SPG), which developed into the communication arm of the Anglican Church, the Roman Catholic Church's Pope Nicholas V approved propagating the gospel to foreign territories beyond the boundaries of Europe as a means of conquest.

---

12. Smith, *John Wesley and Slavery*, 35.

The religious/commercial ideology that Pope Nicholas V popularized in the mid-fifteenth century was later assumed by the Church of England and provided the foundational dogma for the Anglican Church to justify the enslavement of African people and to occupy foreign territories, all under the banner of Protestantism militarily.

Pope Nicholas V issued the Papal Bull *Dum Diversas*, which granted King Alfonso V (nephew of Prince Henry) of Portugal the authority to reduce all Africans, Saracens (Muslims), pagans, and unbelievers to perpetual slavery and the seizure of non-Christian lands in foreign parts. The Roman Catholic Church's Doctrine of Discovery (*Romanus Pontifex*) defined the law of order and provided permission for the seizure of all lands south of Cape Bojador, granting authority to proselytize to Muslims and Indigenous people. This doctrine proved extraordinarily successful in Mexico, Central America, and South America.[13]

The racial ideologies that were well illustrated within the Roman Catholic Church's Doctrine of Discovery were also presented in *The Chronicle of the Discovery and Conquest of Guinea*, written by Gomes Eanes de Zurara (commander in Prince Henry's Military Order of Christ) in 1452.[14]

During the eighteenth and nineteenth centuries, these anti-African racist ideologies were co-opted by the SPG and provided to Anglican missionaries appointed to slave plantations in the Americas and Caribbean Islands. The transportation and trading of enslaved Africans captured along the Gold Coast was the primary economic catalyst for Britain's financial rule over the global production market and England's commercial-military expansion and worldwide foreign missionary zeal, including in the newly forming English colonies of North America. On August 20, 1619, when twenty-to-thirty enslaved Africans aboard the English privateer ship *White Lion* arrived at Point Comfort (now Fort Monroe in Hampton, Virginia) Anglican priests understood that their own racial identity, cultural values, and Protestant religious beliefs were innately superior to that of African and Native American people.

For the Anglican Church to justify its support of the enslavement and annihilation of both the African and Native American, missionaries deemed that Africans and Native Americans needed to be converted to Protestant Christianity, which would provide them with true religion and liberate them from their ignorant spiritual superstitions and savage

---

13. Gerbner, *Christian Slavery*, 13–30.
14. Kendi, *Stamped from the Beginning*, 23.

behavior. From this egocentric frame of thought, Anglican missionaries embarked on an imperial quest to convert the souls and untutored minds of these so-called savages and bring them into the awareness of Christianity and high culture/moral behavior. British settlers now residing in the English colonies of North America had been long indoctrinated to believe in their racial and religious superiority.

Although the British settlers desired to liberate themselves from the overpowering authority of the Church of England, they continued its practices and adhered to the underlying beliefs, traditions, and values of the Church of England for their social identity—both consciously and unconsciously in ways that were socially and theologically exclusive of Africans and Native Americans.

While the Church of England, in conjunction with the newly forming British Empire, was the principal agent in the expansion of the transatlantic slave trade, they learned the practice of slave trading from the Roman Catholic enslavers from Portugal and Spain.

Under the authority of the Roman Catholic Church, Southwestern Europe was already legally vested in and practicing the enslavement of Africans prior to the official establishment of the English colonies in North America and the Caribbean Islands. On August 6, 1444, 240 enslaved African people were transported to Lagos in Portugal. In celebration of the capture of the enslaved people and to illustrate that the Portuguese had joined the Europeans in the trading of slaves, Prince Henry showcased the slave auction.[15] However, the establishment of European and Christian exceptionalism (the belief that Europe and Christianity are exemplary compared to other regions and religious traditions) began with the expulsion of Muslims from Southwest Europe during the First Crusades in 1095 at the order of Pope Urban II.

The idea of European racial and religious superiority, which began to form during the Crusades, became normalized in Western Europe over time and served as the foundational thinking for the Church of England throughout the transatlantic slave trade. The Western Europeans' expansion of the slave trade over the next three and a half centuries continued to give rise to the notion that non-White people worldwide were inferior races that needed to be converted from their idolatry and savagery by acculturating them into the Christian faith and Western European culture.

---

15. Kendi, *Stamped from the Beginning*, 23.

Educated and wealthy Englishmen, influenced by pseudoscientific studies in phrenology, the humanities, and religion, primarily led by academic race theorists, Anglican theologians, foreign business investors, and military personnel, spread a belief that promoted the superiority of Protestant-White England's commonwealth. This doctrine later spread globally to non-Whites. A common thought among the Crusaders, which Protestant enslavers later adopted, was that it was better for freed Africans to be enslaved by Christian slavers than for them to become influenced by Islam.

ANTIGUA: THE BIRTHPLACE OF BLACK METHODISM

After John Wesley had returned to London from the Colony of Georgia, he then traveled to Wandsworth (a borough of London), where he baptized his first Negro converts on November 28, 1758, at the home of Nathaniel Gilbert. Scholars of Methodist history note Wandsworth, England, as the place where the first enslaved Africans were converted to the Methodist faith.[16]

John Wesley's Journal entry for November 29, 1758, is, "Wed. 29.—I rode to Wandsworth, and baptized two Negroes belonging to Mr. Gilbert, a gentleman lately come from Antigua. One of these is deeply convinced of sin; the other rejoices in God her Savior and is the first African Christian I have known. But shall not our Lord, in due time, have these Heathens also 'for His inheritance?'"[17]

Bessie, Sophia Campbell, and Mary Alley (Mulatto woman) were the slaves of Nathaniel Gilbert's plantation. Mary, Sophia, and Bessie traveled with Nathaniel Gilbert from his plantation in Antigua (West Indies) to Wandsworth, England, in search of medical assistance for Gilbert and to meet with John Wesley personally. Professionally, Nathaniel Gilbert was a lawyer trained at Gray's Inn, London, a plantation owner in Antigua, and the Speaker of the House of Representatives for the West Indies.

Feeling ill, Nathaniel Gilbert asked Mary, his five-year-old daughter to bring him a book to read to help him relax. Mary brought him *An Earnest Appeal to Men of Reason and Religion*, a book written by John Wesley that was sent to Nathaniel Gilbert by his brother Francis Gilbert. Upon reading the book, Nathaniel was deeply changed by the experience.

---

16. Graham, *Black United Methodists*, 11.
17. Quoted in Graham, *Black United Methodists*, 11.

Exclusive Theology

After hearing John preach in London, Nathaniel Gilbert wanted to meet John personally. Nathaniel (once agnostic) was so inspired that he converted to Methodism and later became a lay preacher of the Methodist society in Antigua.[18]

Photo, Nathaniel Gilbert Plantation Mansion

Adopting John Wesley's "open air preaching" approach that was very appealing to England's working class, Nathaniel Gilbert preached to his slaves in the courtyard from the back steps of his plantation home several times throughout the week.

18. Methodist Church of Antigua & Barbuda, "Part 1: Beginnings."

Photo taken in November 2021. Courtyard and backsteps to Nathaniel Gilbert's Plantation Mansion. Photo, S. Redmond Collection

As a memorial to Nathaniel Gilbert's "open-air preaching," members of the Methodist Society of Antigua sent a "front step" of Gilbert's plantation house to Wesley's Chapel and Leysian Mission in London, England.

Photo, S. Redmond Collection

The step was altered by Wesley Chapel, London, England, to illustrate that "through Christ, the chain of slavery is broken." The carved-out circle in the center is used to hold water during baptisms. The White line along the edge of the step marked the front steps of Nathaniel Gilbert's plantation home (note: enslaved people were not allowed to cross over the White Line without permission).

Dr. S. Redmond showing Baptismal Font (Wesley Chapel, London, England, July 2019). Photo. S. Redmond Collection

In an interview, Keith Dutton (Heritage Steward of Wesley's Chapel and Leysian Mission) stated that the inscription "circular broken chain and cross" on the stone step was later added by members of Wesley Chapel to illustrate that the "chains of slavery could be broken through the power of Christianity"[19] and that the stone step was in honor of John Wesley's message of anti-slavery. It could be argued that the later alteration to the stone step engraved by members of Wesley Chapel is an attempt at *revisionist history*, motivated by modern Methodists to reinterpret the original historical meaning of the artifact for the purpose of presenting the World Methodist Church and John Wesley as anti-racists and long-term supporters of anti-slavery.

Both assumptions, anti-racist and supporter of anti-slavery, would be somewhat misleading narratives, omitting the history of Methodism and John Wesley's roles in helping to maintain slave societies in the Americas and British West Indies. According to Harold Recinos, professor of church and society at Southern Methodist University, Wesley did not publicly criticize the institution of slavery candidly until he was sixty-nine years old.[20]

19. Dutton, interview with author, Jul. 2019.
20. Harold Recinos, interview with author, Apr. 2019.

Another example of modern Methodists' attempts to revise history is illustrated in Brandon C. Wason's exhibition celebrating the legacy of Margaret A. Pitts, displayed at the Pitts Theology Library, Candler School of Theology, Emory University. Wason illustrated in his exhibition booklet that "Peter Bohler and George Whitefield crossed paths numerous times, and they had collaborated in preaching ministries and jointly created an orphanage and school for African American children."[21]

While Wason highlighted the constructive working relationship of Bohler and Whitefield, he omitted that the African American children he regarded as orphans (*defacto*) residing in the Bethesda Orphanage (which means "House of Mercy") were, in fact, slaves of George Whitefield, who, along with enslaved adults, labored on his Providence plantation in St. Paul's Parish, South Carolina.

It is generally agreed that the "mature" John Wesley argued against the ownership of enslaved people, evident in his published writing "My Thoughts on Slavery" and in his final letter to William Wilberforce, instructing him to continue the fight to end slavery. However, data illustrates that "young" John Wesley (through conscious intent) was in support of plantation owners and a leading contributor in socially engineering a "Culture of White Protestant Supremacy" that persisted throughout the eighteenth century in the British West Indies and in the colonies of South Carolina and Georgia, which North Georgia Methodists have continued to embrace today.[22]

BLACK HARRY HOOSIER'S PLANTATION PREACHING IN NORTH AMERICA AND BRITISH ISLANDS

In 1782, evangelical Harry Hoosier ("Black Harry" or "Parson Harry") was allowed to deliver his first sermon, "The Barren Fig Tree," taken from Luke 13:6–9 to a Black Methodist congregation at Adam's Chapel in Fairfax County, Virginia, under the supervision of Bishop Francis Asbury (father of the American Methodist Church). The sermon was recorded as the first Methodist sermon orated by a Negro.[23] On September 11, 1786, Black

---

21. Wason, *Religion of the Heart*.
22. See Smith, *John Wesley and Slavery*, 44–52; and Wesley, *Thoughts upon Slavery*.
23. McEllhenney, "Harry Hosier."

Harry preached at John Street Church in New York, the oldest Methodist congregation in the United States.[24]

Black Harry's preaching was so celebrated by Whites, free Negroes, and the enslaved that Bishop Asbury, on numerous occasions, had him preach in his stead. In the beginning, behaving in accordance with Bishop Asbury's liking, Black Harry's sermons promoted the message of White supremacy and Black inferiority, which plantation owners supported. According to Bishop Thomas Coke, Black Harry was one of the best preachers in the world.[25]

In 1780, Bishop Asbury regarded Black Harry as a suitable companion to preach to the enslaved because his sermons supported the status quo. As a result of Black Harry's growing popularity and disobedience, Bishop Asbury accused him of becoming too arrogant.

Black Harry was later sold to a Dutch plantation owner on the island of St. Eustatius.[26] Many historians argue that Black Harry overtly encouraged the enslaved to be obedient to their masters, acting in accordance with area slave laws and adhering to the scriptural interpretation of the Methodist Society while covertly (away from the surveillance of Bishop Asbury) meeting with Richard Allen, and Prince Hall (African Masonic Lodge) and other supporters of the Abolitionist movement.[27]

Black Harry's plantation preaching appeared to highlight "a gospel of heavenly salvation" over bodily liberation, and his sermons laid the foundation for Thomas Coke's arrival in St. Eustatius on January 14, 1787. Upon Coke's arrival on St. Eustatius, he found a vibrant and organized Methodist society comprising approximately 120 persons, led by Black Harry.

Moreover, Coke organized the society members into six classes and appointed Black Harry as the leader of the entire body of believers. While Coke was absent from St. Eustatius, authorities prohibited public prayer, making it a criminal offense. Black Harry ignored the injunction and replied to it by stating, "Christ was flogged; why should not I?"[28]

Against the order of the injunction, Black Harry continued to meet with the enslaved in secret and when discovered, he was detained, publicly

---

24. Graham, *Black United Methodists*, 2.
25. Graham, *Black United Methodists*, 2.
26. Graham, *Black United Methodists*, 3.
27. McClain, *Black People*, 45.
28. Gumbs, *Methodism in the MCCA*, 31.

flogged, imprisoned, and sold back to America.[29] Reports illustrate that Black Harry was never ordained and was later expelled from the Methodist Society altogether. Black Harry eventually received his freedom; however, he later became a severely depressed alcoholic and died in 1806.

Painting of Black Harry Hoosier, located at Hoosier Memorial United Methodist Church, Atlanta, Georgia.

29. Graham, *Black United Methodists*, 3.

Chapter 4

John Wesley and the Early Methodists in Georgia

The central difference between Black and White Methodism was and is the refusal of Black people to reconcile racism and social justice with the experience of conversion and new birth. Blacks do not believe it is possible to be sanctified and racist at the same time.

—James H. Cone

It had been 109 years since Englishman and privateer John Hawkins first raided the Gold Coast (1561), burning down villages and kidnapping Africans for trade in the Caribbean Islands on behalf of Queen Elizabeth before the religious societies were established in the late seventeenth century.[1] In the 1670s, Anthony Horneck, an Anglican pietist, started religious societies composed of small groups of laity who fused moralism and devotionalism in addition to promoting an idea of "real holiness and life."[2]

Horneck's religious societies were in demand due to increasing immorality throughout England. Religious societies grounded in piety and motivated by social reform became aligned with the Church of England. In 1691, these religious societies established the Society for the Reformation of Manners (SRM), and members served as secret informants to the justices of the peace and the Church of England. Informants provided information

---

1. Sublette and Sublette, *American Slave Coast*, 80–81.
2. Heitzenrater, *Wesley and the People*, 21.

concerning moral offenses committed by their fellow Englishmen, hoping to transform England's immoral society into communities of holy living.

According to Richard P. Heitzenrater, professor of church history and Wesley studies at Duke Divinity School, these religious societies became centralized at the turn of the eighteenth century and gave rise to organizations such as the Society for Promoting Christian Knowledge (SPCK), which became a model for moralism and devotionalism throughout the British Empire, including the British West Indies. Heitzenrater also explains that Samuel Wesley (John and Charles Wesley's father), the rector of the Epworth parish, became a member of the SPCK movement.

The fact that Samuel Wesley's son, John Wesley, became a corresponding member of the SPCK is of consequence because it highlights the established belief and value systems of the Wesley family and the core ideologies and motivations of the early Methodist movement.[3]

With England (the so-called nation of liberty) swiftly becoming the single largest slave trading nation in Western Europe, the SPCK believed it was important from its very beginning to support missionaries in foreign parts, authorizing them through the power of the Anglican Church to evangelize enslaved Africans residing on plantations in the British West Indies and the Americas.[4]

The mission of Anglican missionaries affiliated with the SPCK and its related organization, the Society for the Propagation of the Gospel in Foreign Parts (SPG), was to provide Christian educational training to the enslaved for their moral improvement and heavenly salvation but designed to benefit plantation owners' commercial ambitions by maintaining social order.

John and Charles Wesley, both foreign missionaries ordained in the Anglican Church, journeyed to the foreign mission stations in the British Colony of Georgia with the sole purpose of propagating the gospel to poor White settlers and to the savages—enslaved Africans and Indigenous people.[5] It was Charles's and John's divine mission to enlighten the minds and convert the souls of the so-called savage Indians and heathen Africans on behalf of the Anglican Church, the SPCK, and the SPG—all united under the rule of one imperial society, the British Crown.

---

3. Heitzenrater, *Wesley and the People*, 21.

4. Heitzenrater, *Wesley and the People*, 21–25.

5. Smith, *John Wesley and Slavery*, 55–62.

Furthermore, the goal of the propagation of the gospel in the Colony of Georgia was to create racial and moral harmony by way of developing docile enslaved people as a means of acculturation, which was to add additional protection for the plantation owners and the White working class against slave uprisings and curtail the slaves' desire to escape the harsh conditions of the plantation. In the process of providing safeguards for plantation owners and White overseers, the Wesleys (as members of the SPCK), whether consciously or unconsciously, aided in the social engineering of a caste system that fostered Protestant supremacy, a racial hierarchy, and escalated British imperialism in the Americas and British West Indies.

In Katharine Gerbner's book, *Christian Slavery: Conversion and Race in the Protestant Atlantic World*, she explains that upon the death of Christopher Codrington (Barbados Plantation owner and appointed governor-general of the Leeward Islands) in 1710, he willed two of his Barbados plantations totaling seven hundred acres, part of the island of Barbuda, and three hundred slaves to the SPG. Further, Codrington's actions transformed the SPG into a slave-owning organization.[6]

John Wesley, being keenly involved in the SPG, was able to obtain financial backing and an organizational platform to communicate his numerous religious publications, which provided practical instructions to missionaries ministering in foreign parts on the means to catechize among enslaved Africans in the British American colonies and the West Indies. The Codrington Plantations were managed on behalf of the SPG, and their operational oversight was supervised by a board of trustees of the society headed by the archbishop of Canterbury (the principal leader of the Church of England) and a committee of Church of England bishops.

Plantations managed on behalf of the SPG were reliant on a regular supply of newly enslaved Africans from West Africa, due primarily to smallpox and dysentery.[7] In 1740, four out of every ten enslaved persons bought by plantations were reported to have died within three years, resulting from mistreatment and ill health. Furthermore, Gerber illustrates in *Christian Slavery* that both Elias Neau (SPG missionary in New York), Francis Le Jau (SPG missionary in Goose Creek, South Carolina), predecessors of Christopher Codrington, and members of the SPG petitioned the

---

6. Gerbner, *Christian Slavery*, 92.
7. Wilder, *Ebony and Ivy*, 84.

Assembly of New York to pass reform laws that would ensure the legality of enslaving people who were Christianized.[8]

These laws (acts of assembly) focused on accommodating and appeasing the enslavers and reassuring them that the conversion of enslaved people did not equate to freedom or social equality. Francis Le Jau reassured plantation owners that the enslaved did not equate their baptism and conversion with physical freedom by vetting the enslaved immensely on their loyalty to their enslavers before they could be baptized and accepted into Christian society.

Further, Francis Le Jau forced all adult enslaved men and women to recite the following declaration prior to being baptized: "You declare in the presence of God and before this Congregation that you do not ask for the holy baptism out of any design to free yourself from the duty and Obedience you owe to your Master while you live, but merely to the Members of the Church of Jesus Christ."[9]

JOHN WESLEY'S METHODOLOGY FOR SLAVE CONVERSION

From its inauguration, the motivation of the SPG, through its financial support of plantation missionaries and lectionary publications (formal prayers, Scripture lectionary, hymns, and sermons), was meant for the docility and acculturation of the enslaved Africans for the purposes of indoctrinating them into cerebral bondage and cultural-racial inferiority, a mission which "young" John Wesley perpetuated as a foreign missionary on behalf of the Anglican Church during his eighteen months of ministry in the British Colonies of Georgia and South Carolina.

Moreover, John Wesley rigorously required the Anglican Church's "Means of Grace" (baptism and the Lord's Supper) to be administered as often as possible during his parish work in the Colony of Georgia. Like the Anglican missionaries before him, Wesley intended to convert enslaved Africans from the sinfulness of West African spiritual traditions such as Udo and to save their eternal souls through the practical methodology of a "leader system."

The leader system divided society members into small groups led by authoritarian teachers who functioned as spiritual guides for enslaved

---

8. Gerbner, *Christian Slavery*, 117.
9. Gerbner, *Christian Slavery*, 125.

people, addressing both heavenly and earthly moral concerns. According to Noel Leo Erskine, professor emeritus of theology and ethics at Candler School of Theology, the class leaders became somewhat more than mere teachers; they were guides who were instructed to lead the enslaved on a strange spiritual transformation, and their power over the small groups was authoritarian to the point of tyranny.[10]

It is worth noting that plantation owners and missionaries feared African spiritual traditions such as Obeah, Myal, and Vodou because they felt that the languages, rituals, and beliefs would inspire the enslaved to unite and revolt. Throughout John Wesley's maturity as a foreign missionary and reiterating his father's support concerning infant baptism, he placed special interest on baptizing the infants of enslaved people who had been Christianized.[11] It was common for adult Christianized enslaved people to misinterpret the connection between baptism, citizenship, and freedom regarding infants.

To reduce the confusion about whether Christian baptism brought about liberty, plantation owners advised the newly converted enslaved people that they and their baptized infants were free within the bounds of the plantation. However, if they ran away from the plantation and the safety of the master, their freedom would be stripped away, placing themselves at risk of being re-enslaved by a cruel plantation owner. By highlighting the liberty within the borders of the plantation, enslavers attempted to illustrate their goodwill; however, their primary desire was to maintain the status quo and reduce the enslaved people's desire for freedom beyond the plantation.

Anglican missionaries stationed on plantations were tasked with teaching Christian virtues and morality to the enslaved, which emphasized the practical duties of charity, honesty, justice, mercy, piety, temperance, sobriety, industry, fidelity, and obedience to their owners, who also served as the earthly representatives of God. Heitzenrater states that "Dr. John Burton informed John Wesley that one purpose of the SPG was the conversion of Negro slaves and that a door was open to this end in Purryburg, South Carolina."[12]

John Burton's letter to John Wesley on September 28, 1735, from Eton College states,

10. Erskine, *Plantation Church*, 91.
11. Heitzenrater, *Wesley and the People*, 200.
12. Heitzenrater, *Wesley and the People*, 67.

> One end for which we were associated was the conversion of negro slave. To date, nothing has been attempted in this manner. But a door is opened, and not far from home. The Purrysburgers [in South Carolina] have purchased enslaved people; they act under our influence, and Mr. Oglethorpe will think it advisable to begin there. You see, the harvest is truly great ["And who is sufficient for these things?"]; this is a point among others to be kept in view.[13]

Moreover, for Anglican missionaries, the building of God's kingdom on earth was directly associated with the agricultural and industrial developments in the Americas and British West Indies, which continued the expansion of the British Empire into foreign lands. God's earthly kingdom would be developed through the spreading of the gospel to foreign parts from the free labor of enslaved Africans and by the selective slaughter of Indigenous people.

The common mindset of the Anglican missionaries, Salzbugers, and Moravians (who were expelled from Germany), and most White settlers in the Colony of Georgia during the 1700s was that the Negro and Indigenous person were both slightly higher than the beast of the field regarding their culture, intelligence, and physical makeup. In addition to the SPG, the notion that the Negroes were inferior was a fundamental thought in the establishment of the Society for the Conversion and Religious Instruction and Education of the Negro Slaves in the British West India Islands in 1794.[14]

Bishop Beilby Porteus (son of Virginian planter Robert Porteus and president of the Society for the Conversion and Religious Instruction and Education of the Negro Slaves in the British West India Islands) provided instruction to the Anglican missionaries in the British West Indian Islands on how to govern their actions regarding the enslaved people, planters, and the social elites. Bishop Porteus advised Anglican missionaries, "You must be careful to give no offence either to the Governor, to the Legislature, to the Planters, the clergy, or any other class of persons in the Island; but to demean yourself humbly, quietly, and peaceably towards all men; not interfering in the commercial or political affairs of the island but confining yourself entirely to the business of your mission."[15]

Furthermore, Bishop Porteus also provided the missionaries with special instructions regarding their engagement with the enslaved population

---

13. Smith, *John Wesley and Slavery*, 37–38.
14. Goveia, *Slave Society*, 264.
15. Goveia, *Slave Society*, 284.

of the island. Bishop Porteus encouraged the missionaries to "appeal first to the emotions of the Negroes, leaving instruction in doctrine and scriptural knowledge to the second stage of moral and religious training."[16] According to Elsa Goveia, there was no doubt that the final object was a change of moral and religious conduct among the enslaved people because of their conversion. Goveia further stated that "the missionary was instructed to do his best to gain the goodwill and affection of his converts to reinforce his spiritual influence over their development."[17] Moreover, the instructions stated,

> You will enter into habits of acquaintance and familiarity with them, will treat them with kindness and condescension, will convince them that you are interested in their happiness and welfare, will watch the most favorable opportunities of instilling principles of virtue and religion into their hearts, will improve to the best advantage the seasons of sickness and affliction, when their minds are most open to serious impressions, and will, in short, endeavor to turn every little incident into an instrument of moral and religious improvement.[18]

From Slave Traders to Abolitionists

In the late 1700s, like John Wesley and William Wilberforce, Bishop Porteus understood the need to convert enslaved people as a means of successfully managing slave societies and promoting England and the Anglican Church to the world as just and humane. However, beneath the surface of England's industrial revolution were the newly developing labor forces in India and Asia, increased slave rebellions throughout the British colonies, and America's demand for liberty. These were all important factors behind Wesley, Wilberforce, and Bishop Porteus' desire for pious social reform and inspiration to abolish slavery.

Prior to these factors, the three British elites were influential in England's monopoly on slavery in the British colonies and as partakers of the goods and services derived from slave labor in the Americas and the Caribbean Islands. Furthermore, they transitioned later in their lives from being active participants in maintaining slave societies and allies of

---

16. Goveia, *Slave Society*, 286.
17. Goveia, *Slave Society*, 286.
18. Quoted in Goveia, *Slave Society*, 286.

plantation owners to employed antislavery activists serving the British Crown. Throughout the 1700s, these British elites held dual identities, being both enslavers and antislavery advocates (slave-trade abolitionists), acting in loyalty to the British Crown. However, for plantation owners in the Americas and British West Indian Islands, these men had betrayed their trust by becoming antislavery advocates.

According to Heitzenrater, John Wesley embraced a negative viewpoint of Native Americans in general. In his journal, Wesley described the Creeks and other Indigenous tribes as gluttons, drunkards, thieves, dissemblers, liars, and worse. He further stated that they showed no inclination to learn anything, least of all Christianity. However, Wesley deemed that, out of all the Indigenous Nations, the Choctaws were the least corrupt, so the Choctaws were the target group Wesley hoped to catechize.[19] John and Charles Wesley perpetuated a theological belief that the Negro and Indigenous person were created by God and endowed with "Free Grace," which they received graciously from God. Through God's Free Grace, the Negro and Indigenous person could be awarded heavenly salvation through Christian conversion and by being obedient to their earthly masters.

In opposition to John and Charles Wesley's Free Grace theology, George Whitefield (Anglican priest), along with Peter Bohler (Moravian), adhered to John Calvin's predestination doctrine, which taught that God had predetermined the fate of lesser creatures such as the Negro and Indigenous person and that these so-called "beasts of the field" were not susceptible to God's salvation due to their lowly status.

Although Wesley's' social and religious understandings may have elevated Negroes and Indigenous people to somewhat human status, which differed from the beliefs of Whitefield and Bohler, Charles and John still embraced racial and cultural bigotries that implied that Negroes and Indigenous people were innately inferior biologically in comparison to Anglo-Saxons and all other Europeans without any possibility of ever becoming equally intelligent as Europeans without first having been acculturated into Western culture. Even then, Whites would continue to evolve at an accelerated rate.

While many Methodist scholars liked to highlight John Wesley's and George Whitefield's emotional dispute over slavery and their parting of ways over the issue of slavery, the two men remained on good terms until Whitefield's death. In fact, John Wesley eulogized Whitefield at Whitefield's

19. Heitzenrater, *Wesley and the People*, 67.

funeral in London in 1770.[20] While Wesley and Whitefield may have disagreed on the humanity of the Negro and whether slavery was aligned with biblical Scripture, the two men wholeheartedly agreed that slave conversion was necessary for the safety of the plantation owners and their property.

In addition, they both agreed with the notion that Africans and Indigenous people were innately inferior, and Anglican and Methodist clergy felt that Christian conversion could minimize slave uprisings and escapes. According to William Pollitzer, "Methodist leaders organized White missions to enslaved people and stressed that Christianity, properly interpreted, could be a safeguard against rebellion."[21]

On October 14, 1735, John Wesley voyaged with his brother Charles (secretary of Indian Affairs and secretary to General Oglethorpe), Benjamin Ingham (friend), Charles Delamotta (friend), and General James Oglethorpe to Gravesend. Seven days later, on October 21, 1735, they voyaged from Gravesend to the Colony of Georgia on the *Simmonds* (merchant ship).[22] The voyage across the harsh Atlantic Ocean took 109 arduous days, including a stopover on the Isle of Wight. The crew arrived in the Georgia colony on February 4, 1736, and Wesley first set foot on American soil on Friday, February 6, 1736.[23] John Wesley served as both chaplain and missionary, and while sailing to the Colony of Georgia, Wesley practiced German to converse with the Moravian passengers.

According to John Wesley, his "chief motive is the hope of saving his soul."[24] Furthermore, as Wesley matured (at age 43), he illustrated in his 1743 writing of the "General Rules," that Africans needed to be spiritually transformed through Christian conversion, which would save them from damnation. In Henry Adams's book, *Methodism in the West Indies*, he states that "Methodism is primarily an evangelistic agency." Adams's quote was derived from the eleventh rule of John Wesley's "Rules of a Helper." Therein, Wesley says,

> You have nothing to do but to save souls, and without doubt, this simple policy has, in the long run, secured a greater and surer advance in moral and civil reformation than a direct interference with existing conditions or political questions as such. There is no

---

20. Wason, *Religion of the Heart*, 57.
21. Pollitzer, 136.
22. Smith, *John Wesley and Slavery*, 38.
23. Smith, *John Wesley and Slavery*, 39.
24. Smith, *John Wesley and Slavery*, 38.

doubt that the efforts to promote the moral and religious improvement of the slaves, without interfering with their civil condition; did more for the West Indian negroes than any attempt on the part of the missionaries at "interfering with civil condition."[25]

As illustrated in his "General Rules," John Wesley's missionary enthusiasm was solely focused on the need to evangelize and convert the enslaved Africans and Indigenous people for their moral and spiritual reform, which assisted in creating docile enslaved people befitting slave societies and justified the murder of hundreds of thousands of Indigenous people.

Historians such as Albert J. Raboteau, professor of religion at Princeton University, illustrated that the SPG missionaries who were appointed to the colonies of Georgia and South Carolina had no yearning to liberate the Africans from bondage, but rather, their motivation was to cultivate docile enslaved people for plantation owners.[26] In addition to cultivating enslaved Africans, missionaries belonging to the SPG such as Charles Wesley, worked to convert Native Americans to Christianity.[27]

In July 1736, John and Charles Wesley traveled from Savannah, Georgia, to Charleston, South Carolina, which was the brothers' first journey to Charleston, and the brutal realm of slavery they witnessed would change their views on slavery forever, more so for young Charles than older brother John. Charles left for England in anguish after serving only five months in the colonies.[28]

In Charles's private journal dated August 2, 1736, he explained,

> Nor is it strange, being thus trained up in cruelty, they should afterward arrive at so great perfection in it; that Mr. Star, a gentleman I often met at Mr. Lasserre's, should as hem himself informed L[asserre], first nail up a negro by the ears, then order him to be whipped in the severest manner, and then to have scalding water thrown over him, so that the poor creature could not stir for four months after. Another much-applauded punishment is drawing their slaves' teeth. One Colonel Lynch is universally known to have cut off a poor negro's legs; and to kill several of them every year by his barbarities.

---

25. Quoted in Adams, *Methodism in the West Indies*, 17.
26. Raboteau, *Slave Religion*, 291–318.
27. Smith, *John Wesley and Slavery*, 40.
28. Smith, *John Wesley and Slavery*, 41–42.

> It was endless to recount all the shocking instances of diabolical cruelty which these men (as they call themselves) daily practice upon their fellow-creatures; and that on the trivial occasions. I shall only mention one more, related to me by a Swiss gentleman, Mr. Zobuberbuhler, an eyewitness, of Mr. Hill, a dancing-master in Charlestown. He whipped a she-slave so long, that she fell at his feet for dead. When, by the help of a physician, she was so far recovered as to show signs of life, he repeated the whipping with equal rigour, and concluded by dropping hot sealing-wax upon her flesh. Her crime was overfilling a teacup.[29]

John, who was not as emotionally disturbed by the brutality as his younger brother Charles, was requested by Rev. Alexander Garden (SPG affiliate and Anglican bishop of London commissary) to preach the morning service the following day. During the morning service, John Wesley noticed an estimated three hundred enslaved Negroes in attendance, and he later retraced a conversation in his journal that he had with one of them. John Wesley writes, "O God, where are thy tender mercies? Are they not over all thy works? When shall the Son of Righteousness arise on these outcasts of men, with healing in his wings?"[30]

John Wesley's journal entry references the low status of the enslaved and the extremely harsh treatment of the slaves. John does not demand that the enslaved be freed, but rather, he summons the enslavers to be more humane regarding the treatment of their slaves. On April 23, 1737, John Wesley could not depart from Charleston, South Carolina, due to stormy weather, so Rev. Thompson, minister of St. Bartholomew (near Ponopon), offered John a horse for transportation and instructed his slave to guide John to his residence. There, at Rev. Thompson's estate, John met a slave woman named Nanny. John held a conversation with Nanny, whom he thought to be more intelligent than some of the others because she was formerly a house slave of an Anglican minister in Barbados. Finding that Nanny was a good listener, John talked to her for some time regarding the Christian doctrines of good and evil.[31]

Concerning the conversation, John Wesley wrote in his journal, "The attention with which this poor creature listened to instruction is inexpressible. The next day, she remembered readily answering every question

---

29. Smith, *John Wesley and Slavery*, 42.
30. Wesley, *Journal*, 1:40.
31. Smith, *John Wesley and Slavery*, 47.

and said she would ask him what made her show her how to be good."[32] Throughout John Wesley's three journeys to Charlestown, South Carolina, between July 1736 and December 1737, he was requested as a special guest of South Carolina's most prestige slave plantation owners to dine at their estates—Alexander Skene, Hugh Brian, Samuel Eveleigh, Alexander Garden, William Bellinger, and Colonel William Bull.[33]

Methodist historian Warren Thomas Smith, in his book *Wesley and Slavery*, illustrates John's admiration for Hugh Brian's compassion for his slaves. Quoting Smith, "Wesley was patently impressed by Brian's kind treatment of his slaves and mentioned him thirty-seven years later in writing, *Thoughts upon Slavery.*"[34]

Moreover, William Bellinger and the other plantation owners were highly impressed with John Wesley's preaching and his plantation missionary efforts to the enslaved and understood him to be an ally of the institution of slavery. Throughout his travels in the Colony of South Carolina, plantation owners frequently provided John with personal enslaved people as travel guides and personal servants to accompany him. According to Smith, Bellinger instructed one of his slaves to guide John to Purrysburg, South Carolina.[35] Purrysburg was the first settlement in the Colony of South Carolina to introduce slavery.

On April 15, 1737, while residing at Colonel Bull's plantation. John was so charmed by the estate that he referred to the plantation as "the pleasantest place he has yet seen in America. "[36] Colonel Bull, in response to the 1739 Stono Rebellion, introduced the Negro Act of 1740. The Negro Act of 1740 made it illegal for enslaved Africans to move abroad, assemble in groups, raise food, earn money, and learn to write. In addition, the Negro Act of 1740 gave enslavers the right to kill rebellious enslaved people. The act remained in effect until 1865.

Moreover, Colonel Bull proposed to the British King's Royal Council that Indigenous people be employed to track down runaway slaves.[37] The Negro Act of 1740 was a codification of White supremacy. On September

---

32. Wesley, *Journal*, 1:48.
33. Smith, *John Wesley and Slavery*, 35–54.
34. Smith, *John Wesley and Slavery*, 50.
35. Smith, *John Wesley and Slavery*, 50.
36. Smith, *John Wesley and Slavery*, 46.
37. O'Neall, *Negro Law*, 1–68.

10, 1735, Samuel Eveleigh, another of John Wesley's associates, issued an address to the trustees of Georgia entitled "Reasons for Slave Labor."

Eveleigh argued that the Colony of Georgia's financial future relied on the introduction of slavery.[38] These plantation owners were John's long-term personal friends, fellow Anglican priests, and SPG associates. In general, South Carolina plantation owners valued "young" John Wesley's plantation missions and considered him a knowledgeable friend to both the plantocracy and the British Crown. John Wesley was appointed by the SPG and sought after by these plantation owners (also members of the SPG) to proselytize to their enslaved people as a means of encouraging moral behavior designed to curtail slave revolts and increase work production on the plantations, enhancing plantation owners' profit margins.

In Nick Lindsay's book, *And I'm Glad: An Oral History of Edisto Island*, he illustrates that John Wesley founded the mission station on Edisto Island, where Calvary African Methodist Episcopal Church is currently located. Lindsay further explained that the mission station, in its beginning, had all White members but did not flourish, which led the Whites to give up the station to Black people.[39]

According to historian Charles Spencer, South Carolina's Lowcountry was a primary focus of the early Methodists, including John Wesley, Charles Wesley, George Whitefield, Bishop Thomas Coke, and Bishop Francis Asbury.[40] Each of these Methodist forefathers visited and preached in the city of Charleston, South Carolina. Spencer further highlighted that both John and Charles traveled to Charleston in 1736 and that John visited Charleston twice in 1737, leaving behind rumors that he had stopped in Edisto and founded a church there (later known as Calvary AME Church).[41]

In 1791, Beverly Allen was appointed Methodist missionary to Edisto Island, which ended in scandal and the murder of a US marshal at the hands of Allen.[42] While there is no evidence of Methodists establishing a White Methodist church on Edisto Island before the Civil War, Methodists continued to evangelize and engage in missionary work to the enslaved at eleven plantations and chapels across the island, converting 345 adults and

---

38. Baker, "John Wesley's Last Visit," 265–71.
39. Lindsay, *And I'm Glad*, 79.
40. Spencer, *Edisto Island*, 111.
41. Spencer, *Edisto Island*, 111.
42. Spencer, *Edisto Island*, 111.

catechizing 180 children.[43] The South Carolina Lowcountry was highly attractive to early Methodists because it was rich, fertile ground for the newly developing plantation aristocracy and provided evangelical opportunities for the church.

Historians point to Charleston, South Carolina, as the "Ellis Island" of the North American slave trade. Gadsden's Wharf, Port of Charleston was the largest slave port in the United States.[44] Early Methodist fathers such as John Wesley and George Whitefield, as well as William Capers and many other missionaries from competing Protestant denominations, understood the township of Charleston and its surrounding areas to be bountiful for religious missions, plantation ownership, and capital investments. Both George Whitfield (Providence Plantation) and William Capers (Bull Head Plantation) owned slave plantations in the Charleston area. Attempting to locate a single plantation in the South Carolina Lowcountry is equivalent to searching for a single tree in the Blue Ridge Mountains—plantations were plentiful throughout South Carolina's Atlantic Coast.

JOHN WESLEY: PERPETUATION OF THE INSTITUTION OF SLAVERY

Through John Wesley's authoritarian leadership and the practical theology evident within his numerous religious publications, Methodist enslavers could cultivate the minds of their enslaved to see Christian conversion as a doctrine of social holiness that highlighted a Calvinistic work ethic and heavenly salvation in exchange for physical liberation that would most likely have been gained through longstanding slave insurrections and revolts. In Warren Thomas Smith's book *John Wesley and Slavery*, he highlights a conversation recorded in Wesley's journal on March 1, 1756, between Wesley and Samuel Davies (fourth president of Princeton University), which illustrated Davies's receipt of Christian education books from John Wesley for Negroes in Virginia.[45]

Davies, owner of enslaved people himself, believed that enslaved people deserved direct access to the gospel equal to that of their masters. Davies justified his position of enslaving people by arguing that he was a benevolent master—this attitude was consistent with the Presbyterian

---

43. Spencer, *Edisto Island*, 111.
44. Preservation Society of Charleston. "Gadsden's Wharf."
45. Smith, *John Wesley and Slavery*, 61.

doctrine of the day, which insisted that slavery was a political matter and not a concern of the church. According to Davies, "Of all the books sent by John Wesley, none pleased the slaves more than the Psalms and Hymns, which enabled them to gratify their peculiar taste for psalmody."[46] Davies's demand for the Christian educational books was in response to the growing population of Negroes residing in Virginia, which had reached one hundred fifty thousand—half the population of Virginia.

Although the "mature" John Wesley argued against slavery, he was in support of converting the enslaved, which, in return, benefited plantation owners and assisted in developing and maintaining the social-racial order that allowed slavery to flourish during the colonial period.

In conjunction with John Wesley's leadership and Christian publications (his first publication of a collection of psalms and hymns was published in Charleston, South Carolina, in 1737) that provided enslavers the educational tools they needed to catechize and convert their slaves into obedient Christians, in 1747 John wrote and published a medical handbook: *Primitive Physick*. *Primitive Physick* was infused with John's belief in holistic salvation (mind, body, and soul), whereby he provided his readers with easy and natural methods for curing common diseases.

Primitive Physick was of great use to plantation owners and slavers in caring for the physical health of their enslaved individuals, and it helped them avoid incurring additional costs by hiring expensive physicians or veterinarians. While it is common for Methodist scholars to insinuate that John Wesley's publications highlight his devout love for all of humanity, one could equally argue that John Wesley's publications helped to safeguard and perpetuate the institution of slavery, creating financial profit for British plantation owners in the Americas and the West Indies.

According to Henry Adams, "By the year 1838, eighty-three Methodist missionaries occupied the West Indian mission field, and 42,928 members were enrolled upon its registers and by far, the greater number had been slaves."[47] The successful growth of slave conversions and the increase in production that plantation owners experienced were a direct result of John Wesley's devotion, leadership, and numerous publications.

The missionary zeal for the enslaved during visits to Antigua by Bishop Francis Asbury, who arrived in Antigua on February 22, 1775, and Thomas Cokes, who arrived in Antigua on December 25, 1786, was reinforced by

---

46. Smith, *John Wesley and Slavery*, 61.
47. Adams, *Methodism*, 15–16.

Exclusive Theology

John Wesley's desire for good health and social harmony on British governed plantations throughout the island. The missional and evangelical zeal that Bishop Asbury and Cokes demonstrated in Antigua among the enslaved was also evident in Georgia. On April 9, 1788, Bishop Asbury conducted the first Methodist Annual Conference at the fork of the Broad River in Wilkes County, Georgia. Ten people were present, including Hope Hull, who is now regarded as the "Father of Georgia Methodism." Bishop Asbury was dedicated to the evangelization of Georgia, making seventeen trips to the state.[48]

While many Methodist historians argue that Nathaniel Gilbert freed his many slaves and provided them with land before his death, Keith Dutton, church historian at Wesley Chapel, London, refutes this claim. According to Dutton, although Nathaniel Gilbert was sensitive to the social conditions of the enslaved population, Gilbert did not emancipate his slaves upon his death because, as mentioned before, freeing enslaved people in the British Islands was not a lawful act.

Enslaved people were constituted as property under British Property Law.[49] After the death of Nathaniel Gilbert, France Gilbert (Nathaniel's brother) was given ownership of the Gilbert Plantation, enslaved people included. In addition to British Property Law forbidding plantation owners from emancipating their slaves in the British West Indies, in 1736, before John Wesley converted Nathaniel Gilbert's three enslaved women in Wandsworth, England, Prince Klaas (Kwaku, his African name) along with 87 other enslaved people attempted to organize a revolt against thirty-eight hundred White residences on the Island. The plantation owner discovered the plot, and Prince Klaas was executed via the wheel along with the other 87 supposed insurrectionists.[50]

Further, David Gasper illustrates numerous instances on the island of Antigua where plantation owners (serving as both plantation masters and government officials), acting in accordance with the Slave Code, received compensation from the state for the execution of enslaved people accused of physically harming or resisting the punishment of their masters. According to Gasper, in 1714, Richard and Baptist (two enslaved people)

---

48. Georgia Historical Society, "First Methodist Church."
49. Dutton, "Chapel Font."
50. Dash, "Antigua's Disputed Slave Conspiracy."

were executed for murdering John Haynes, and their owner, John Roe, was awarded compensation for their deaths.[51]

Moreover, during that same year, Mingo (an enslaved person) was also executed for laying hands on his master, Humphrey Davis, for which Davis petitioned for Mingo's execution and received compensation.[52] Throughout the West Indies, slave insurrections were a constant threat to plantation owners and the financial welfare of soon-to-become Great Britain, so enslaved people's mobility was extremely limited.

Nathaniel Gilbert is credited with the success of evangelizing and converting large numbers of "saltwater" Africans (enslaved people born in Africa) and bred enslaved people in the West Indian Islands into Christianity, and for providing a racial hierarchical structure of Methodism that promoted Black inferiority and White superiority among the island residents. This racial hierarchy could not have been accomplished without the ongoing support of Wesley's leadership and publications. Moreover, Gilbert's lowly worldview of people of African descent and their need for Christian salvation to redeem them from heathenism was very much a part of John Wesley's thinking, although Wesley later advocated for emancipation, which was motivated by the British Crown's desire to end violent labor protests throughout England over the negative impact slave labor had on employee working conditions and wages.

For Gilbert and Wesley, slavery was both a blessing and a curse for plantation owners and Britain. However, for British expansion, it was considered a necessary evil by the Anglican Church and the British Empire. On the one hand, the institution of slavery was considered theologically problematic and socially inhumane. On the other hand, the enslaved could be converted to Christianity, and Britain could further increase its socioeconomic expansion through the means of slavery.

As John Wesley's journal entry from November 29, 1758, illustrates, "I rode to Wandsworth, and baptized two Negroes belonging to Mr. Gilbert, a gentleman lately come from Antigua. One of these is deeply convinced of sin; the other rejoices in God, her Savior, and is the first African Christian I have known. But shall not our Lord, in due time, have these heathens also 'for His inheritance?'"[53]

---

51. Donoghue, *Black Breeding Machines*, 289.
52. Donoghue, *Black Breeding Machines*, 289.
53. Quoted in Smith, *John Wesley and Slavery*, 64.

Wesley's journal entry leads one to suppose that he believed that through the means of the institution of slavery and Christianity, the heathen Africans could also experience God's salvation. In 1786, there were 1,890 Negro members of the newly formed Methodist Episcopal Church, and 1,000 of these Negroes were residing in Antigua, while only two Whites had become Methodists during this period.[54]

Furthermore, by 1796, over ten thousand enslaved people had been converted to Methodism throughout the West Indies. In 1834, at the point slavery was abolished on the island of Antigua, the Anglican and Methodist missionaries had proved so successful in their conversion of the enslaved and maintaining social control that not one incident of violence had been reported leading up to emancipation—it was a peaceful transition of power.

According to Brian Dyde, the Anglican and Methodist missionaries were so effective in their social engineering practices, particularly for enslaved mothers and their children, that even the low infant mortality rate (less than one infant in twenty births died) was attributed to the work of missionaries.[55] The success of plantation missions could not have been possible without the practical knowledge and leadership of John Wesley, as well as the evangelical work of Black preachers and laypersons who served as mediators between the plantocracy and the enslaved.

JOHN WESLEY'S *PRIMITIVE PHYSICK*

In addition to holy Scripture, John Wesley's interest in the well-being of the whole person (the mind, body, and soul) was best understood through his ongoing engagement in missional theology and his study of the *Psychology of Health* that embodied scientific reasoning, which inspired Wesley to write and publish a medical text in 1747: *Primitive Physick: Or, an Easy and Natural Method of Curing Most Diseases*. *Primitive Physick* was concerned with the spiritual and physical health of the poor in Methodist societies in England, Ireland, and America.[56] Methodist plantation owners in the American colonies and the West Indies, whose desires were to improve their own family's health and the health of their enslaved, particularly that of the enslaved women, would reference readings such as *Primitive Physick* for the betterment of their plantations. The health of enslaved women

---

54. Graham, *Black United Methodists*, 19.
55. Donoghue, *Black Breeding Machines*, 277.
56. Malony, "John Wesley's Primitive Physick."

was essential to the overall well-being and long-term profitability of the plantation.

Furthermore, the reproductive systems of young, enslaved women were the primary means for maintaining stable labor populations and growth on plantations. No matter how large or small, almost all slave plantations participated in slave breeding. For Methodists, adhering to Wesley as their spiritual leader and now understanding the relationship between maintaining good health and profit, Methodist plantation owners began to invest in their slaves' health care in addition to their spiritual well-being. In care of enslaved women's reproductive health, Southern medical physicians in training, who were enrolled in medical schools such as Atlanta Medical College (currently Emory University School of Medicine) and Augusta Medical College, would often receive their surgical experience by mutilating the bodies of enslaved women without the use of anesthesia.[57] In the antebellum South and British West Indies, many Methodist plantation owners were considered, in some regards, to be more humane than other religious sects. However, Methodists were vested in medical practices, which included the mutilation of enslaved women and men.

Prestigious Southern Methodist colleges like Emory University, later belonging to the "Magnolia Conference," can trace the history of their medical schools to the brutal actions of slave breeding and the bloodletting of the reproductive systems of enslaved women. The primary motivations of these elite Southern Methodist–affiliated medical colleges and Methodist plantation owners were to increase their financial profits and elevate their social status at the expense of the enslaved. The health care of enslaved women and men was simply a by-product or a means to an end for the medical practitioners and plantation owners.

In addition to overseeing the medical care of the enslaved, many of these Southern medical doctors, being plantation owners themselves, were also interested in the spiritual enlightenment of their enslaved, which, for owners, translated into docile enslaved people and profit gains. These medical professionals understood the connective power of mental/spiritual and physical health, and how these two disciplines, if applied successfully, could not only maintain a healthy slave population but could also provide safety for themselves against slave rebellions.

By implementing a holistic-practical theology that promoted mental, spiritual, and physical health, plantation owners hoped to create a moral

57. Schwartz, *Birthing a Slave*, 227–56.

Christian foundation for their enslaved and for the outside world, which would highlight slavery as being both humane and divinely sanctioned by God. With the hiring of Methodist ordained and lay preachers (many of whom were also medical doctors) to uplift the moral values and beliefs among the enslaved, the day-to-day running of the plantation proved very profitable for both the plantation owners and the church.

In general, Methodist preachers and plantation owners were viewed by most enslaved people as good Christians and humane owners, for whom the enslaved had developed a sense of love and loyalty. Moreover, Wesleyan theology, which taught Christian perfection (entire sanctification), was the ideal theological perspective for plantation owners and for the majority of the enslaved who would later claim Methodism as their faith tradition. Methodism upheld Anglican values and beliefs of individual righteousness and social holiness without jeopardizing financial profits, which plantation owners and England so strongly desired.

In addition, Methodism also emphasized the importance of good health and heavenly salvation, which the enslaved understood, at a basic level, to be an act of inclusion and acceptance. This status was in comparison to the Moravian plantation owners, whom the Methodists understood to be their brethren, who deemed that the enslaved were innately created for a lifetime of earthly bondage, acting in accordance with God's divine order.[58]

JOHN WESLEY INSPIRES CONTEMPORARIES AND GENERATIONS OF METHODISTS

John Wesley's experience as a foreign missionary evangelizing enslaved Africans and Indigenous tribes in the Colony of Georgia inspired his contemporaries, including George Whitefield and Nathaniel Gilbert, to view Methodism as an industry-friendly movement. For plantation owners, Methodism embodied the social-behavioral procedures useful for plantation management, which White clergymen and slaveholders felt the African and Indigenous person needed for their awakening from spiritual and cultural ignorance. As a pastor, Gilbert preached a message of "heavenly salvation" to his enslaved from the rear porch steps of his mansion. Gilbert introduced Methodism to the West Indies, which was comprised primarily of Negroes, particularly enslaved African women.

---

58. Bethabara, "Stories of Bethabara's Enslaved."

John Wesley and the Early Methodists in Georgia

While Wesleyan scholars have historically presented John Wesley and Methodism as embracing an anti-slavery position, the research illustrates that Methodism was a leading religious dogma used to expand the plantocracy, slave breeding, and racism in the West Indies and the Americas. Both George Whitefield (British Colony of Georgia), Nathaniel Gilbert (Island of Antigua), and other Methodist enslavers would regularly petition John Wesley for financial support, medical advice, and Christian educational publications in their efforts to catechize their enslaved, creating an entire slave society.[59]

In response to the plantation owners' requests for assistance, John Wesley would readily provide his wisdom and services. The same catechism practices that were implemented on Methodist-owned sugar cane plantations throughout the Caribbean Islands were also employed by Methodist plantation owners in Georgia, South Carolina, and Virginia.

Herchel H. Sheets illustrates that John Wesley must have known, too, about Whitefield's purchase of five hundred acres of land in Pennsylvania to establish a school for enslaved people.[60] Moreover, slave ownership was not limited to individual plantation owners such as Whitefield and Gilbert only. Many Methodist congregations took part in the ownership of enslaved people and free labor. On June 10, 1783, prominent tobacconist planter James Aymar sold Peter Williams Sr. (cofounder of the African Methodist Episcopal Church Zion) and his family for forty pounds to John Street Methodist Church in Manhattan, New York. Peter Williams Sr. served as the church sexton until November 4, 1785, when he was able to purchase his freedom from the trustees of John Street Methodist Church.[61]

Wesley stated that he "hoped to learn the true sense of the gospel of Christ by preaching it to the heathen."[62] In general, White Protestant superiority was the core belief held among Anglican missionaries in the Americas and the West Indies on both sides of the antislavery–proslavery debate. The idea of racial, ethnic, and cultural supremacy united plantation owners with their White brethren who desired to abolish slavery. Slavers and abolitionists may have differed over the issue of institutional slavery, but for the most part, both sides shared the belief that Africans and Native Americans were created inferior to Whites and did not warrant full social

---

59. Sheets, *Methodism in North Georgia*, 37.
60. Sheets, *Methodism in North Georgia*, 37.
61. Asbury, "Journal and Letters," ch. 1.
62. Smith, *John Wesley and Slavery*, 38.

equality. John Wesley was no exception to this thinking, and neither were many of the White Georgia Methodists who came after him throughout the Five Phases of Methodism in Georgia, which are as follows:

- Associated Methodist Church (1828–1830)
- Methodist Protestant Church (1830–1916)
- Methodist Episcopal Church, South (1916–1939)
- Methodist Church (1939–1968)
- United Methodist Church (1968–present)

Chapter 5

From Plantation Missions to the Rise of the Central Jurisdiction

In 1738, replacing John Wesley as the foreign missionary, celebrity evangelist George Whitefield journeyed to the developing Colony of Georgia (the first colony to be founded without slavery), which was organized through a philanthropic group connected to the SPG and SPCK.[1]

Prior to 1750, the trustees of the Georgia Colony banned slavery in the colony until Methodist clergyman George Whitefield advocated for the introduction of slavery. Whitefield published "Letter to the Inhabitants of Maryland, Virginia, North and South Carolina," criticizing plantation owners for keeping their slaves ignorant of Christianity.

Furthermore, Whitefield attempted to appeal to the hearts of the enslavers and argued that Christian slaves would be more faithful and docile after their true conversion. Whitefield's letter to plantation owners has been described as the first formal defense of slavery in the Atlantic world.[2] According to Herchel H. Sheets, Georgia had outlawed the importation of enslaved people from other states, but the law was not enforced and did not prevent enslavers from relocating to Georgia and bringing their enslaved with them.

By 1790, the enslaved population comprised 35.9 percent of the state's total population of 82,548, and by 1830, it had increased to 42.6 percent of the total population of 516,823. Sheets illustrates that the total number

---

1. Gerbner, *Christian Slavery*, 189.
2. Gerbner, *Christian Slavery*, 189.

of Black people in Georgia in 1830 was 220,017, and of that number, only 2,420 (1.1 percent) were free Blacks.[3]

Throughout the 1830s, Georgia Methodists had unequivocally denounced the abolition of slavery. The Georgia Conference regarded the conduct and activities of Northern abolitionists and all other slave abolitionists to be meddlesome, reckless, and un-Christian in opposition to the true biblical gospel that upheld slavery and the authority of states' rights.

On November 18, 1836, during the Georgia Annual Conference of the Methodist Protestant Church, a resolution was passed to address clergy members and lay delegates regarding the issue of slavery. Bishops presiding over the conference claimed that slavery was not a moral evil, but rather, the abolitionists were the primary problem.[4] Furthermore, the attendees were to instill an attitude of obedience and Christian faithfulness into the enslaved. Modern practices of exclusive theology held among conservative, White, North Georgia United Methodists regarding race, sexuality, and ethnicity were also illustrated in the proslavery theology of White Georgia Methodists during the 1800s.

Moreover, the homophobic and racialized attitudes and behavior traits that are hidden beneath the surface in today's United Methodist Church were passed down from earlier Anglican/Methodist foreign missionaries such as John Wesley and George Whitfield. John Wesley was constantly aware of the success his practical and systematic theology had in proslavery societies, largely due to the financial gains earned by Methodist plantation owners, the establishment of new Methodist societies, and the number of slave conversions.

Today's North Georgia United Methodists' practice of exclusive theology is deeply rooted in White Protestant supremacy and conservative politics adopted from earlier Georgia Methodists who were pro-slavers. The transatlantic slave trade was abolished by both England in 1807 and the United States in 1808.[5] However, during the 1790s and early 1800s, America's Southern states entered a golden age, which depended upon local slave breeding and interstate slave trading. The increased need for slaves resulted from the global demand for cotton ("white gold"), which was produced at an increased rate through the invention of the cotton gin, patented at Yale

3. Sheets, *Methodism in North Georgia*, 37.
4. "Minutes."
5. Kendi, *Stamped From the Beginning*, 136.

College (now Yale University) by alumnus Eli Whitney in 1794.[6] Whitney relocated to the Mulberry Grove Plantation (the state's oldest plantation built in 1736) near Savannah, Georgia.

The invention and introduction of the cotton gin led to the increased number of slaves in Georgia by more than 300 percent and made plantation owners immensely wealthy and politically powerful. Captain John Cuthbert originally owned the plantation. However, after his death, the property was willed to his sister Anne Cuthbert. In 1739, Anne became the first woman to own and operate a slave plantation in the colony of Georgia.[7] Furthermore, in 1785, in honor of General Nathaneal Greene's efforts during the American Revolutionary War, the Mulberry Grove Plantation was awarded to him. Following General Greene's death, the plantation was left to Catherine Greene, his widow.[8]

The implementation of the cotton gin, in conjunction with local slave breeding and interstate slave trading, revolutionized the Southern economy. The cotton gin enabled Southern planters to produce at a much faster rate, and as a result, increased the demand for younger enslaved people to harvest the white gold. For plantation owners, slave breeding was less stressful because they did not have to worry about the language and cultural barriers that came along with saltwater enslaved people.

However, even with bred enslaved people, the issue of slave uprisings was always a pressing concern for plantation owners and the White commonwealth because it was common for bred enslaved people to inherit the desire for liberation from their African ancestors, and they would often destroy the crops as a means of protest and rebellion. Historically, plantation owners were constantly fearful of slave revolts, primarily amongst saltwater enslaved people demanding freedom.

For plantation owners, it was much more difficult to subjugate enslaved Africans who were once free and make them docile, obedient, and productive slaves. In addition, the overhead cost and dangers associated with transporting enslaved people from West Africa to the West Indies and the Americas had become too expensive and dangerous. Slave breeding within the boundaries of America was more financially beneficial long-term, and the risk of slave revolts, plantation owners believed, could be lessened through the introduction of a systematic theological approach that

6. Kendi, *Stamped From the Beginning*, 126.
7. Nicholson, "Subsumed by Industry."
8. Mulberry Grove Foundation, "Timeline of Mulberry Grove."

would be taught from conception and reinforced throughout adulthood. The systematic theological approach was intended to instill practical habits that would impart Protestant Christian moral beliefs and work ethics, which could be managed by plantation owners and missionaries throughout the enslaved child's natural life and be passed down generationally from mother to child. This systematic theology was grounded in a racial caste scheme that was designed to reinforce notions of White supremacy, good Protestant Christian society, and inferior-docile behavior for the enslaved.

According to Albert J. Raboteau, "Enslaved people distinguished the hypocritical religion of their masters from true Christianity and rejected the slaveholder's gospel of obedience to master and mistress."[9] In the late 1700s, in conjunction with the invention of the cotton gin and the increase, primarily in Northern Virginia, North Carolina, and the Caribbean, of plantations breeding enslaved people, Negro preachers were also necessary for the profitability of plantations, the reduction of slave revolts, and for the successful Christian conversion of bred enslaved people. The Negro preachers were highly effective in gaining trust among their fellow enslaved individuals and were able to convey the desires of plantation owners to the enslaved.

White Methodist clergy and missionaries (many owning plantations and enslaved people themselves) understood Negro preachers to be a vital asset to the long-term success of the plantation by serving as the masters' agents and by being moral examples to their fellow enslaved. Slavery was always a political-religious issue for Methodists in the Americas and the West Indies because the institutions of slavery placed financial profit in direct conflict with the moral Christian lesson of "love God and love neighbor," illustrated in the Gospel of Matthew (22:37–40).

However, Methodists were able to find a political-religious loophole that would justify their aspirations for financial profit gained through free slave labor and their understanding of biblical Scripture. During the 1780s and 1790s, Methodists globally, including a few Georgia Methodists, were adhering to John Wesley's theological claims that "slavery was morally indefensible—to say nothing of its being completely at variance with the Christian gospel."[10]

In short, the Methodists began claiming that the institution of slavery was immoral and sinful. However, with the economic revitalization that the cotton gin provided, Methodist plantation owners worldwide quickly

---

9. Raboteau, *Slave Religion*, 294.
10. Smith, *John Wesley and Slavery*, 91.

reversed course, arguing that slavery was a political matter that should be administered according to state legislation and that slavery was not an issue of the church. Holding dearly to this proslavery stance, they demanded an immediate increase in enslaved people.

According to Wilkes County, Georgia historian Robert M. Willingham (also a historian of Washington First United Methodist Church, Washington, Georgia), "By 1844, in the South within the Methodist Church, 200 traveling preachers held 1,600 slaves, approximately 1,000 local preachers held 10,000 slaves, and about 25,000 members held 207,900."[11]

As mentioned previously, the transatlantic slave trade had been abolished in America in 1808, thirty-six years earlier; however, due to the enslaved average lifespan of an enslaved person being seven years, Methodist enslavers relied heavily on slave breeding and interstate trading to maintain their slave populations and plantation vitality.

BISHOP WILLIAM CAPERS: SUPERINTENDENT OF PLANTATION MISSIONS

Methodist forefathers of plantation missions, bishops William Capers (Owner of Bull Head Plantation, Berkeley County, South Carolina) and James Osgood Andrew, both North Georgia slave plantation owners, offered little-to-no interest in emancipating the enslaved, but they instead looked to catechize their enslaved through the use of rudimentary Christian instructions (not including reading and writing). This taught the bonded persons to have moral discipline in their duties and to be obedient servants of God and to their earthly enslavers, which extended to all White citizens no matter their social status.[12]

Bishop Capers was born on January 26, 1790, to Mary and Major William Capers in St. Thomas Parish near Charleston, South Carolina, on his family's rice plantation. Bishop Capers's grandfather, John Singeltary, was an early convert to Methodism in South Carolina, and in 1808, William Capers would follow in his grandfather's footsteps, converting to Methodism at a camp meeting. Bishop Capers founded the Asbury Mission for the Creek Indians, where he served seven years as superintendent and was later appointed the secretary of the Southern Missionary Department of the Methodist Episcopal Church, South.

11. Willingham, *History*, 12.
12. Richey et al., *American Methodism*, 72.

Exclusive Theology

In 1840, Bishop Capers, an enslaver, had extended the mission to enslaved people in every Southern state, and by 1844, eighty missionaries under his supervision oversaw more than twenty-two thousand enslaved people residing on plantations.[13]

As the superintendent of Missions to Creek Indians and enslaved people for the South Carolina Conference, which covered South Carolina, Georgia, and Alabama, Bishop Capers was committed to the Christian education and moral conversion of the Creek Indians and enslaved people for the safety and economic betterment of his fellow plantation owners, Methodist parishioners, and clergy. For Southern plantation owners, Bishop Capers was the perfect choice to serve as superintendent of the slave missions due to his family's history as rice planters and plantation owners, which provided him with practical experience in plantation and slave management. Bishop Capers, like John Wesley and Methodist plantation owners before him, looked to impart moral habits that would inspire obedience and good behavior in the enslaved through the means of Christian education and conversion.

Further, William Capers Sr. and Bishop Francis Asbury were associates, and during Bishop Asbury's travels to Charleston, South Carolina, he would visit with William Capers Sr. at his Bellevue plantation (Georgetown County, South Carolina). In addition to being a third-generation Methodist, Bishop Capers was provided with a comprehensive understanding of Methodism through his father's close association with Bishop Asbury and later serving as an apprentice to Methodist preacher and circuit rider William Gassaway.

Southern plantation owners needed someone who was both familiar and loyal to their racial ideas and Southern social values and beliefs and skillful at catechizing enslaved people. Like George Whitefield early in Georgia's Methodist history, Bishop Capers could champion the causes of plantation owners and successfully convert Negroes into a submissive religiosity.

---

13. Huff, "Capers, William."

Bishop William Capers. Photo, the General Board of Global Ministries of the United Methodist Church

In 1828, the total number of Black attendees of the Methodist Episcopal Church was 59,056 among its 421,156 White members, the larger percentage of whom were enslaved people residing on Southern plantations.[14]

With the large number of enslaved persons belonging to Protestant planters, plantation owners of different denominations were constantly in fear of slave rebellions and afraid of losing financial profits. Plantation owners, such as Charles Cotesworth Pinckney (an Episcopalian and owner of Santee River Plantation in South Carolina) and Colonel Lewis Morris (owner of a Plantation on the Edisto River), appealed to the likes of Bishop Capers to tour their plantations and assess the moral condition of their slaves.

Upon Bishop Capers's assessment of the enslaved moral status, he would offer recommendations and provide names of missionaries to the planters, which he deemed could improve the morality of the enslaved, in return lowering the risk of slave revolts and creating higher financial profits for the plantation. In addition to the Southern Methodist slaveholders, to impede the abolitionist movement and to halt slave rebellions, the Methodist Episcopal Church (Northern states), during the Missouri Compromise of 1820, effectively ended the prohibition that prevented Methodist preachers and circuit leaders from enslaving people.

Moreover, in 1824, Northern Methodists ventured even further in their efforts to compromise with Southern Methodist plantation owners by

---

14. Richey et al., *American Methodism*, 72.

assisting in the organizing of the American Colonization Society (ACS).[15] The ACS, originally known as the Society for the Colonization of Free People of Color of America, supported chiefly by the Congregational, Presbyterian, and Methodist churches in the North, wished to send educated freed Blacks who were participants in the antislavery movement to Liberia and other parts of Africa as foreign missionaries.[16] They hoped that freed Blacks engaged in foreign missions far away on the African continent would break up the underground information highway between freed Blacks residing primarily in the North and the enslaved in the South. As a result, the Methodists hoped that antislavery agitation and enslaved persons' rebellions would greatly decrease. Northern Methodist church leaders such as Wilbur Fisk (president of Wesleyan University) and Nathan Bangs (secretary of the Missionary Society and editor of the Methodist Episcopal Church's widely published magazine, the *Christian Advocate*) gave their full support to the ACS.[17]

Despite Northern and Southern Methodists' diligent attempts to curtail the actions of abolitionists in the North and halt slave rebellions in the South, the most famous slave insurrection took place in Southampton County, Virginia. On August 21–22, 1831, plantation preacher Nat Turner (Baptist lay minister) and nearly seventy followers led a two-day rebellion consisting of both freed and enslaved Blacks, killing approximately sixty White plantation owners and families.[18] Soon after that, Whites organized militias and mobs and attacked Black folks in the surrounding area, killing approximately 120 Blacks—men, women, and children.[19]

In response to Nat Turner's rebellion, Bishop Capers continued to argue that under Christian conversion, slaves were more docile and certainly less prone to revolt. Bishop Capers deemed that teaching enslaved people to write and read the Bible for themselves posed a great threat to White citizens and all of society. In 1833, to guide plantation missions and prevent slave revolts, Bishop Capers drafted and published an instructional manuscript, *A Catechism for Little Children*, which would be kept in White hands (preachers, planters, and spouses). This guide was edited for use with

---

15. Richey et al., *American Methodism*, 72.
16. Robinson, "American Colonization Society."
17. Richey et al., *American Methodism*, 72.
18. Sublette and Sublette, *American Slave Coast*, 443.
19. History.com Editors, "Nat Turner."

enslaved adults and was published as an official document of the MECS until after the Civil War.[20]

In addition to Bishop William Capers's publication, other Southern Methodists also published works illustrating how to provide religious instruction to the enslaved, such as Holland N. McTyeire (*Duties of Christian Masters*, 1859), William A. Smith (*Lectures on the Philosophy and Practice of Slavery*, 1856), Richard H. Rivers (*Elements of Moral Philosophy*, 1859), and Bishop James O. Andrew (*Four Letters on the Religious Instruction of Negroes*, *New Orleans Christian Advocate*, 1856).[21]

According to Russell E. Richey, by 1843, under the Episcopal leadership of Bishop William Capers and Bishop James O. Andrew, seventeen missionaries assigned to slaveholding plantations catechized 6,556 slaves and provided Christian teaching to 25,025 enslaved children. In addition, Richey stated that one missionary assigned "in Georgia on the Savannah River Mission reported in 1835 itinerating weekly to nine plantations, catechizing orally 165 children, praying 'with the old and sick in their houses or hospitals,' and lecturing or preaching 'every night, and three or four times each Sabbath, beginning at sunrise.'"[22]

Bishop Capers's and Bishop Andrew's desire to increase the number of slave conversions had proven successful, particularly with enslaved women and children.

Bishop James Osgood Andrew. Photo, Oxford Historical Society

20. Richey et al., *American Methodism*, 73.
21. Richey et al., *American Methodism*, 73.
22. Richey et al., *American Methodism*, 73.

At Candler School of Theology, Emory University, the name Bishop James Osgood Andrew is reasonably familiar among United Methodist historians and scholars. James Andrew (May 3, 1794–March 2, 1871) was the son of Georgia's first itinerant John Andrew. Bishop Andrew was born in the township of Washington in Wilkes County, Georgia, and was converted to Methodism at a camp meeting held at Broad River Valley at the age of eighteen.[23] Soon after, young Andrew entered the conference as a Methodist minister. James O. Andrew was elected to the episcopacy at the 1832 General Conference and served as president of the Emory College board of trustees.

Further, Bishop Andrew was a strong supporter of White Southern traditions and was actively involved in providing religious publications aimed at evangelizing Indigenous people and combating Catholic authority in Latin America.[24] Bishop James O. Andrew gained notoriety in both the Northern and Southern states among Methodists for his reluctance to free his slaves, in particular an enslaved biracial girl—referred to as Kitty Andrew by White folks of Oxford and known to local Black residents as Catherine Boyd.[25]

---

23. Willingham, *History*, 13.
24. Willingham, *History*, 13.
25. Avis Williams, personal interview with author, Sept. 14, 2022.

MISS KITTY AND THE METHODIST CHURCH SCHISM OF 1844

Catherine "Miss Kitty" Andrew-Boyd (1822–1851). Photo, Oxford Historical Society

Not only was Bishop Andrew's first wife a slave owner, but so was his second wife, Leonora Greenwood (and hence, he was legally a slaveowner too). According to the 1840 census reports, Bishop Andrew, a resident of Newton County, Georgia, was the owner of thirteen enslaved people, most notably an enslaved person named "Miss Kitty." Kitty Andrew Shell (later married to Nathan Shell) was born in 1820 and died in 1851 and was the only enslaved person buried among Whites at the Oxford Historical Cemetery. A memorial stone was placed at the base of a tree to mark the location where she was buried. Kitty's burial stone is located near Bishop Andrew's burial plot, numbered 171A.[26]

---

26. Oxford Historical Society, "Catherine."

Exclusive Theology

Catherine "Miss Kitty" Andrew-Shell Burial Stone, Oxford Historical Cemetery, Oxford, Georgia. Photo, S. Redmond Collection

Catherine "Miss Kitty" Andrew-Shell is perhaps the most unrecognizable and central figure behind the national division of the Methodist Episcopal Church in 1844, which lasted for nearly a century until the Methodist Church reunified in 1939.[27] Moreover, the church schism ignited a division between the Northern and Southern states, giving birth to the American Civil War (April 12, 1861 to April 9, 1865).[28]

Kitty was a twelve-year-old Mulatto enslaved person given to Ann Amelia MacFarlane (Bishop Andrew's wife) by Mrs. Powers of Augusta, Georgia.[29] The agreement between Mrs. Powers and Bishop Andrew

27. Oxford Historical Society, "Catherine."
28. Sheets, *Methodism in North Georgia*, 69.
29. Mills, "James Osgood Andrew."

stipulated that once Kitty reached the age of nineteen, she would be given her freedom and sent to the Colony of Liberia in West Africa.[30]

It was customary for the ACS to oversee the repatriation of formerly enslaved people to West Africa, so this was the likely agency that would assist in Kitty's resettlement. In an interview, Avis Williams (lifelong Oxford, Georgia resident and Emory College alumna) suggested that Kitty may have served as Bishop Andrew's concubine, and they possibly conceived three children together—two boys and a daughter.[31] During Kitty's enslavement to Bishop Andrew, the Methodist Episcopal Church as a national organization had become opposed to slave ownership, primarily in the Northern states.

According to Avis Williams, Kitty refused the offer to repatriate to Liberia because she was not originally from Africa and would miss her family and friends, so she wished to remain in Georgia.[32] In 1844, under Georgia law, Bishop Andrew could not legally offer Kitty her freedom within the state of Georgia. Like plantation owner Nathania Gilbert in Antigua and other Methodist plantation owners, Bishop Andrew informed Kitty that she was free within the boundaries of his estate. Although Bishop Andrew gave Kitty her unofficial freedom within the bounds of his estates, she still was required to perform her daily duties and maintain their slave-master relationship.

Moreover, regarding Kitty's refusal to be repatriated to Liberia, historical records indicate that it was not uncommon among educated freedmen to decline the ACS's offer to return to Africa. Many of the enslaved feared being separated from their families and believed that the ACS was attempting to resettle them in foreign parts to terminate the abolitionist movement by limiting antislavery propaganda developed by freedmen and White antislavery activities being secretly transported to slave societies throughout the Southern states.

Members of the ACS believed they could kill two birds with one stone by repatriating the freedmen to West Africa and by stopping the spread of antislavery opposition while simultaneously using the freedmen to establish Christian societies in West Africa.[33] Many White Northern Methodists working in conjunction with their White Southern Methodist brethren were also conspiring to bring about an end to the abolitionist movement in the Northern states and desired to maintain slavery in the Southern states through their affiliation with the Freedmen's Aid Society. In short, enslavers

30. Sheets, *Methodism in North Georgia*, 69.
31. Avis Williams, personal interview with author, Sept. 14, 2022.
32. Avis Williams, personal interview with author, Sept. 14, 2022.
33. Kendi, *Stamped from the Beginning*, 145–46.

feared that freed Blacks would either help the enslaved to run away or, worse, encourage them to revolt against their enslavers.

Miss Kitty Andrew Shell's Cottage (City of Oxford, Newton County, Georgia). Photo, S. Redmond Collection

Miss Kitty's Cottage is currently located in the rear of First Methodist Church in Oxford, Georgia, which is a quarter of a mile north of Emory College and the Emory College Confederate Officers' Cemetery. Additionally, the messaging on the plaque above was written by the largely White Newton County, Georgia, Historical Committee.[34]

If Kitty's dedication and loyalty to the Andrew family are sincere, then it's an example of the effectiveness Methodism had on many house-enslaved people in North Georgia and elsewhere across the South. Through the Wesleyan teachings of prevenient grace, justification, and sanctification that placed a high demand on Christian morality and dedicated work ethics, Methodist plantation owners and Negro preachers were not only able to evangelize to the enslaved people successfully, they were truly able to effectively indoctrinate enslaved children into Christianity (a form of slave religion) and plantation culture with little-to-no worry that the children may have been pre-exposed to any African spiritual beliefs and cultural values such as Obeahism, Shango, and Udo (Vodou).

Slave breeding offered the plantation owners a clean slate to educate the enslaved children without any outside threats and in accordance with what was to be beneficial to the plantation—economic profits. Not only had American Southern plantations benefited from the docile obedience and work ethic of the bred enslaved people, but so had the entire Western world. The institution of slavery (primarily through slave breeding) in the American South was vital to the establishment of the British Empire; through mass cotton production, British soldiers were supplied with cotton uniforms, which perpetuated British military dominance across Europe during the winter months.[35]

In addition, the British sold and shipped American-produced cotton throughout Europe and the global market, establishing their financial stronghold worldwide. While the British were establishing financial-political power globally, they were simultaneously destabilizing and colonizing North Africa by means of stoking divisions among Indigenous African tribes, massively deporting enslaved people across the Atlantic Ocean, and engaging in endless wars across Northern Africa for which they gained healthy profits from the trade of weapons and other materials with Muslim merchants.

The spread of Methodism in the American colonies and the West Indies proved to be highly effective in the rise of British imperialism because

---

34. Digital Library of Georgia, "Kitty's Cottage Historical Marker."
35. Sublette and Sublette, *American Slave Coast*, 24.

Methodism, like its Protestant predecessor the Anglican Church, justified slavery, capitalism, war, nationalism, classism, and racism, all in support of British expansionism. While Methodism sought to elevate the White race spiritually and socially, the church embraced the idea of racial inferiority regarding non-Europeans. The idea of racial and cultural superiority had quickly become institutionalized and normalized in Western Europe and throughout the New World for both Whites and POC. And, in the American South throughout the 1800s, slave breeding became associated with social status whereby Southern social elites (medical doctors, clergy, lawyers, etc.) were taking full advantage of the opportunities provided by means of slave breeding (sports entertainment, sex slaves, medical experimentation, and so forth). Georgia Methodists were at the forefront of this slave-breeding prosperity movement.

THE EDUCATION OF THE NEGRO

In addition, in the 1860s, Southern and Northern Methodists such as Atticus Green Haygood, Lovick Pierce Jr., and Richard S. Rust were able to look past their political-geographical differences and compromise to develop educational systems and institutions that would continue the promote the racial ideas of Black inferiority and White superiority and initiate racial segregation for generations to come. Atticus Green Haygood, retired Confederate army chaplain, John F. Slater Fund director, and president of Emory College, Oxford, Georgia, and Richard S. Rust, Freedmen's Aid Society field agent, were two of the leading persons who coordinated the development of educational curriculums for the founding of Negro Normalcy Schools.

According to Haygood, "There should be separate schools for Negro children. It is best for all parties. However, it may be in other sections or countries; it is not best to mix the races in Southern schoolrooms."[36] The educational curriculums were aimed at creating a "melting pot" effect, a carryover from plantations whereby Negroes were trained to assimilate and to accept their role as inferior on the plantation in racially segregated spaces.

Negro educational institutions funded through the Freedmen's Aid Society, such as Rust College, Clark College, and Dillard (Straight University), were not solely developed for the purpose of Negro social upliftment or inclusivity. These ideas of upliftment and inclusivity were publicly denoted by Black and White Methodist elites to gather financial and social support.

36. Haygood, *Our Brother in Black*, 144.

However, the primary agenda for the Negro Normalcy School was to maintain oversight of the Negro's progression and to continue racial separation across the deep South. While it was necessary for Northern and Southern Methodists to coordinate together to oversee the "Negro problem," both sides continued to distrust the motives of the other.

Southern Methodists, with Haygood leading the charge, argued that Northern Methodists had too much influence over Negro education in the South. Haygood, Lovick Pierce (the father of Methodism in Georgia), and other leading Southern Methodists argued that the educational curricula designed in the North and taught in the South did not correspond with the Southern beliefs and values of racial separation and Negro inferiority.

Pierce displayed a sincere passion for the introduction of education for White women of Georgia with the founding of Wesleyan College (the first chartered college for women in America) on December 23, 1836, in Macon, Georgia.[37] However, the education system that he deemed Negroes should have would be one that reinforced the racial exclusive values and beliefs of the old South.[38]

Haygood, former Sunday school secretary of the Methodist Episcopal Church, South, had proven successful in writing and producing Sunday school literature throughout the denomination, particularly in his home state of Georgia.[39] In addition, Haygood could develop graded materials and uniform lessons, skills needed in the development of religious-vocational curriculums—one for White students and one for Black students. With Haygood's educational background and the loyalty of his fellow Southern Methodists, along with Rust's Northern financial support and insight, they were able to develop and implement educational curriculums that would give birth to the Jim Crow Era, particularly in the field of education.

Rust Chapel United Methodist Church (an African American congregation that's named in honor of Richard S. Rust) in Oxford, Georgia, was established in 1867 for the Black attendees who once attended "Old Church" Methodist Episcopal Church, South in Oxford, Georgia, alongside their masters. The Old Church was established in 1841, and its congregation consisted of wealthy White plantation owners and professors affiliated with Emory College who resided in Newton County, Georgia.

---

37. Sheets, *Methodism in North Georgia*, 61.
38. Sheets, *Methodism in North Georgia*, 61.
39. Sheets, *Methodism in North Georgia*, 80.

Exclusive Theology

According to an interview conducted with Anderson Wright (Rust Chapel historian and Sunday school teacher), the Black attendees of Old Church Methodist Episcopal Church, South, served primarily as house enslaved people and domestic laborers for the professors and administrators at Emory College before and after the Civil War.

Further, Wright illustrated that the Black attendees of Old Church and later Rust Chapel served as a model community to show how Haygood and Rust envisioned Negro communities functioning throughout the new South and for Methodist colleges designed for Negroes. Following the Civil War, the Methodist religious and educational leaders not only pushed for the continued development of a permanent inferior Black underclass, but they also instituted the need for racially segregated churches and schools. While the public inkling was to uplift the Negro race through providing liberal arts and vocational education grounded in religious instruction, the connoted motivation was still to acculturate and assimilate Negroes further into Protestant White values and belief systems that safeguarded White privilege and continued to enforce racial ideas of Black inferiority.

For example, in Georgia, by the fall of 1866, Blacks had financed entirely or in part 96 of the 123 day and evening schools.[40] However, White educators and politicians still campaigned to develop and oversee Black academic curriculums and have oversight of the educational centers in general. The basic concept of the educational curricula combined Protestant Christian moral instruction with domestic servitude and vocational labor. These same components were the cornerstones of maintaining productive plantations prior to the emancipation of enslaved people. The recently emancipated Negroes of Georgia wanted funding for education but did not want White Methodists from the North or South overseeing their children's education because they desired separation from their former enslavers after being confined and abused for over two and a half centuries.

However, both the Northern and Southern White Methodists realized the potential danger of self-educated Negroes, and as a result, worked through the newly developed Freedmen's Aid Society to minimize future threats. Although Southern White Methodists were very reluctant to partner with their Methodist brethren from the North, they saw the Freedmen's Aid Society as a compromise and as a means of controlling Negro educational institutions in the Southern states.

---

40. Anderson, *White Rage*, 29.

Through the collaboration of Haygood and Rust, as many as thirty-eight mission colleges for Negro teachers and ministers had been established throughout the South between 1866 and 1892.[41] As illustrated previously, on the one hand, these newly created Negro mission colleges (HBCs) appeared to uplift the race. However, on the other hand, they reinforced the Jim Crow laws (racially segregated educational systems) that Southern White conservatives desired.

In addition, this provided White educators and religious leaders the authority to dictate Negro education for the first fifty years of the colleges' existence. In the New South, in 1882, an estimated 750,000 Black and White children had come under the instructions of these White benevolent teachers.[42] According to Herchel Sheets, by 1888, the *Wesleyan Christian Advocate* had over 7,000 subscriptions, with 3,470 of these from the North Georgia Conference.[43] The *Wesley Christian Advocate* was placed into Negro educational institutions as a means of providing moral instructions.

In the early 1880s, the board of managers of the Freedmen's Aid Society of the Methodist Episcopal Church, in conjunction with the Southern Educational Society of the Methodist Episcopal Church, South, established the Woman's Home Missionary Society.[44] The purpose of the society was to minister to and evangelize Negro women, encouraging them to establish and maintain Christian homes. Elizabeth Rust (wife of Richard Rust) was a vocal advocate for the Woman's Home Missionary Society, and her dedication to establishing mission schools for Negro girls was embraced by White Methodist women in the North and South.

For Southern White Methodist women, the Woman's Home Missionary Society merely provided them with a source for domestic servants. The Freeman's Aid Society and Woman's Home Missionary Society had done great work preparing Negroes to become teachers, ministers, and domestic servants. The education offered through the Freemen's Aid Society still transmitted the idea that Black people needed to embrace White Southern Christian values and beliefs as a means of acculturating into good White society.

For many White North Georgia Methodists, these religious societies went too far in their efforts to educate the Negro, which threatened the social status of the White commonwealth. Rebecca Felton (Early Methodist

41. Thomas, "Methodism's Splendid Mission," 139–56.
42. Born, "Richard S. Rust."
43. Sheets, *Methodism in North Georgia*, 91.
44. Brawley, *Two Centuries*, 67–136.

Exclusive Theology

feminist and an affiliate of United Daughters of the Confederacy), native of Decatur, Georgia, and wife of Methodist minister William Harrell Felton (US House of Representatives), spoke vigorously throughout her long life about the dangers of educating Black folks and the need for lynching.

On August 11, 1898, Rebecca Felton addressed the Georgia State Agricultural Society in Tybee, Georgia, whereby she stated, "The more money that Georgia spent on Black people's education, the more crime Black people committed."[45] In addition, Felton spoke publicly on numerous occasions to large, influential audiences in support of lynching Black men, who she claimed had a "desire to rape defenseless White women left alone on rural farms throughout the South. In 1922, the Board of Temperance and Social Service reported that all too often, Georgia led the nation in the number of lynchings and that from 1889 to 1930, there were more than 450 lynchings in the state, not including legal lynchings."[46]

While Mrs. Rebecca Felton was arguing that education motivated Blacks to commit crime and supported the lynching of Black men, early Black Methodist womanists such as Ida B. Wells-Burnett and Mary Jane McLeod Bethune-Cookman were diligently advocating for the education of Black people, and these brave women spoke publicly against the illegal and legal lynching of both Black females and males.

Rebecca Felton's ardent hatred of Black people was largely shared by her fellow White North Georgia Methodists, who illustrated their support by electing her as the first female to serve in the US Senate on November 21, 1922. In conjunction with now Senator Felton, North Georgia Methodist William J. Simmons was dedicated to the cause of White supremacy and racial segregation. On Thanksgiving Day 1915, William J. Simmons (imperial wizard of the Invisible Empire of the Knights of Ku Klux Klan) began a new era of the Ku Klux Klan after they had all but vanished after the Civil War and Reconstruction by marching a band of White men with burning crosses to the top of Stone Mountain, Georgia.[47]

The act of White supremacist intimidation was duplicated on August 11, 2017, at a "Unite the Right" rally when a band of conservative White men marched through the campus of the University of Virginia wielding burning tiki torches and chanting White nationalist slogans protesting the removal of the city's Confederate sculpture of Robert E. Lee. Thirty-two-year-old

---

45. Felton, "Mrs. Rebecca Felton Speech."
46. Sheets, *Methodism in North Georgia*, 143.
47. "Klan Is Established."

Heather Heyer was killed, and dozens of other protestors were injured by White supremacist James Alex Fields Jr. when he violently drove his car into a crowd of counter-protestors during the "Unite the Right" rally in Charlottesville, Virginia.[48]

Simmons's wish was to rebuild and inaugurate the new Ku Klux Klan and to impose fear on non-White Christian communities across America, particularly in the South where Black people resided in large numbers. The primary goal of the Klansmen was to stoke fear in Black sharecroppers, hoping to scare them from voting and migrating out of the South. Two years prior to Simmons's cross-burning ceremony on top of Stone Mountain, the second General Missionary Conference of the Methodist Episcopal Church, South, convened in what is now known as Lake Junaluska, North Carolina (formerly the Methodist Episcopal Church, South Retreat Center). Lake Junaluska was named after Chief Junaluska, a Cherokee chief who was credited with saving the life of Major General Andrew Jackson (seventh president of the United States) at the Battle of Horseshoe Bend.

Chief Junaluska later stated that he regretted saving President Jackson's life since Andrew Jackson issued the Treaty of Fort Jackson (also known as the Treaty with the Creeks, 1814), requiring the Muscogee (Creek) Indians to surrender their land (twenty-three million acres) and forcing them to relocate westward. On May 28, 1830, President Jackson signed the Indian Removal Act, the beginning of the "Trail of Tears." Between 1830 and 1850, approximately 60,000 Native Americans (Cherokee, Creek, Seminole, Chickasaw, and Choctaw Nations) were forcibly removed from their lands in the Southeastern areas of the United States. Between 13,200 and 16,700 Native Americans perished during the long journey west of the Mississippi River.[49]

President Jackson deemed that the Creek Indians would never completely acculturate into White society, which led him to initiate their relocation westward in commemoration of Chief Junaluska. Members of the Methodist Episcopal Church, South, who also held membership in the Klan, thought it was befitting to name the retreat center after Chief Junaluska.

Today, a statue of Chief Junaluska and a flaming (lighted) cross stand across the street from the Bishop Walter Russell Lambuth Inn as a constant reminder of Chief Junaluska's action to rescue Jackson from certain death, and Jackson's dedication to White supremacy for future White United Methodists to view in admiration. Lake Junaluska serves as a central

---

48. Burke and Sotomayor, "James Alex Fields."
49. History.com Editors, "Trail of Tears"

destination for the United Methodist Church's Southeastern Jurisdiction, which covers all the former Confederate states.

In 2005, over twenty Klansmen from Georgia, Texas, North Carolina, and elsewhere threatened to convene at the retreat center to protest a gay-inclusivity meeting sponsored by Troy Plummer, executive director of Reconciling Ministries. Over 550 people registered to attend the Reconciling Ministries' annual conference. One member of Reconciling Ministries, clueless about the Klan's connection with the retreat center, asked, "What concern is Lake Junaluska to the Klan?"[50] Similarly, very few present-day church members and clergypersons serving in the United Methodist Church can identify the historical relationship between the Methodist Church and the Ku Klux Klan.

However, during an interview with the late Linnie Booker (Booker frequently and regularly visited Lake Junaluska as a youth and Methodist pastor), she stated that she was told by a fellow White member of the United Methodist Church that "Black people have the AME, AMEZ, and CME, so White people need a church that represents them—the United Methodist Church."[51]

THE CREATION OF THE CENTRAL JURISDICTION, 1876-1974

As a result of viewing the Methodists as more humane Christians with higher values and morals, after the emancipation of slaves the newly freed men remained loyal to Methodism with the creation of the Central Jurisdiction. Following the Civil War, four Black Methodist Annual Conferences were established from 1876 to 1971, forming the Central Jurisdiction in Georgia, which is now part of the North Georgia Annual Conference of the United Methodist Church.

(1) The Savannah Conference (1876–1952) developed in the Northern Methodist Protestant Church.

(2) The Atlanta Conference (1897–1952) was organized on January 21, 1897, after dividing from the Savannah Conference in 1896.

---

50. Outtraveler Staff, "KKK to Protest."
51. Booker, interview with author, May 5, 2018.

(3) The Colored Methodist Protestant Conference (1880–1939) developed out of the Methodist Episcopal Church, South.

(4) The Georgia Conference of the Methodist Church (1952–1971) was developed at the reuniting of the Savannah Conference and Atlanta Conference in July 1952.[52]

These four Black Methodist Conferences developed out of Black Methodists' longing for autonomy following their emancipation from slavery, and White Methodists demanded racial segregation in churches and the larger society in general.

According to John H. Graham, in 1890, before the great Negro migration to the North began at the end of World War I, 92 percent of Black people resided in rural farming locations throughout the Deep South. Further, Graham illustrates that in 1910, Mississippi and South Carolina reported greater numbers of Black Methodists than the other Southern states. The Upper Mississippi Conference and the Mississippi Conference combined to claim 45,573 Black Methodists, and the South Carolina Conference reported 55,707 Black Methodist members.[53]

According to Herchel H. Sheets, the first session of the North Georgia Conference of the Methodist Episcopal Church, South was held from November 27 to December 2, 1867, in Atlanta, where Bishop George Foster Pierce served as the presiding officer and Bishop Atticus G. Haygood served the Black members. In the South Georgia Conference, reports illustrate the total membership as being 26,543 (19,626 White and 6,917 Black).

However, Sheets illustrates that by 1868, the North Georgia Conference had only 4,119 Black members, having lost 2,566 during that year. Sheets noted in the conference's minutes, "Many Colored members, not reported with North Georgia Annual Conference, remain to be reported at the Colored Annual Conference organized by Bishop Pierce in Augusta, Georgia, on January 6th, 1869." By the end of the twentieth century, membership within the North Georgia Conference had more than doubled, reaching a total of 99,009, but it had become an all-White membership.[54]

Although Black Methodist numbers declined across the deep South after World War I due primarily to Southern Blacks migrating North in search of more humane working conditions and to escape the harsh racial

---

52. Sheets, *Methodism in North Georgia*, 211–37.
53. Graham, *Black United Methodists*, 79.
54. Sheets, *Methodism in North Georgia*, 77.

environment in the South, most Black people still resided below the Mason-Dixon line where they continued to be victimized by state-enforced Jim Crow laws supported by the Methodist Episcopal Church, South.

The Central Jurisdiction, the only Methodist jurisdiction to be based solely on race, came into existence in 1940 after the Uniting Conference convened in Kansas City, Missouri, on May 10, 1939.[55] The Methodist Church (with the uniting of the Methodist Episcopal Church, Methodist Episcopal Church, South, and Methodist Protestant Church) became a reality, and the development of the Central Jurisdiction, which had commenced in the minds of both White Northern Methodists and Southern Methodists dating back to the General Conference of 1864 was also now a reality.

According to Graham, the period between 1864 and 1900 was the timeframe of the nation and the church's institutional development following the American Civil War.[56] On May 2, 1864, the General Conference of the Methodist Church was held in Philadelphia, Pennsylvania. At the conference, members were convinced that the Union army would be victorious in defeating the Confederate army and would occupy the Southern states.

In planning for institutional development in the Southern states, Methodist delegates were asking, "What is to become of Negroes?" and "How might we minister to them?" What developed out of these questions was the establishment of eight Black Mission Conferences. The Mission Conferences are listed below, with founding dates provided in parentheses:[57]

- Delaware Mission Conference (July 29, 1864)
- Washington Mission Conference (October 27, 1864)
- Mississippi Mission Conference (December 25, 1865)
- South Carolina Mission Conference (April 2, 1866)
- Tennessee Mission Conference (October 11, 1866)
- Texas Mission Conference (January 3, 1867)
- Georgia Mission Conference (October 10, 1867)
- North Carolina Mission Conference (January 14, 1868)

In the 1868 General Conference, delegates voted to rescind a portion of its 1864 legislation, and by this action, these Mission Conferences were

---

55. Davis, *Methodist Unification*, 1.
56. Graham, *Black United Methodists*, 33.
57. Graham, *Black United Methodists*, 35–45.

awarded the status of Annual Conferences. The thirteen Annual Conferences are listed below with founding dates are in parentheses:

- The Mississippi Conference (January 7, 1869)
- The Louisiana Conference (January 13, 1869)
- The Lexington Conference (March 2, 1869)
- The Florida Conference (January 19, 1873)
- The West Texas Conference (January 22, 1874)
- The Central Alabama Conference (October 18, 1876)
- The Savannah Conference (November 1, 1876)
- Little Rock Conference (February 21, 1879)
- East Tennessee Conference (October 25, 1880)
- The Central Missouri Conference (March 24, 1887)
- The Upper Mississippi Conference (February 5, 1891)
- The Atlanta Conference (January 22, 1896)
- The South Florida Conference (January 25, 1925)

This period of institutional development was a continuation of White superiority and the practice of exclusive theology, which inspired the original formation of Methodism and provided the foundational ideologies for the development of the Central Jurisdiction. On January 22, 1896, in Griffin, Georgia, the Savannah Conference was divided into two separate conferences—the Savannah Conference and the Atlanta Conference (present-day North Georgia Annual Conference). The Atlanta Conference was officially established on January 21, 1897, in the Lloyd Street Church (now Central United Methodist Church) in Atlanta by Bishop Cyrus D. Foss. The Atlanta Conference consisted of sixty-five ministers, 141 churches, and 13,502 church members across four districts.[58]

Although Northern Methodist seminaries had opened their doors to Black students, very few Blacks students attended. In 1883, in honor of Elijah H. Gammon, Gammon Theological Seminary was founded in the Bible department of Clark University in Atlanta, Georgia.[59] Gammon Theological Seminary ("School of the Prophets") became the primary training

---

58. Graham, *Black United Methodists*, 45–46.
59. Graham, *Black United Methodists*, 54–55.

institution for Black Methodist clergy and laypersons in the Atlanta Conference and for Black Methodists seeking ministerial education in the other twelve Negro annual conferences.

With racial separation being the primary motivation for segregated churches, educational institutions, and society at large, White Methodists assisted in establishing affiliated Black Methodist congregations throughout the North Georgia Conference. In 1867, Black/Colored Methodist Congregations, such as the Alpharetta Colored Methodist Church (now St. James United Methodist Church) in Alpharetta, Georgia, and Rust Chapel Colored Methodist Church in Oxford, Georgia, were established across the North Georgia Conference. Alpharetta Colored Methodist Church was founded at 109 Cumming Street in Alpharetta, Georgia, and was chartered by eight formally enslaved families (the Rucker, Manning, Chandler, Burse, Wells, Strickland, Morris, and Teasley families) that had once attended church with their masters.[60]

While White Methodists pushed for racially segregated churches, they continued to demand direct oversight of Black Methodist congregations and loyalty from Black pastors, which some Methodist scholars and church historians would argue is still the de facto practice today.[61]

May of 1920 marked a new beginning for Black members in the Methodist Episcopal Church, or so Black Methodists thought, with the election and consecration of two Black bishops: Bishop Robert Elijah Jones of the North Carolina Conference and Bishop Matthew Wesley Clair Sr. of the Washington Conference. In addition, Robert Jones and Matthew Wesley, Clair Sr. became the first two Black Methodists to be elected as general superintendents and consecrated bishops on May 20 of that same year.

The General Conference also approved women to become local licensed preachers in the Methodist Episcopal Church. On June 12, 1920, Mary E. Jones of Indianola, Mississippi, and a member of the Upper Mississippi Conference Greenwood District, became the first Black woman granted a local preacher's license.[62] However, it was not until 1956 that women were granted ordination with full clergy rights. Not until 2016, with the consecration of Sharma Lewis (a graduate of Gammon Theological Seminary), was a Black woman elected bishop in the Southeastern Jurisdiction.

60. St. James Alpharetta United Methodist Church, "Our Story."
61. Dunlap-Berg, "Black Clergy, Laity Share."
62. Graham, *Black United Methodists*, 80–89.

In 1918, during the Joint Commission meeting held in Savannah, Georgia, leading Black Methodists Bishop Robert Elijah Jones and Irvine Garland Penn (Rust College alumni and officer of the board of education for Negroes of the Methodist Episcopal Church) played an important role in maintaining the color lines by reassuring their White counterparts (both in the North and South) that they were in no way demanding social equality. Penn stated that "he himself had written the color line into the MEC book of discipline."[63] Bishops Jones and Penn comforted Southern White Methodists by rendering their support to the efforts of Booker T. Washington, who upheld the racial color line.

Bishop Jones, in his first speech at Baltimore, often repeated on the floor of the Joint Commission that he supported a racial color line and had no fears about it. In addition, Penn added that he had written the color line ideology into the Methodist Episcopal Church *Book of Discipline*.[64]

While Black Methodists were beginning to celebrate their superficial upward mobility within the Methodist Episcopal Church throughout the nation, the color line and social inequality were still very much a reality. This reality was not lost on Southern White Methodists, who widely supported the development of the Central Jurisdiction for racial segregation and institutional control. In opposition to the Central Jurisdiction, the "Committee of Five," which included James S. Thomas (Atlantic Coast Area), Richard Erwin (Baltimore), John H. Graham (Nashville/Birmingham), W. Astor Kirk (New Orleans), and John J. Hicks (Saint Louis), demanded *de facto* inclusiveness on all levels of the church.[65]

A vocal critic of the Central Jurisdiction, Joseph E. Lowery (dean of the Civil Rights Movement and member of the Southern Christian Leadership Conference) transferred from Alabama to the Georgia Conference in 1968. Lowery pastored eighteen years at Central United Methodist Church and six years at Cascade United Methodist Church (Atlanta, Georgia). Lowery commented, "It is determined that all necessary steps will be taken to eliminate any structural organization in the Methodist Church based on race at the earliest possible date and not later than three months prior to the 1972 General Conference."[66]

---

63. Davis, *Methodist Unification*, 84.
64. Davis, *Methodist Unification*, 84.
65. Graham, *Black United Methodists*, 98.
66. Graham, *Black United Methodists*, 103.

The Southern Christian Leadership Council's (SCLC) Joseph Lowery, circa 1987. Photo from the SCLC Records, Manuscript, Archives, and Rare Book Library, Emory University.

While many Black Methodists understood the Central Jurisdiction as providing some degree of autonomy and a safe space whereby they could fellowship among themselves in secret, the overarching institutional structure of the Methodist Church persisted in adhering to White superiority and racial exclusion and continued to relegate Black Methodists into an enclaved system of racial inferiority. In opposition to Lowery's hopes of bringing about closer to the Central Jurisdiction, Warren G. Booker Sr. of Lexington, Mississippi, indicated that "with the ending of the Central Jurisdiction, the only thing Black Methodists will be able to do within the newly formed United Methodist Church is to polish the shoes of White Methodists."[67]

According to Graham, all efforts to save the Central Jurisdiction failed, and on April 23, 1968, at approximately 9:30 a.m., Bishop Reuben Mueller and Bishop Lloyd C. Wicke introduced the Plan of Union. By this declaration, the Central Jurisdiction came to an end.[68] With the end of the Central Jurisdiction, Black Methodists had mixed emotions and confusion regarding their future within the United Methodist Church.

As a result of Black Methodists feeling voiceless within the newly developed United Methodist Church organizational structure, a group of Black United Methodist clergy organized the Black Methodists for Church Renewal (BMCR), designed to continue to be a voice of Black Methodists within the United Methodist Church. Moreover, the BMCR's vision and mission were created to "communicate the new self-image and attitude of the Black community to the United Methodist Church and argue that renewal must come through the redistribution of power."[69] However, my sense, having discussed the matter with leading lay persons and clergy members is that the BMCR continued to adhere to the exclusive theological and conservative values and beliefs of White United Methodists on issues such as ordaining gay persons.

---

67. Linnie J. Booker, personal interview with author, Oct. 2016.
68. Graham, *Black United Methodists*, 107.
69. Black Methodists for Church Renewal, "Our History."

Chapter 6

The Lost Cause in North Georgia

FOLLOWING THE CIVIL WAR and the abolishment of slavery in 1865, supporters of the Confederate army in North Georgia and throughout the Southern states felt a tremendous loss and witnessed their way of life change rapidly. Northern Georgians, with their financial and social status devastated at the hands of the Union army, quickly attempted to overcome their shortcomings in combat and to commemorate the Confederate soldiers. Southerners, including North Georgians, reconciled the defeat by adhering to social beliefs, values, and symbols they referred to as the "Lost Cause."[1]

According to Arthur Remillard, assistant professor of religious studies at Saint Francis University, the Lost Cause offered nostalgic White Southerners a "true history" of the Old South and the Civil War.[2] The Lost Cause was a set of social principles as well as redemptive narratives (heroic stories) that interconnected with their religious, political, and social values during the post–Civil War era, which were foundational to the antebellum South. These social principles and redemptive narratives provided the North Georgia Methodists with an ideal of a "good society," which illustrated a loyalty to Protestantism, Confederate symbols, conservative politics, and institutional racism that continued to promote racial/ethnic separation.

In North Georgia and across the Deep South, White Christian conservatives, although seeking to conform to the ways of the New South, continued to outwardly express their discontent about racial inclusion and Northern involvement in the South. The Methodist Episcopal Church, South's bishop and Emory College president, Atticus G. Haygood, became

1. Remillard, *Southern Civil Religions*, 1–3.
2. Remillard, *Southern Civil Religions*, 11.

one of the "New South's" most influential orators and editor of *The Wesleyan Christian Advocate*.[3]

As a seminary student at Candler School of Theology, Emory University, the name Bishop Atticus Greene Haygood was regularly mentioned in United Methodist studies courses and could be viewed on buildings and street signs at Emory College in Oxford, Georgia. However, not until reading Carter G. Woodson's book, *The History of the Negro Church*, wherein Woodson gives praise to former Confederate army chaplain Bishop Haygood for his leadership as director of the John F. Slater Fund that helped to finance Negro education, did I realize that Negro Normal Schools were developed from the partnership between White Northern missionaries and Southern segregationists. The partnership functioned to safeguard racial separation by establishing educational policies designed to enforce judicial supervision over Negro educational institutions throughout the deep South. As Woodson notes,

> Dr. A. G. Haygood, a distinguished churchman among the Methodist, deserves here some mention. He represented, in a large measure, the best thought in the South concerning the Negro. He came forward to impress upon the South the claims of the Negro on the "sympathy and helpfulness of all who were more fortunate, especially those who called themselves the followers of Jesus Christ." This sentiment he set forth in a book, *Our Brother in Black*, struck the North with agreeable surprise and led the South to think more seriously of another solution to the so-called Negro Problem.[4]

For White Northern missionaries and Southern segregationists, the primary goals for the development of Negro educational institutions were not aimed at fostering social equality between the races but rather to enable the advancements of the Northern industry while continuing to reinforce the Southern systems of inequity. And the promotion of a Christian-centered education that focused on Negroes' moral behavior would serve to uplift industry and social ethics.

In the years following the Civil War and Reconstruction, Bishop Haygood (president of Emory College from 1875 to 1884 and director of the John F. Slater Fund) pushed to maintain social oversight of the Negro race

---

3. Sheets, *Methodism in North Georgia*, 67.
4. Woodson, *History*, 150–51.

in the Deep South, particularly in the public areas of citizenship, education, and voting. Regarding the freedmen's right to vote, Bishop Haygood argued,

> We find ourselves face to face with as difficult a problem as was ever committed to any people of any age. Take any view possible of the history of the emancipation and enfranchisement of the negroes, and this portentous fact remains nearly a million men, who had been enslaved, were made voters before they could read. They were to vote upon the most difficult and complicated of all questions, questions of public policy involving the interests of half a continent and of nearly fifty million people, before they could read or understand the Constitution under which they were governed.[5]

Bishop Haygood began to learn the methods of the Freedmen's Aid Society by observing Richard S. Rust (secretary of the Society) during Rust's visit to Oxford Colored Church, Oxford, Georgia.[6] Bishop Haygood partnered with the Freedmen's Aid Society to fund racially segregated schools and assisted with the development of educational curriculums that focused on teaching Christian morals, liberal arts, vocational education, and self-reliance, which were all important if the New South wanted to meet the demands of industry, sharecropping, and social responsibility.[7]

North Georgia Methodists and former Confederate elites such as Bishop Atticus G. Haywood and Gustavus J. Orr (state school commissioner of Georgia) believed it necessary for White Southern teachers to assist with educating Negroes. While appearing to be socially progressive on the issue of race relations, Bishop Haygood scorned the idea of White northerners educating the newly emancipated Negroes in the South, fearing that they may offer Negroes a more condescending education that opposes Southern traditions, which may foster discontent and lack proper edification.[8]

Both Haygood's and Orr's Southern progressive ideas regarding the "Negro Problem" mirrored those of earlier Anglicans/Methodists such as George Whitefield, Nathaniel Gilbert, and John Wesley. All these clergymen understood themselves, not to be oppressors of the Negro race but rather devoted "friends" of the Negro race inspired by God to uplift the race morally. Their primary goal was to further catechize and acculturate the Negro

5. Haygood, *Our Brother in Black*, 78–79.
6. Haygood, *Our Brother in Black*, 230.
7. Haygood, *Our Brother in Black*, 145–58.
8. Haygood, *Our Brother in Black*, 150.

race into a racial caste system aimed at maintaining a cheap labor force. In addition to fearing northern missionaries' influence on Southern Negroes through the introduction of liberal arts education, North Georgia Methodists also worried that Northern whites would gain control of the new freedmen's vote, which would further impede upon their Southern institutional systems that upheld White supremacy and increase the socio-political power of the Negro race in the South. Bishop Haygood, in his book *Pleas for Progress*, illustrates, "The Negro is here and here to stay. He is a citizen armed with that thunderbolt of political power, the ballot. That it was given to him unwisely because untimely and without conditions as to the use of it; that as a rule, he is unfit to be a voter—all this I understand well."[9]

Bishop Haygood's hypothesis regarding Negroes being unfit to be voters was based on the 1870 US Census, which showed that the Negro illiterate vote in Georgia was 100,551 and 116,516 in 1880, compared to the White illiterate vote in 1870 of 21,899 and 28,571 in 1880. In addition, to the accelerated increase in the Negro illiterate vote, which outpaced that of the White illiterate vote by 24.5 percent in 1880, Bishop Haygood also compared the nationwide population growth between the White race and the Black race. Bishop Haygood stated that "the increase in the total population of the United States from 1870 to 1880 was 30.06 percent; the increase of the White race, aided enormously by foreign immigration, was 28.82 percent. The increase in the Negro population, unaided by foreign immigration, was 34.78 percent." Furthermore, he added, "One hundred years ago, there were in this country about 700,000 Negroes; now there are 7,000,000. That is, they have multiplied ten times in a century. How many will there be in 1983?"[10]

From 1883 to 1890, Haygood served as an agent for the John F. Slater Fund and the chief spokesman for the "New South." In 1887, North Georgia Methodists helped to issue an "All White Democratic Primary" in Georgia, designed to strip "Americanized African" voters—a term Haygood employed[11]—of their voting rights.[12] Bishop Haygood had a conundrum—commemorating the customs of the Old South while envisioning the advent of the New South.

9. Haygood, *Pleas for Progress*, 10.

10. Haygood, *Pleas for Progress*, 11–12.

11. See Haygood, Our Black Brother, 6–7, 17, 24, 241. This is the earliest (1881) usage I have found of the term "Americanized African" in reference to Black people.

12. Ashmore, "Thoughts on White Supremacy."

Exclusive Theology

On one hand, Bishop Haygood wanted to restrict Negroes from their constitutional right to vote. On the other hand, he was vigorously fundraising and providing institutional oversight via the John F. Slater Fund to Hampton College and Tuskegee College. Also, Bishop Haygood noted the progress that Richard S. Rust was reporting in the *Thirteenth Annual Report*, which illustrated that the Methodist Episcopal Church had legally chartered six institutions for Black Americans with collegiate power by 1870 (Central Tennessee College, Nashville, Tennessee; Shaw University (present-day Rust College), Holly Springs, Mississippi; Clark University, Atlanta, Georgia; Claflin University, Orangeburg, South Carolina; New Orleans University, New Orleans, Louisiana; and Wiley University, Marshall, Texas.)[13] Bishop Haygood noted that "there are few churches or schoolhouses in all the South, built for the use of the Negroes since the war, in which the money of Southern White people has not been freely invested. Hardly any of the Negro institutions were built without Whites Southern Methodist aid: some chiefly through their help."[14]

However, Susan Y. Ashmore, professor of history at Oxford College of Emory University, argues that "no records were found showing that Southern Methodists had contributed funds toward Negro education as Bishop Haygood had stated."[15] Historically, Bishop Haygood and North Georgia Methodists deemed that providing a Christian education to the once enslaved Negroes helped to uplift the Black race from their own savagery of the "Dark Continent" and protected the social boundaries of White supremacy. Bishop Haygood's relationship with the enslaved was that of a paternal slave owner, who expressed a mutual obligation of loyalty and community care between the White race and the Black race while maintaining the social order of White superiority and Black inferiority.

Bishop Haygood, a loyalist to his Southern brethren, was aided by White Northern industrial philanthropists and missionaries in his efforts to explore Negro labor for himself and was supported by formerly enslaved people looking to improve their social condition through education. This support enabled him to envision a New South that embodied tolerance, acceptance, and urged reconciliation. However, Bishop Haygood's New South was merely a modification of the antebellum South.

---

13. Haygood, *Our Brother in Black*, 174–76.
14. Haygood, *Our Brother in Black*, 239.
15. Ashmore, "Thoughts on White Supremacy."

The Lost Cause in North Georgia

In opposition to Northern missionaries, a few White North Georgia Methodists reluctantly took up the challenge to educate Negroes. However, they did so as a divine calling and social responsibility, believing in their Southern belief of White superiority, which demanded racial separation between Blacks and Whites. Throughout the Southern states, Jim Crow laws were established to maintain the racial boundaries between Whites and Blacks in educational institutions and the larger society.

While Bishop Haygood publicly expressed the need for Negroes' education through both liberal arts and vocational education, he also put forth the strongest argument of his fellow Southern elites for Blacks and Whites to be educated in segregated schoolhouses, which later led to economic and racial inequalities in both public and private schools. According to Bishop Haygood, "Race-separation should not cease at the expense of the White child's sincerity or of the Black child's self-respect. Sincerity and self-respect are more important than sitting together, even granting the advantages that have been claimed for the plan."[16]

Overall, North Georgia Methodists, in concert with Bishop Haygood and Gustavus John Orr (state commissioner of education), also constructed ideological boundaries between themselves and their White counterparts in the North. North Georgia Methodists perceived their way of life as exceptional in comparison to that of Whites in the North, whom they deemed to live in perpetual sinfulness and hypocrisy. For post–Civil War Southern Methodists, a just and religious society was one in which Christ was depicted as being of Western European ancestry.

For Southern Methodists throughout the Deep South, Christ was a White evangelical Protestant who preached a gospel message of Southern patriotism, industrialism, capitalism, slave ownership, American exceptionalism, and states' rights. Furthermore, Southern Methodists deemed these social constructs righteous, a form of civil religion that went beyond individual interests and served a higher good.[17]

Today, throughout North Georgia many White United Methodists maintain a similar ideology as their Southern ancestors did a century ago regarding a good society. Both their politics and religious ideas are expressed through racial reasoning, whereas American exceptionalism and Protestantism are representatives of the "American way of life" and what it means to be socially conservative. The late Robert Bellah (Elliott Professor

---

16. Haygood, *Our Brother in Black*, 145.
17. Remillard, *Southern Civil Religions*, 1–14.

of sociology at the University of California, Berkeley) explained that "the 'American way of life' . . . has a religious dimension, derived from a common history and institutionalization through national myths (George Washington crossing the Delaware), symbols (the Statue of Liberty), and rituals (Memorial Day ceremonies)."[18]

Bellah's "American way of life" theory is also represented among many conservative Whites in North Georgia's religious dimension, which also derives from their common history and institutionalization through Southern myths (Old South of Lost Cause), symbols (carving on Stone Mountain of Robert E. Lee, Thomas "Stonewall" Jackson, and Jefferson Davis), and rituals (Confederate Memorial Day). Furthermore, non-Whites who adhere to the "Southern Way of life" are acceptable within conservative White political and religious societies if they abide by the social standards of what it means to be a good American and evangelical Protestant—social standards that the founding fathers of Southern slave plantations established. In general, White, conservative, North Georgia United Methodists understood the Southern Founding Fathers' motivations for constructing a Southern way of life as being grounded in White superiority, Southern patriotism, and Protestantism.

Embracing the tradition of the Southern way of life, in November of 2012 during a Sunday-morning sermon, the pastor of Union Hill United Methodist Church stated to the congregation that "it was time for President Obama's library to be constructed in Chicago because he would lose the 2012 presidential race."[19] Historically, Union Hill United Methodist Church has been used as a voting precinct. For the 2012 presidential election, the voting results were posted outside the front doors of the church for public viewing. On November 6, 2012, as I was reviewing the presidential election results posted on the front door of the church, the pastor rushed outside and snatched the election results down from the door.

Moreover, later that morning, the pastor's mother entered my office and asked if I thought that President Obama was the antichrist. I replied, "What is an antichrist?" She responded: "President Obama is trying to destroy America, and he is a Muslim." Her comments were not at all surprising due to the pastor's (her son) reaction to the presidential election results and his previous statements regarding then-Senator Obama. In general, members of the congregation suspected President Obama of

---

18. Remillard, *Southern Civil Religions*, 3.
19. I observed the worship service and documented the pastor's sermon in Nov. 2012.

being a Muslim terrorist born outside of the United States and who had illegally acquired a US birth certificate. For conservative, White, North Georgia United Methodists, the notion that President Obama was not a US citizen connoted that he was ineligible to serve as commander in chief and had somehow stolen the presidential election. Furthermore, the pastor and other members of the congregation deemed that President Obama was an illegal immigrant radicalized by Islamic extremists to undermine America's good society while simultaneously issuing a new era of socialism.

In addition to the conservative, White, North Georgia United Methodists, White conservative Republicans throughout the United States supported the ideology that immigrants, Muslims, Asians, African Americans, Latinos, and homosexuals all represent what was deemed the "faces of evil." In Carol Anderson's book *White Rage*, she illustrates that "while the number of Whites who voted remained roughly the same as it had been in the 2004 election, two million more African Americans, two million additional Hispanics, and six hundred thousand more Asians cast their ballots in 2008."

Furthermore, Anderson stated, "What was even more unsettling to the GOP was the youth and relative poverty of those who had now joined the ranks of voters. Those making less than $15,000 a year nearly doubled their turnout to the polls, going from 18 percent in 2004 to 34 percent in 2008."[20] With the steady increase of young, lower income, and non-White voters, the idea of the "faces of evil" throughout the 2008, 2012, and 2016 presidential elections illustrated to conservative White America that their way of life was under direct threat by outsiders and if White conservatives did not take immediate action to reverse this trend, White America would be lost forever.

Throughout the Republican National Committee's (GOP) 2016 presidential nomination debates, frontrunner Donald Trump and, to a lesser degree, Ben Carson added to the "faces of evil" by debating that terrorism, immigrants, and refugees were all synonymous following the terrorist attack in Paris, France, in November 2015.[21] The "faces of evil" was a conservative ideology that intertwined conservative politics and apocalyptic theology. GOP debates served to motivate further White conservatives (including White, conservative, North United Methodists) to view immigrants, particularly those from Latin American countries and refugees of occupied Muslim nations in North Africa, as threats to America. As a

20. Anderson, *White Rage*, 139.
21. CBS News, "South Carolina Republican Debate."

result, White conservatives further immersed themselves in far-right ideologies that mimicked the beliefs and values of past right-wing political-religious groups that upheld White Christian Nationalism. With the "faces of evil" as motivation, White conservatives demanded more legislation on issues concerning immigration, religious freedom, gun expansion, and gay marriage while continuing to argue for legal limits to be placed on the federal government's authority in state affairs.

During a conversation with the Staff Parish Relations Committee (SPRC) chairperson of Union Hill United Methodist Church, he deemed that "the federal government has become institutionally weak and morally corrupted under the Obama Administration and too authoritative regarding states' rights."[22] For White conservatives, God's petition for humanity was not to include those who represented the "faces of evil" in the kingdom of heaven but rather to exclude them through the means of legislation that endorsed gun expansion, the construction of national border walls, public shaming, physical violence, and state's rights. White conservatives adopted an apocalyptic theology whereby their "good society" was being abolished by the social evils that President Obama was spearheading.

In addition, the pastor of Union Hill United Church argued that "Liberal-mainline United Methodists who embrace a theology of social justice and human equality were not truly following the message of Christ at all, but rather, they had been converted to socialism primarily due to their elitist liberal arts education—the kind education that was being demonstrated at Candler School of Theology, Emory University."[23]

So, not only did White, conservative, North Georgia United Methodists believe that America was being corrupted by the "faces of evil," but they also felt that their children were at moral risk by attending public educational institutions, whereby their children would be forced to embrace liberalism over that of conservatism. With the fear of social liberalism and the constant increase in the Latino and African American student population in North Georgia public educational institutions, many White North Georgia conservatives withdrew their children from public schools in exchange for homeschooling.

---

22. SPRC chairperson, Union Hill United Methodist Church, personal conversation with the author, Sept. 2016.

23. Pastor, Union Hill United Methodist Church, personal conversation with author, Jun. 2014.

The Lost Cause in North Georgia

According to a Pew Research Center survey from October 2022, "About seven in ten Democrats and Democratic-leaning independents (72 percent) said K–12 public schools were having a positive effect on the way things were going in the United States, and about six in ten Republicans and GOP leaners (61 percent) said K–12 schools were having a negative effect."[24] Between the years of 2012 and 2015, several parents of Union Hill United Methodist Church chose to homeschool their children and enroll their college-age young adults into local and regional conservative colleges instead of sending them to large or midsize universities such as the University of Georgia and Emory University, fearing that their children and young adults would become victimized by liberalism. The parents often complained that the public schools were not safe environments for their children and that the public schools' curricula were not in accordance with biblical Scripture.

Union Hill's pastor, after dropping out of both the University of Georgia and Candler School of Theology at Emory University, frequently referred to the Candler School of Theology as being liberal, promoting homosexuality, and having bad theology. He often referred to seminary schools as a "cemetery (place of the dead)" as a means of shaming those who were seminary trained. Moreover, although Candler School of Theology serves as the primary United Methodist seminary in Georgia and has a historical connection to the Confederacy, many White, conservative, United Methodist and Baptist pastors claimed that the seminary had become too liberal in both its biblical and social worldview, particularly regarding feminism/womanism and the LGBTQ+ community. It was common to hear White, conservative, United Methodist clergy who held appointments in the North Georgia Conference and who were alumni of Candler School of Theology justify Emory University's Southern Confederate heritage while condemning its contemporary endorsement of multicultural inclusion and gender-sexual awareness. Less than ten miles away, at Gammon Theological Seminary (the only African American United Methodist Church seminary in the United States), students often regarded the Candler School of Theology as being too liberal and racially motivated.

While Emory University, on the surface, appears to be establishing a safe space for diversity and inclusion, its past affiliation with the Southern Confederacy and the institution of slavery are still motivational factors for many White conservative United Methodist students attending seminary

24. Hatfield, "Partisan Divides over K–12."

at the Candler School of Theology who can trace their family's heritage to the antebellum South. Georgia has progressed socially since the Civil War in the early years of the 1860s and the Civil Rights Movement of the 1960s. However, with the continuous growth of cultural/racial diversity, White, conservative, North Georgia United Methodists throughout the North Georgia Conference are responding by embracing a theology of exclusion within their local churches in relation to POC and gay persons, which is evident in the number of church disaffiliations.[25]

THE PERSONHOOD OF CHRIST AND HIS MESSAGE TO SOUTHERN METHODISTS

Historically, racialized depictions of Christ and angelic figures have played a vital role in the systematic oppression of POC globally and provided a false sense of racial superiority for White people, which persists today. Throughout the North Georgia Conference of the United Methodist Church, no matter the demographic makeup of the congregation, images depicting Christ as being a White male with blue eyes and blond hair are traditionally displayed in plain view, whereby the congregation is constantly reminded of the presence of Christ and his European likeness. However, if one were to visit Central United Methodist Church (Southwest Atlanta), one would see a depiction of an angelic figure with its face painted black hanging high in a stained-glass window at the rear of the sanctuary overlooking the choir seats and pulpit. The story behind the image is that Rev. Dr. Lowery painted the face of the angel black after the assassination of his close friend, Dr. Martin Luther King Jr. in 1968 as a means of destroying images of white supremacy as a means of black pride and social protest.[26]

---

25. North Georgia Conference, "Disaffiliation Process and Information."

26. Rev. Dr. Brain Tillman's Easter Sunday Sermon. Central United Methodist Church. April 20, 2025.

The Lost Cause in North Georgia

Black Face Angel: Central United Methodist Church,
Atlanta, Georgia. Photo, S. Redmond

Out of the nearly two hundred United Methodist churches that I have visited since 2005 in the North Georgia Conference, Central United Methodist Church and Bethel United Methodist Church were the two that I toured that depicted an angelic figure as being of African ancestry or non-White. At Union Hill United Methodist Church, an image of a White Christ is displayed on the wall within the youth room.

In the spring of 2014, while participating in an immersion journey to El Salvador with Harold Recinos (professor of church and society, Perkins School of Theology, Southern Methodist University), it was common to see depictions of Christ as an El Salvadorian revolutionary and as a violently beaten martyr displayed in local churches throughout the capital of San Salvador and the surrounding countryside. Throughout the history of the Western world, oppressed POC have re-envisioned the Westernized physical appearance of Christ and reinterpreted his message through their cultural experiences as a means of solidarity, justice, and peace.

In North America and the Caribbean, Afrocentric-focused Black churches not only transformed Christ's physical appearance from being of Anglo-Saxon origin, but Jesus' message was also reinterpreted in ways that challenged the traditional Anglican interpretations that have maintained White theological beliefs and values. Noel Erskine illustrates that "the roots of the Black Church are in Africa, and this church functions at the center of social life for Africans in the Americas."[27] For the Black church, Jesus' message not only condemned the act of enslavement, but it also elevated the enslaved over that of the master by depicting Jesus and the Hebrew people to be of African ancestry. Due to the enslaved, low socio-economic position, the Black church taught a moral theology of human equality, anti-racism, love, and social justice by proclaiming the biblical view of humanity that expressed all persons are equal under God.[28]

Furthermore, Black folks' interpretation of Jesus' message opposed social norms that caused social injustice, such as capitalism, nationalism, and industrialization, resulting from the oppressed labor forces upon which America was built. The physical image of Jesus being depicted as a Black man and Mother Mary as a Black woman were outward expressions of Black folks' internal belief in their own Black power and Black consciousness.[29] James Cone, father of Black liberation theology, argues in his book *God of the Oppressed*, "It was Scripture that enabled enslaved people to affirm a view of God that differed radically from that of the enslaver. The enslavers intended to present a 'Jesus' who would make the enslaved person obedient and docile. Jesus was supposed to make Black people better-enslaved people, that is, faithful servants of White masters. But many Blacks rejected that view of Jesus not only because it contradicted their African heritage but because it contradicted the witness of Scripture."[30]

For scholars such as Peter Paris and James Cone, Jesus had been systematically oppressed and was crucified (lynched) in the same way Black people had been in the Americas and the Caribbean. In sharing the Black experience in the Americas and the Caribbean, Native Americans and Latino people presented similar accounts of their history of subjugation and scriptural interpretation of Jesus' message as a marginalized-oppressed people who had suffered systematic oppression at the hands of White supremacy.

Harold Recinos, in his book *Good News from the Barrio: Prophetic Witness for the Church*, illustrates,

> The evangelism of the crucified Lord teaches us to read the Scripture and guide life in terms of oppositional political frameworks of

27. Erskine, "Plantation Church," 95.

28. Paris, *Social Teaching*, 14.

29. For an example, see the Shrine of the Black Madonna Cultural Center in Atlanta, Georgia.

30. Cone, *God of the Oppressed*, 31.

consciousness. For instance, when Mary speaks about God in the Magnificat, the core idea of her song is the power of a God who acts in history through saving actions that reverse inequalities in the social order. Mary's song points to a set of political ideas such as the liberating power of God, problems with the social arrangements in society, and human hope in the coming of the One who breaks the economic and political conditions holding people in bondage.[31]

Additionally, Recinos highlighted Jesus' message to be a ministry of compassion and followers of Christ should engage in missional ministries as an expression of their love and faith in God, and not for industrialization and colonialization.[32] In general, Latino Christians (Barrio Christians) have historically comprehended Jesus' message to be one of communal love and social equality. According to Recinos, "Barrio Christians use the gospel both to evangelize others individually and to discern the work of God in local contexts." Furthermore, Recinos adds, "Barrio evangelism declares God's blessing comes when people serve Jesus by feeding the hungry, satisfying the thirsty, visiting the sick, welcoming the stranger, clothing the naked, going to the imprisoned, and offering more life to those denied it. Latino Christians announcing the good news assume service to the least of God's people leads away from self-absorption and toward genuine discipleship that shows the nearness of the reign of God."[33]

Latino Christians, in conjunction with African American Christians, rarely illustrate Christ's message as one that adheres to nationalism and racism. With the continuous growth of the Latino population in North Georgia, White conservatives feel threatened not only by their physical and political presence but also by their scriptural reinterpretation of Jesus' message, which highlights a demand for human equality and social justice before racial reconciliation can be fully achieved. In opposition to the ways in which Blacks and Latinos reinterpret Jesus' message, many White, conservative, North Georgia United Methodists interpret Scripture through the lens of old Southern tradition that continues to project Southern Whites as a superior race and POC as being outsiders who need to be enculturated and acculturated into the larger White, good society.

Southern Christian conservative organizations send tens of thousands of short-term missionaries into marginalized communities annually, and in

---

31. Recinos, *Good News from the Barrio*, 80–81.
32. Recinos, *Good News from the Barrio*, 80–86.
33. Recinos, *Good News from the Barrio*, 55.

many respects, these short-term missionaries feel as if their divine calling as North American Christians is to take civilization and materialism into the host communities. As previously mentioned in chapter 1, while participating in a youth minister's meeting held at Orange United Methodist Church in Canton, Georgia, members discussed engaging in a youth international mission project. During the discussion, a youth minister illustrated that the purpose of foreign missions is to "evangelize them before they attempt to get us." This youth minister had served for over sixteen years as a youth minister and had led numerous international youth mission journeys. His opinion and reputation within his local church and throughout the North Georgia Conference were greatly respected, although he understood foreign missions from the perspective of modern colonialization and human subjugation.

In addition to the youth minister, the pastor at Union Hill United Methodist Church, during one-on-one conversations, would regularly refer to the Indigenous people of Georgia (Cherokee) as having been savages and pagans. Months prior to Union Hill United Methodist Church's first international mission journey to Eleuthera, Bahamas, the pastor and a layperson informed local Cherokee County schools and nearby United Methodist Churches of our upcoming mission journey and asked if they would donate reading materials for the schoolchildren of Eleuthera. Numerous schools and United Methodist Churches throughout Cherokee County responded by donating nearly 150 elementary learning booklets. In every booklet donated, nearly all the characters consisted of one racial group—White people. When this issue was brought to the attention of the pastor and layperson, they stated that the Bahamian children were poor and simply needed learning materials and that the racial makeup of the characters in the reading materials did not matter. The idea that the host community was racially and socially inferior was predetermined by the pastor and layperson prior to having any cross-cultural/background knowledge of the Bahamian community.

In ongoing conversations with other local clergy persons in host communities, and from reading the experiences of long-term missionaries regarding working with White, conservative short-term missionaries, the greatest point of concern was the negative attitudes and rude behavior of White short-term missionaries when serving marginalized communities internationally.

REDEEMING THE WORLD THROUGH MISSIONS

According to Steve Corbett and Brian Fikkert, authors of *When Helping Hurts: How to Alleviate Poverty Without Hurting the Poor and Yourself*, the number of short-term missionaries "were 120,000 in 1989, 450,000 in 1998, 1,000,000 in 2003, and 2,200,000 in 2006. The number reflects a tsunami of epic proportions, a tidal wave of American short-term missionaries flooding the world. The cost? America spent $1,600,000,000 on short-term missions (STMs) in 2006 alone."[34]

Based on my missional experiences and reading journals and reviews of other scholar-practitioners in the field of cross-cultural short-term missions, I discovered that host communities often complained that short-term missionaries had little to no relevant cross-cultural knowledge about the community they desired to serve. As a result, the short-term missionaries would both knowingly and unknowingly offend the host community.

Corbett and Fikkert point out that the issues STMs have with cultural differences are not surface things such as "dress, food, architecture, art, etc., but rather on the differences in the value systems that silently drive people to respond in predictable patterns. These value systems involve quite a range of things, including people's view of who or what is in control of their lives, the nature of risk and uncertainty, the organization and role of authority, the nature of time, and the role of individuals versus groups."[35]

After welcoming numerous unprepared short-term mission teams, which displayed a lack of cross-cultural awareness and knowledge of the communities in which they hoped to serve, marginalized communities and host organizations began to complain about STMs' negative behavior and how this behavior causes anxiety for both the hosts and communities.

As a means of curtailing STMs' negative behavior, some hosting organizations found it necessary to implement behavior policies to manage the issue. For example, the Bahamas Methodist Habitat, as part of its process for accepting short-term mission teams, requires mission team leaders to complete a behavior compliance form for each participant to help reduce negative behavior.[36] For many host communities and disaster relief/recovery organizations, short-term missionary teams (particularly youth groups) are viewed as an opportunity to get international exposure and make money.

---

34. Corbett and Fikkert, *When Helping Hurts*, 161.
35. Corbett and Fikkert, *When Helping Hurts*, 162–63.
36. Bahamas Methodist Habitat, "Short Term Missions."

In addition to Bahamas Methodist Habitat, the United Methodist Volunteers in Mission (UMVIM) requires that the mission team leaders attend a half-day mission seminar led by a conference UMVIM coordinator.[37]

In my opinion, many of the UMVIM coordinators may have served in foreign areas and have years of missionary experience. However, they have done so with a Westernized worldview themselves. Moreover, due to having a Westernized worldview and the lack of cross-cultural intelligence training, many of these UMVIM coordinators are not aware of their own biases in relation to engaging people from different racial and ethnic cultural backgrounds.

The focus of a well-developed, cross-cultural intelligence educational curriculum should be designed to train short-term mission leaders on how to prepare their missionaries to identify the beliefs and value systems of the host community and introduce the prospective missionaries to methodologies that will assist them in modifying their behavior prior to serving and while in action. In general, most current cross-cultural training curriculums focus on issues such as fundraising, completing insurance documentation, travel logistics, and basic evangelical practices—reading and interpreting biblical Scripture.

In my opinion, very few training materials/models focus on educating short-term mission leaders on methods to identify beliefs and value systems of the host communities that exist beneath the surface, and as a result, mission team leaders simply teach their short-term missionaries about geographical aspects and how to financially prepare for a mission trip (and not a mission journey that inspires spiritual transformation) to a foreign destination whereby the host communities are generally understood to be materially poor, uncultured, and godless.

While White conservative, evangelical (this includes White, conservative, North Georgia United Methodists) short-term missionaries engaged in cross-cultural missions will refute the notion that "manifest destiny" is still the primary motivation to participate in cross-cultural missions, the feeling in many host communities is that they would rather receive financial assistance to do the work themselves than deal with unprepared short-term mission teams. Studies illustrate that short-term missionaries/volunteers serve an important role in helping materially poor countries recover from disasters by providing funding and volunteer skilled labor.[38]

---

37. UMVIM, "Trainings."
38. National Voluntary Organizations Active in Disaster, "Impact by the Numbers."

As mentioned earlier, for many cross-cultural host communities, short-term mission teams play a crucial role in their overall economic stability; therefore, they have developed methods for managing the stress of working with short-term missionaries. Instead of viewing short-term missionaries through a lens of providing social justice, typically cross-cultural host communities view them as short-term residential guests and tourists. Short-term mission teams register to stay on the host campus, where meals, lodging, and transportation are provided (an all-inclusive stay), with the hope that they will be spiritually transformed during their missional experience.

With this understanding, cultural hosts create advertisement and marketing campaigns that highlight the geographically beautiful areas and relaxing natural amenities such as sandy beaches, historical sites, and native eateries, all as a means of providing an exciting trip in exchange for financial profits and marketing. Furthermore, it has become a tradition for hosts to schedule a site visit to local elementary schools, where students perform songs and short plays for the short-term missionaries as a means of soliciting donations from individual members of the mission team on both a short-term and long-term basis.

Moreover, hosts typically structure the daily agendas of the mission teams in such a way that missionaries have little to no real contact with the native people. Depending on the overall behavior and attitude of the mission team, once they arrive on-site, the host might require that their mission project be on-site for the entirety of their visit, only visiting the outside community the day before they are scheduled to return home. Traditionally, the day before the mission team is scheduled to depart, the host allows them to visit local tourist shops. With tens of thousands of short-term missionaries from the United States scheduled to engage in cross-cultural missions annually worldwide, and with a high percentage of them traveling from predominantly White Protestant conservative communities across the South, many cross-cultural hosts identify within them a real absence of empathy for POC or their culture.

In some respects, many White short-term missionaries regard missions as an extension of their national patriotism. For example, it was common for youth and adults alike serving at Union Hill United Methodist Church to render prayers and testimonies prior to engaging in missions to local cross-cultural communities that illustrated America as being particularly blessed by God over that of materially poor nations. This White

Exclusive Theology

supremacist attitude is largely attributed to their Southern traditions, perceived US military strength, and understood wealth. In this view, a nation's military might and wealth are directly attributed to being in good favor with God, so nations lacking military might and wealth are in critical need of Protestant Christian intervention as a means of cultural upliftment and God's divine blessings.

Furthermore, White Protestant conservatives assume these materially poor nations (i.e., Haiti, El Salvador, Yucatan, etc.) will continue to remain cursed and outside of God's goodness until they fully acculturate into capitalism and submit to Western exceptionalism. Moreover, any notion or heuristic by all individuals or entire communities is outwardly illustrated as being evil and a direct threat to God's Eurocentric "good society." As a means of constructing greater sociopolitical boundaries that are geared toward excluding undesirables from gaining socioeconomic equality, White Protestant conservatives have intertwined their religious zeal with racism and nationalism, which is illustrated through the historical slogan "Don't Tread on Me."[39]

"DON'T TREAD ON ME"

The Gadsden flag, imprinted with the "Don't Tread on Me" slogan, was prominent across rural North Georgia and among White Protestant conservatives during Donald Trump's 2016 presidential campaign and throughout his first term. As if out of nowhere, the Gadsden flag began to appear on stickers, flags, and other merchandise easily purchased in rural communities and at gas stations along interstate highways.

Initially, I was unaware of the slogan's fundamental meaning as it related to the Tea Party movement or its connection to the history of Georgia Methodists or the Confederate cause. However, I did notice that the Gadsden flag had become increasingly visible in Douglasville and other nearby towns surrounding Metro Atlanta during the early to mid-2000s. In Douglasville, on numerous occasions, I witnessed the Gadsden flag being flown in conjunction with US veterans' military flags and Confederate battle flags. The flag and slogan had become visible at local public schools, on neighbors' cars, and was flown on homes. My earliest perception was that "Don't Tread on Me" was somehow associated with nationalism and patriotism. Not until serving at Union Hill United Methodist Church in

---

39. Walker, "Shifting Symbolism."

Canton, Georgia, did I gain a more in-depth understanding of the implicit belief and value systems symbolized in the Gadsden flag for White, conservative, North Georgia United Methodists and how these beliefs and values were formalized in antebellum traditions, which sustained an exclusive theology of ethnic and racial separation.

As marginalized communities seek to be included in the commonwealth of the global community, White conservatives, with equal vigor, support neoliberal agendas and reject all social actions that promote racial and socio-economic equality. Publicly, however, they desire to appear culturally welcoming and theologically inclusive. Others (non-White people) who lie outside of White conservatives' "good society" can be further exploited and marginalized through systematic institutional racism and classism in ways that are visible, lawful, and easily normalized. The slogan "Don't Tread on Me," which lay beneath the rattlesnake (divided into thirteen parts, representing the original thirteen colonies) on the Gadsden flag, has emerged as a symbol of White conservative patriotism and religious-social intolerance. The Gadsden flag, for many White Christian conservatives, is also a symbol of their faith and represents an American ethos.[40]

As a symbol of America's political libertarian traditions, the flag tells a story of social rebellion against dictatorship. For Southern conservatives who embrace the ideologies of the Tea Party movement, it highlights a golden age in Southern history when White people's livelihoods were profitable and representative of a good society. Overall, White conservatives understood cultural diversity and multiculturalism as being a direct threat to their conservative values and beliefs and unpatriotic, so marginalized groups, regardless of their religious or national affiliation, were considered immoral and a danger to the American social order of White superiority and non-White inferiority.

During multiple one-on-one interviews with White, conservative, North Georgia United Methodists, I learned that many of the interviewees had very different viewpoints on racism and the history of African enslavement from what was common among mainstream historians. While supporting politically and religiously conservative ideologies, the majority of White, conservative, North Georgia United Methodists who were interviewed opposed any claims of having a racialized worldview or of being affiliated with organizations that espoused racial aspirations. Furthermore, they would even argue that they are "color blind" and that White liberals

---

40. Volle, "Gadsden Flag."

and POC are the primary proponents of racializing America today and using the race card.

In addition, many White conservatives would suggest that the issues (incarceration, drug-infected communities, etc.) that impact African American and Latino communities today have little or nothing to do with slavery, colonization, or systemic racism, but rather, these issues are due to these groups' innate absence of intelligence and their laziness. Moreover, White conservatives had issued arguments throughout the transatlantic slave trade that Africans sold themselves into bondage, not Europeans. Because of slavery, Africans were liberated from paganism and are now uplifted into civilized human beings because of their indoctrination into Christianity and close affiliation with European culture.

Considering White Southern conservatives' worldview, which is outwardly expressed through the representation of the Gadsden flag, the underlying motivation to engage in cross-cultural missions and outreach is grounded in racial, social control, and White superiority rather than in genuine love for God and neighbor.

Chapter 7

Obama and Multiculturalism in North Georgia

On May 14, 2012, the cover page of *Newsweek* declared Obama to be "The First Gay President." Andrew Sullivan, *Newsweek* political writer, asserted that "President Obama's support for gay marriage should come as no surprise."[1] President Obama's support of same-sex marriage and the belief among White Southern conservatives that Obama was a foreign-born Muslim resonated profoundly within their consciousness and was in direct opposition to their Protestant faith. For conservative, White, United Methodists in North Georgia, President Obama was forcing them, against their will, to live in a multicultural and inclusive society—sinfulness.

In my view, President Barack Obama was more reviled in the deep rural South among White Protestant conservatives than anywhere else in the nation, primarily due to his African heritage and multicultural worldview, which Southern White conservatives understood as being countercultural to their beliefs and values. In addition to his race and worldview, President Obama's personality was not one of docility; nor was he submissive to the insults and negative criticism hurled at him and his family by presidential candidate Donald Trump.

On August 2, 2016, President Obama stated that the GOP's 2016 presidential nominee, Donald Trump, was "unfit" and "woefully unprepared" to be president of the United States after Trump had publicly criticized the

---

1. Sullivan, "First Gay President."

family of Muslim US soldier Captain Humayun Khan, who had been killed serving in Iraq.[2]

Throughout Donald Trump's 2016 presidential campaign, he continued to demean many non-White and non-Christian Americans with his divisive and derogatory statements, which present other racial, ethnic, and religious groups as being a threat to the "true" Americans—White Protestant conservatives.[3] Trump's racially divisive language was reminiscent of conversations I had with many of the laity at Union Hill United Methodist Church, in addition to the pastor.

For many White, conservative, North Georgia United Methodists and Tea Baggers throughout North Georgia, President Barack Obama was a clear representation of the antichrist whose sole purpose was to annihilate America's good society. The mere notion of President Obama serving as commander in chief of the United States was a direct insult to traditional White Southern racial values and beliefs. On November 2, 2008, I sat in Dugan's Bar in downtown Atlanta, watching the reactions of White people across the street when Senator Obama won the 2008 presidential election. Inside Dugan's Bar, Black folks were cheering loudly and celebrating Obama's presidential victory in a fashion that illustrated a change had come for POC in America.

However, in the sports bar directly across the street, White people were yelling angrily and cursing aloud and were visibly upset at the presidential election result. In that moment, I never considered how electing a Black man as president would impact ethnically and racially diverse communities. However, witnessing firsthand the responses of both Blacks and Whites on that presidential election night provided me with a more in-depth understanding of how entrenched racism was in America, particularly in Georgia and the Deep South.

Instead of the 2008 presidential election serving to build racial and ethnic bridges between White people and POC, it seemed to have inspired even greater racial and ethnic intolerance, whereby all non-White and multicultural communities were now understood to be in boundless opposition to the future of White America. This "spirit of intolerance" was on display throughout the United States, and as a result, White conservatives publicly voiced hatred toward President Obama and expressed their anger

---

2. Smith and Jacobs, "'Unfit to Be President.'"
3. Jones, "Trump, 'True' Americans Triumph."

at their local multicultural communities. And Union Hill United Methodist Church was no exception.

As mentioned earlier, the Sunday morning after President Obama was re-elected in 2012, the pastor's mother entered my office and asked, "Do you think that Obama is the antichrist?" I responded, "No," and asked her to explain what she meant by antichrist. As expected, she could not truly answer my question, so she just stood there with tears in her eyes as if the world were coming to an end. As the only non-White person attending and serving at Union Hill United Methodist Church, parishioners would frequently vent their racial frustrations to me and ask me questions about African American culture.

For many White conservatives, President Obama's ethnic heritage and racial identity were automatic indicators that he was innately inferior to Whites and their cultural norms and that his status as the US president was a direct result of affirmative action. Furthermore, they believed that liberal Whites (primarily from the North) were the puppet masters dictating President Obama's every thought and action. In addition, White conservatives deemed that all of President Obama's lifetime achievements were due to liberal Whites who were behind the scenes providing him with underserved opportunities, resulting from their support of affirmative action. In fact, they believed that all POC were innately inferior to Whites. However, due to affirmative action and what they deemed as federal government handouts such as welfare, Section 8 housing, and minority-based educational scholarships, POC were being awarded unfair opportunities more so than Whites who were more qualified and deserving.

White conservatives argued that affirmative action was an act of reverse racism being upheld through the federal government and White liberal democrats. In general, White conservatives gave little consideration to the long-term negative impacts caused by slavery, Jim Crow legislation, and segregation of African Americans. In addition, they understated how White people historically have greatly benefited from state, federal, and corporate handouts that built tremendous wealth for them as a result of four centuries (1400s through the 1800s) of free slavery, labor, and discrimination.

For White conservatives, President Obama was an overt illustration of what was inherently wrong with modern-day America. Moreover, President Obama was out of place serving as commander in chief and in direct opposition to the US Constitution and the future ambitions of the nation's founders—a nation that was racially and ethnically designed for the upliftment and generational welfare of White Protestant Christians only.

With America becoming increasingly culturally diverse, many White conservatives began to contemplate what the country's future would resemble for their White children and generations to come if something did not immediately happen to reverse the current trends. In 2012, when White conservatives failed at making President Obama a one-term president, it became evident to them that their way of life was no longer the ideal lifestyle for most Americans.

Intuitively, they witnessed what they considered was once a great nation now fall into the hands of a "Marxist" whose goal was to eradicate Western civilization.[4] To further the narrative that Obama was both a Marxist and Muslim during the 2012 presidential campaign, Donald Trump routinely questioned President Obama's citizenship by suggesting that his birth certificate had been falsified.[5] Trump's accusations were understood to be absurd and motivated by racism for many multiculturalists.

Following President Obama's 2012 re-election, Wikileaks founder Julian Assange asserted that President Obama was a "wolf in sheep's clothing."[6] For White conservatives in the United States and Europe, Assange's assertion gave credence to their earlier notions that President Obama was untrustworthy.

When President Obama was re-elected for a second term, many liberals believed that the hatred toward the president would subside among White conservatives over time, but that did not transpire. Instead of White conservatives' hatred waning over time as leftists had earlier argued, it intensified into violence across the nation, and displays of hatred for President Obama became normalized in conservative media outlets and pulpits across the North Georgia Conference of the United Methodist Church. Union Hill United Methodist Church was no exception. White conservative congregations such as Union Hill United Methodist Church and Douglasville First United Methodist Church were encouraged to see their Southern racial traditions and evangelical exegetical interpretation of Scripture as one harmonious divine truth without any possibility of being immoral and sinful.

4. Associated Press, "Is Obama a Socialist?"
5. ABC News, "How Donald Trump Perpetuated."
6. Agence France-Presse, "Julian Assange."

CONSERVATIVE MEDIA JUSTIFICATION OF RACISM

White conservatives primarily relied on Fox News political commentators such as Bill O'Reilly and Sean Hannity for their sociopolitical truths, which also embodied conservative religious ideologies. White conservatives regarded both CNN and MSNBC as being too liberal and as representatives of President Obama's devilish agenda. However, POC understood Fox News to be the public representative and political voice of social divisiveness that was inflaming systemic racism and violence toward non-White groups.

Many multicultural communities felt that Fox News justified racism and even inspired violence against POC, particularly when it came to issues of police brutality and murders committed by White police officers that involved African Americans and Latino Americans. In the shooting death of Trayvon Martin, a seventeen-year-old Black young man, by George Zimmerman, Fox News commentators quickly took to Zimmerman's defense by stating that the shooting was in self-defense, although Martin was unarmed and a minor.[7]

Not at all surprising, the then-pastor of Union Hill United Methodist Church told me over lunch that he was in support of the court's decision to acquit Zimmerman. Following the murder of Trayvon Martin, it became normal for the mainline news networks to report the murder of African Americans by White police officers seemingly daily, and in each case, conservative news networks robotically justified the murders, particularly when the murder involved the killing of a Black male.

Conservative news networks commonly shared their negative commentaries about the poor state of African American communities, with a particular interest in Chicago, President Obama's hometown. For White conservatives, the ongoing gang violence in Chicago's African American communities illustrated President Obama's lack of leadership and was evidence to them that African Americans were innately violent and naturally drawn to a lifetime of crime. White conservatives consciously ignored any possibility that the violence and crime that existed within Black and Brown communities could have stemmed from centuries of unresolved issues that resulted from generational poverty, racial exploitation, segregation, and slavery.

On one hand, White conservatives believed that the issues African Americans faced were innate to Black culture and all self-inflicted. However, on the other hand, those African Americans who were educationally and

---

7. Fox News, "Trayvon Martin Attacked George."

financially affluent became so through acculturation and affirmative action. As mentioned previously, African Americans were considered innately inferior to Whites, and President Obama was no exception to the rule. Not only was President Obama considered to be racially inferior according to White conservatives, but he was also deemed to be a radical Muslim and an illegal immigrant born outside of the United States of America.

In 2011, Donald Trump used both his sociopolitical popularity and conservative news networks to try to force President Obama into displaying his birth certificate to the public. This act gave rise to the Birther movement.[8] In conjunction with Donald Trump's foolish claim that President Obama was not a US citizen, many White conservatives in the North Georgia Conference also felt that President Obama was a Muslim and an illegal immigrant seeking to undermine the US Constitution and overthrow capitalism.

Furthermore, President Obama's claim of America being a pluralist nation and accepting of religious diversity stoked fear in the minds of conservative parishioners in both the United Methodist Church and the newly forming Wesleyan Covenant Association (WCA) and Global Methodist Church (GMC) that America was no longer under the control of White evangelical Protestants. The WCA served as an advocate for the formation of the GMC after several years of collaboration. The GMC developed from conservative churches seeking to leave the United Methodist Church, primarily due to disagreement over LGBTQ+ issues.[9]

The notion of America being lost to secularism and immigrants was particularly adhered to by White conservative baby boomers (those born between 1946 and 1964), who were the majority in the United Methodist Church, WCA, and GMC. Donald Trump's 2015 presidential campaign slogan, "Make America Great Again," touched the hearts of White conservative Methodists because it echoed their fears that the American Constitution and Protestantism were under siege by foreign terrorists and that President Obama was the ringleader of this neo-secular-far-leftist movement aimed at demolishing America's White privilege.

The members of Union Hill United Methodist Church embraced this apocalyptic narrative and felt that if something radical were not done immediately to overturn this leftist shift, the country would be lost forever. Many White conservatives, North Georgia United Methodists, and WCA

8. ABC News, "How Donald Trump Perpetuated."
9. See Global Methodist Church, "Our Formation."

pastors capitalized on the distress by furthering this apocalyptic narrative that America's end is near by preaching that homosexuals, immigrants, and Muslims were all in opposition to the teaching of the gospel and American values and beliefs.

Although the pastor of Union Hill United Methodist Church's tenure came to an end before Donald Trump announced his bid for the presidency, his sermons were in direct line with Donald Trump's sociopolitical viewpoint throughout his 2016 run for the White House. Donald Trump's television popularity and direct opposition to President Obama made him a perfect Republican candidate for White, conservative United Methodists, Tea Baggers, and the WCA. The pastor of Union Hill United Methodist Church, like that of Donald Trump, used racial identity as a methodology to stoke the fear of White folks to believe that POC had caused harm to the well-being of White America.

This thinking laid the platform for the WCA to disaffiliate from the United Methodist Church and to be in opposition against what they perceived to be a threat to their good White supremacist society. On November 29, 2016, more than three weeks after the presidential election in which Donald Trump defeated Hillary Clinton, I met with the Union Hill United Methodist Church's SPRC chairperson for lunch. During our lunch meeting, he shared his thoughts on President Obama's legacy during his time in office. The chairperson repeatedly referred to President Obama as a failure and praised Donald Trump for using harsh language throughout his campaign to become President.

Furthermore, he suggested that President Obama was a weak leader and that he had also failed the Black community most of all. The SPRC chairperson pointed to the Black-on-Black violence in Chicago and the Black unemployment nationally as evidence of President Obama's failure as president. However, the SPRC chairperson failed to acknowledge that Black-on-Black violence in Chicago and the unemployment rate for Blacks nationally pre-dated Obama's presidency and were due to unresolved issues stemming from centuries of enslavement and socioeconomic inequality.

In my opinion, the SPRC chairperson knew that his statements were offensive; however, he felt comfortable making them, no matter the racial overtone. The racial tone and outward comfortability with which the SPRC chairperson spoke were quickly becoming the new normal for White conservatives and were reflective of how President Donald Trump presented himself to the public.

DONALD TRUMP'S ASSAULT ON MULTICULTURALISM

One week into his first term as president, Donald Trump issued Executive Order 13769 ("Muslim ban") that barred citizens of seven majority-Muslim countries (Syria, Iraq, Iran, Yemen, Libya, Somalia, and Sudan) from entering the United States for the next 90 days and suspended the admission of all refugees for 120 days.[10] President Trump's executive order immediately caused global protests and chaos among people from multicultural backgrounds. Also, after Trump's first week in the Oval Office, he deepened rifts with Mexican president Enrique Peña Nieto by insisting that Mexico would pay for a border wall between America and Mexico as a means of stopping illegal immigrants from entering the United States.[11]

Domestically, Trump unblocked the Dakota Access Pipeline project, which set the stage for a new confrontation with the Standing Rock Sioux and environmentalists.[12] At large, liberals pushed the "go green agenda," aimed at promoting environmental sustainability; however, conservatives supported Trump's agenda to drill for gas and oil on federal land. While protestors, both foreign and domestic, voiced anger against Trump's executive orders, White conservatives praised and justified Trump's executive orders by suggesting that they would further America's economic growth and keep foreign terrorists from entering America posing as refugees.

The pastor (Mexican-born) of Shepherd of the Hills United Methodist Church in Douglasville, Georgia, stated that several of his parishioners spoke with him on numerous occasions regarding his sermons that addressed issues involving immigration policies from the pulpit, which the parishioners deemed political and unwanted. In an interview, the pastor provided me with three responses that his parishioners gave him during their discussions concerning his sermons that highlighted Jesus' message of caring for and being welcoming to the refugee/stranger:

- Preaching about immigration in the pulpit is political and thus inappropriate, which makes people leave the church.

- Immigrants abuse the welfare system and do not pay taxes. US citizens are at stake when it comes to undocumented immigrants taking benefits that are solely for US citizens.

---

10. CNN Politics, "Full Text."
11. Ortiz, "Trump, Mexican President."
12. Milman, "Standing Rock Sioux Tribe."

- Immigrants should use appropriate and legal means to come to the United States.[13]

Many parishioners' worldviews at Shepherd of the Hills United Methodist Church regarding refugees and immigrants mimicked those at Union Hill United Methodist Church and were the norm among White, conservative, North Georgia United Methodists. On Interstate 75 North in Dalton, Georgia, a highway billboard read in bold White letters: "Trump, Pray For Our Nation—Take Our Country Back." And, not far from Dalton, Georgia, near Benton, Tennessee, off Highway 411, Rick Tyler, a Republican campaigning for congress, displayed a billboard that read "Make America White Again."

Rick Tyler, during a radio interview with WTVC, stated that his billboard "Make America White Again" plays off presumptive Republican presidential nominee Donald Trump's "Make America Great Again" slogan. Further, Tyler's webpage stated that the "Make America White Again" billboard was the first one of many planned for the area (North Georgia) in the months leading up to the November election. Tyler also stated that he had ideas for other billboards, such as "Fight Federal Tyranny / Stop the Muslim Invasion" and "Mamas, don't let your babies grow up to be MISCEGENATORS."[14]

In a different interview, Tyler told WRCB radio station (a local NBC News affiliate) that the signs were meant to convey a message that America should go back to the 1960s, *Ozzie and Harriet*, and *Leave it to Beaver* time when there were no break-ins, no violent crime, and no mass immigration.[15] Tyler's billboard "Make America White Again" was a rallying cry for WCC throughout North Georgia that America was being taken over by immigrants, gays, Muslims, and POC.

Overt symbols such as Tyler's billboard and the Tea Party's "Don't Tread on Me" flag were constant visual reminders to White Christian conservatives that outsiders were threatening America's White Christian values.

While such racially motivated symbols were visual throughout North Georgia's rural communities, more covert messages were also being consumed by White conservatives that went largely unnoticed by multicultural America. Andrew Breitbart and Stephen Bannon (Tea Party activist and

---

13. Pastor, Shepherd of the Hills United Methodist Church, personal interview with author, Oct. 2017.
14. Evon, "Make American White Again."
15. Jaffe and Siemaszko, "Outrage."

chief strategist to President Trump) were inspiring White conservatives through Breitbart News Network, a far-right news feed that pushed racist, sexist, xenophobic, and anti-Semitic propaganda into the households of White conservatives and alt-right advocates.

Stephen Bannon produced documentaries and films, such as *In the Face of Evil* and *Fire From the Heartland: The Awakening of the Conservative Woman*. These productions aimed to motivate White Christian conservatives to see multiculturalism as their enemy. *Fire From the Heartland* primarily targeted rural conservative White women (aka Mamma Grizzly) with a promotion that illustrated the future of America as being unsafe for their children unless they joined the conservative fight. Bannon developed movies and documentaries that were racially provocative, and the films demanded that White conservatives weaponize themselves against what they believed to be foreign illegals. Bannon's movies and documentaries did not air in large movie theaters for all of America to see. Instead, the films were recorded on videotapes and made available for purchase.

These low-budget films were very popular among White conservatives because they highlighted the immediate need to take America back from President Obama's immoral foreign illegals and to reclaim America as a majority White Protestant nation. While White conservatives made up the majority of persons who shared this racialized vision of America, some financially mobile Latino American and African American conservatives agreed with their White conservative counterparts that under President Obama's administration, the nation had become too liberal.

The former Latino American pastor of Midway United Methodist Church in Douglasville, Georgia, said that he was a supporter of Donald Trump and that he was seeking to become the head of the Republican Party in Douglas County. When asked to complete a research survey for the pastor's doctoral dissertation, he told me that Douglasville had become "too blue and too Black."[16] In other words, Douglasville had become largely Democratic, and African Americans represented the greater portion of the city's population. In addition to his derogative views concerning African Americans, the pastor also illustrated that he was not in support of gay persons becoming ordained clergy in the United Methodist Church.

Although the pastor was a Latino American himself and wanted Midway United Methodist Church to develop a Hispanic ministry, his

---

16. Pastor, Midway United Methodist Church, personal interview with author, Jun. 2017.

political views and aspirations seemed to suggest that he would be in support of harsh immigration legislation that largely targeted persons from Mexico and other Latin American countries. The pastor's comments modeled those conservative views embraced at Union Hill United Methodist Church, Shepherd of the Hills United Methodist Church, and Douglasville First United Methodist Church, and by the pro-Trump mob that stormed the US capitol building on January 6, 2021, to disrupt the certifying of the Electoral College votes that declared Joe Biden winner of the 2020 US presidential election.

While I do not believe that White, conservative, North Georgia United Methodists wanted to incite armed physical violence against US government officials, many of them did share in Trump's theory that the 2020 presidential election had been stolen and that America was falling into the political hands of foreign socialists. The "March to Save America" occurred when President Trump instructed an angry majority of the White mob to march to the US capitol and violently attack the federal building. The mob consisted of thousands of Trump supporters wearing military-style clothing and waving such flags as the Confederate battle flag, the Tea Party flag, and the MAGA flag. The pro-Trump mob left six people dead, including one US capitol police officer, Brian D. Sicknick.[17]

Furthermore, the pro-Trump mob vandalized the US capitol by looting offices and urinating and defecating in the hallways. The mob was not only angry about the outcome of the presidential election, which Biden won through a national "Democratic blue wave," but also at the results of Georgia's two US Senate runoff races, for which Democrats Raphael Warnock and Jon Ossoff ousted senators David Perdue and Kelly Loeffler.[18]

During the January 6 attack, the pro-Trump mob was looking to assassinate Nancy Pelosi, the Speaker of the House, and lynch Vice President Mike Pence for honoring the election results and going forward with the exchange of power. As quickly as Trump rose to political power, seemingly his fall from political grace was even faster after being defeated by Joe Biden in 2021, so liberals believed.

However, Trump would regain the Republican Party's support again in his 2024 presidential campaign. After Trump's defeat in 2021, the fallout was traumatic for White conservatives across the North Georgia Conference. Once again, White, conservative, North Georgia United Methodists,

---

17. Levenson et al., "What We Know."
18. Wise and Duehren, "Mob Storms Capitol."

like the heartbreaking experience of their Methodist forefathers and mothers following the Civil War, were vested in a lost cause.

In conjunction with the congregations of Douglasville First United Methodist Church, Midway United Methodist Church, and Union Hill United Methodist Church, several Black United Methodist churches affiliated with the North Georgia Conference of the United Methodist Church also supported church legislation aimed at excluding gay persons from ever becoming ordained clergy. The former Atlanta College Park district superintendent and previous pastor of Hoosier Memorial United Methodist Church denounced homosexuality and claimed that it was incompatible with biblical Scripture.

While serving as pastor of Hoosier Memorial United Methodist Church, the former district superintendent forced a male youth who regularly dressed in gender-affirming clothing into a restroom as he entered the church and proceeded to tell him that "he was a boy and not a girl." The former pastor informed the youth that he would be arrested if he caused any more problems in the church. Although the pastor's actions were reported to the church's nurturing committee chairperson as required by the United Methodist Church's safe sanctuary policy, no disciplinary actions were ever taken. Although the youth had been an active member of the church for over five years, he never returned to Hoosier Memorial after the incident with the pastor, and no one seemed to question his whereabouts.

While many African American United Methodist clergy in the North Georgia Conference may have supported President Obama's multicultural agenda concerning race and gender equality, many of them practiced an exclusive theology when it came to accepting gay parishioners as ordained clergy. While it was acceptable for gay persons to function in roles such as choir directors and church administrators, the United Methodist Church *Book of Discipline* (2016) excluded them from becoming ordained elders and deacons. The church claimed that the practice of homosexuality was incompatible with Christian teaching.[19]

EXCLUSION OF THE LGBTQ+ COMMUNITY

In 2014, the Pew Research Center's *America's Changing Religious Landscape* study illustrated that 60 percent of United Methodists said homosexuality

---

19. *Book of Discipline*, 226.

should be accepted by society.[20] However, this did not appear to be the reality in the United Methodist Church throughout the North Georgia Conference. Although Metropolitan Atlanta's surrounding suburban and urban communities had rapidly become more multicultural, the congregational demographics of the United Methodist Church across the North Georgia Conference became increasingly White over three years, rising from 92 to 96 percent White, according to Gregory S. Williams of Golden Memorial United Methodist Church, Douglasville, Georgia.[21]

In addition to becoming increasingly White, churches appeared to be overwhelmingly heterosexual. The overall population of the church's membership had decreased primarily due to ageism, which impacted non-White congregations at a higher rate. While the North Georgia Conference of the United Methodist Church (largely comprised of White conservatives) considered itself as being a denomination that supported an inclusive theology and having an "open table" philosophy, its clandestine behavior, which was a result of its Anglican imperialistic and Southern traditions, still engaged ethnic minority and LGBTQ+ communities in traditional, Southern, White conservative fashion, supporting White supremacist cultural values and beliefs.

During my first year serving as youth director at Shepherd of the Hills United Methodist Church (SOTH), the congregation consisted of approximately sixty-eight total parishioners (fifty-seven White, fifteen parishioners of the LGBTQ+ community, ten African American parishioners, and one Mexican American). Fourteen of the fifteen parishioners who represented the LGBTQ+ community were White. The church council consisted of fourteen parishioners, including me. Serving on the church council were twelve Whites, two African Americans, and one Mexican American. Within the youth ministry, there were ten youths in total—seven White and three African Americans. Within my first year at SOTH as a youth director, LGBTQ+ parishioners initiated a safe haven ministry with the goal of organizing SOTH as a member of the Reconciling Ministries Network (RMN).

As a result of the increasing diversity within the church's leadership and the newly established safe haven ministry, some of the church's longstanding parishioners began issuing threats that they would stop attending SOTH, and several individuals and entire families eventually did stop attending. The chairperson of the church council emailed a three-page

---

20. Pew Research Center, *American's Changing Religious Landscape*.
21. Gregory S. Williams, personal conversation with author, Sept. 2017.

complaint letter to the members of SOTH, highlighting the concerns that he and other parishioners had with the LGBTQ+ parishioners' desire to establish an RMN at SOTH. The chairperson's email highlighted reasons why SOTH did not need to associate itself with RMN and suggested that if LGBTQ+ parishioners continued to campaign for the church's inclusion into the RMN, the church's membership would continue to decline and that SOTH would not survive financially.

Prior to the chairperson's email, during the church council meeting the previous month in late April 2017, the church council voted to reduce the part-time staff's (office administrator and youth minister) monthly compensation by 50 percent. The following Sunday, during the announcements to the congregation, the finance chairperson illustrated that the church council was hoping to have the Rome-Carrollton district pay the pastor's pension.

The finance chairperson further announced that tithes and offerings had decreased for the first two financial quarters of the year and that parishioners needed to be more accepting of LGBTQ+ individuals and live out the mission and vision statements of the church, which emphasized the need to be inclusive of all persons without judgment. While SOTH's congregation was becoming more culturally diverse, its overall membership and financial giving were speedily declining because of the church's internal cultural conflicts. The growing cultural changes within SOTH's congregation were a microcosm of a larger cultural and demographic shift occurring in Douglasville, Georgia, and throughout North Georgia.

The greatest impact on LGBTQ+ status in the United Methodist Church occurred from February 23 to 26, 2019, at the Special General Conference in St. Louis, Missouri, at the America's Center Convention Complex. In St. Louis, Missouri, the conservative delegates (the majority) voted against allowing LGBTQ+ persons to serve as ordained clergy and against current United Methodist clergypersons performing same-sex marriages.[22]

This decision illustrated that the United Methodist Church was moving further away from being an inclusive mainline denomination to that of an evangelical denomination that openly practiced exclusivity. In 2019, the United Methodist Church in North America was 94.6 percent White, with most of its members residing in the Southeastern Jurisdiction. Within a few days after the decision to ban LGBTQ+ persons from serving as ordained clergy, I spoke with several LGBTQ+ members who had long

22. Gryboski, "United Methodist Church Upholds."

served at SOTH, and they informed me that they had decided not to attend SOTH any longer and were requesting that their names be removed from the church's membership roll.

White conservative United Methodists serving in the North Georgia Conference saw the decision as a victory. On February 26, 2019, the day of the vote, the pastor of Douglasville First United Methodist Church, during our staff meeting, continued to provide us with minute-by-minute updates on what was occurring at the Special General Conference. As soon as the decision was made, he announced to staff members that the Traditional Plan had won (438 to 384 votes) over the One Church Plan (including LGBTQ+ persons) and the Connectional Conference Plan (the development of a new denomination). The next morning, the pastor emailed the staff the message below, providing little empathy for the LGBTQ+ community, which had existed within the United Methodist Church for decades.

> Staff-
>
> The four-day Special Session of our United Methodist Church General Conference has passed the Traditional Plan that affirms our current stances and adds penalties, hoping to reduce defiance. The Judicial Council will still need to weigh in on the constitutionality of the plan.
>
> I have a video message on our church's Facebook page.
>
> Overall, the status quo holds, and we continue in ministry to connect people to Jesus, make disciples, and transform the world.

The pastor of Douglasville First United Methodist Church and other, largely conservative White United Methodist Churches in the North Georgia Conference understood the cultural shifts as threatening to their conservative traditions and politically motivated by Democratic liberals who wished to seize political power over the entire United Methodist Church. So, as a counter-response to increased diversity within some local churches and the perceived threat of a liberal takeover, White conservatives practiced withholding their financial tithes and offerings and limited their volunteer time in protest. While diverse groups demanded acceptance within their local United Methodist Churches, they did not have the financial ability to maintain the churches without financial assistance from White conservative members.

Exclusive Theology

BLACK METHODISTS' RESPONSE TO TRUMPISM

During the Obama administration, White conservative ideologies were being challenged globally by diverse communities. However, after the election of President Trump, White conservatives and diverse groups swiftly reverted to their ethnically and racially separate spaces. In the fifth edition (July 2017, General BMCR 50th Celebration) of the Black Methodists for Church Renewal (BMCR), the *Southeastern Jurisdiction Informer* stated that "BMCR supported 'Black Lives Matter'" and that they were outraged and lifting their voices of concern on several issues that continued to impact and plague African American communities: violence, immigration, LGBTQ+ injustice, mass incarceration, poverty, lack of access to health care, illiteracy, and failing public school systems. Furthermore, BMCR also stated that it "affirms and is committed to the upliftment and dignity of Black and Brown people and recognizes their gifts."[23] While the BMCR demanded social equality and equity for marginalized people and hoped to build multicultural bridges, White conservatives throughout North Georgia were their primary opponents.

For White conservatives, social justice and multiculturalism were not only components of a political leftist agenda; they were also understood to be an attack on Protestantism and White America's core values and beliefs. Trump, head of the Republican Party and now president, overtly politicized racism and made Eurocentric nationalism seem normal. In opposition to Trump's agenda to "Make America Great Again," political protestors on the left were deemed as invoking violence and were labeled as criminals. However, Trump regarded hate groups such as the Ku Klux Klan, Proud Boys, and other White supremacy groups to be "very fine people."[24]

During a rally held in Huntsville, Alabama, in September 2017, Trump referred to National Football League (NFL) players who were kneeling during the playing of the national anthem in protest of police brutality and the murder of Black men by White police officers as "sons of bitches." In addition to calling NFL players "sons of bitches," Trump further stated that the "NFL players should be fired for kneeling and for disrespecting the national anthem."[25] For many, Trump's insult and the call for the NFL players to be fired by team owners for protesting violated the players' constitutional

23. Ferree, "General BCMR."
24. Dunn, "Fact Check."
25. Van Dyke, "This Miami Dolphins Player."

rights and was a political strategy to silence oppositional protests aimed at his racialized agenda.

However, throughout Trump's speech in Alabama, he remained silent about the issue of police brutality and the murder of Black men by White police officers, though in an earlier speech the previous month, he jokingly instructed police officers to slam suspects' heads against their police vehicles upon arresting them. Minority groups and political leftists understood Trump's speeches to be racially motivated and as issuing "dog whistles" to White supremacists that they had a friend in the White House.

Trump's public opposition to the removal of Confederate soldier statues and his slow repudiation of White supremacists in the Charlottesville, Virginia, riot tapped into White, conservative, Southern traditions that long deemed that North America is a White Protestant nation. For White conservatives in North Georgia, Trump was their knight in shining armor, and he could do no wrong. Trump validated their Eurocentric ideas of racial supremacy, Protestantism, and North American nationalism to such a degree that White conservatives did not feel it necessary to voice their political philosophies publicly, but rather, they were surely convinced of their power as the silent majority.

In 2018, while attending the Forum for Theological Exploration held in Indianapolis, Indiana, I attended a lecture session led by Jonathan Wilson-Hartgrove, during which he spoke in-depth about topics such as Trumpism, slaveholder religion, and racial blindness. During his lecture, Wilson-Hartgrove presented his newly published book *Reconstructing the Gospel: Finding Freedom from Slaveholder Religion*. In chapter 3 of the book, he illustrates how evangelical minister Franklin Graham (son of the late Billy Graham) of North Carolina traveled across the nation, speaking to predominantly White Christian audiences at state capitol buildings and asking them to "Vote Your Values" during the 2018 presidential election.

According to Wilson-Hartgrove, Graham highlighted to his White conservative audiences that Obama's administration had assaulted religious liberty and that "progressive" was a euphemism for atheists.[26] Moreover, after it was announced that Trump had won the 2018 presidential election and had also won North Carolina convincingly, Graham attributed the victory to a "God factor," meaning that God was in support of the values that upheld racial, religious, and nationalist notions of human superiority, inferiority, and separation.

26. Wilson-Hartgrove, *Reconstructing the Gospel*, 49.

Exclusive Theology

Both White conservatives in the North Georgia Conference and North Carolina Conference of the United Methodist Church shared in a belief that God was and still is in support of an America that denies human civil rights to non-Whites, gay persons, immigrants, and Muslims. "Vote Your Values" was a dog whistle to Trump supporters and all White North Americans to unite and restore America ("Make America Great Again") to its so-called golden age because the values and beliefs in which the country was founded were now on the decline and being threatening by a multicultural alliance bent on destroying the country from within.

In response to the perceived threat to North American traditional values and beliefs, White, conservative North Georgia United Methodists joined the fight to take America back and save the United Methodist Church from being overtaken by the antichrist and godless foreigner. The fight for North America, Protestantism (as represented by the United Methodist Church), and Whiteness had reverberated throughout all of society and every agency of the North Georgia Conference of the United Methodist Church.

White Protestant superiority and the practice of exclusive theology, which continued to reinforce a culture of violence, were evident at all organizational levels of the United Methodist Church (local churches, districts, annual conferences, extension ministries, general boards, colleges, and universities). However, the early development of the United Methodist Church's history of racial violence can be traced as far back as the rise and expansion of the Church of England and American Methodism. John Wesley, through his support of foreign missions and the creation of Methodist doctrine (constitution, *Book of Discipline*, and liturgy), instituted into the thinking of Methodists in North Georgia and around the world value and belief systems grounded in Protestant White supremacy that continued to be influential and have inspired racialized behavior in modern times and perhaps into the unforeseen future.

Chapter 8

Conclusion

AS A RESULT OF the growing diversity of many small rural communities, White conservative United Methodist Churches throughout Cherokee County and across the North Georgia Conference of the United Methodist Church were seeking to develop multicultural materials and outreach ministries aimed at communities of color. However, while seeking to create multicultural outreach ministries, these small United Methodist Churches were rooted in Southern White socioreligious values and belief traditions that exhibit behaviors that uphold racism and an exclusive theology—a theology founded on the ideas of White Protestant supremacy and Eurocentric superiority.

White, conservative, North Georgia United Methodists embodied socioreligious beliefs and values that were racially and multiculturally exclusive, which lay beneath the surface and helped shape their behavior toward others. These denoted socioreligious values and beliefs were in opposition to the social principles illustrated in the "Social Principles" of *The Book of Discipline of the United Methodist Church.*

The White conservative values and beliefs have been inspirational, both religiously and socially, for North Georgia Methodists since the formation of the North Georgia Conference in 1866 and will likely continue under the episcopal leadership of Presiding Bishop Robin Dease (the first African American woman bishop to preside over both the North Georgia Conference and the South Georgia Conference). During a conversation with Bishop Dease, she stated, "While a significant number of White, conservative, North Georgia United Methodists disaffiliated over the past few years, there continue to be a large number of White conservatives in the North Georgia Conference that internalize racism."[1]

In 2015, Pew Research estimated that 3.6 percent of the US population, or 9 million adult adherents, self-identify with the United Methodist Church, revealing a much larger number than the registered membership. In addition, Pew's 2014 *America's Changing Religious Landscape* study reported that 94 percent of United Methodist members were White and 6 percent non-White.[2]

---

1. Bishop Robin Dease, personal conversation with author, Mar. 17, 2024.
2. Pew Research Center, *America's Changing Religious Landscape*, 20–23.

Appendix

2020 Map of the Eight Districts of the North Georgia
Conference of the United Methodist Church

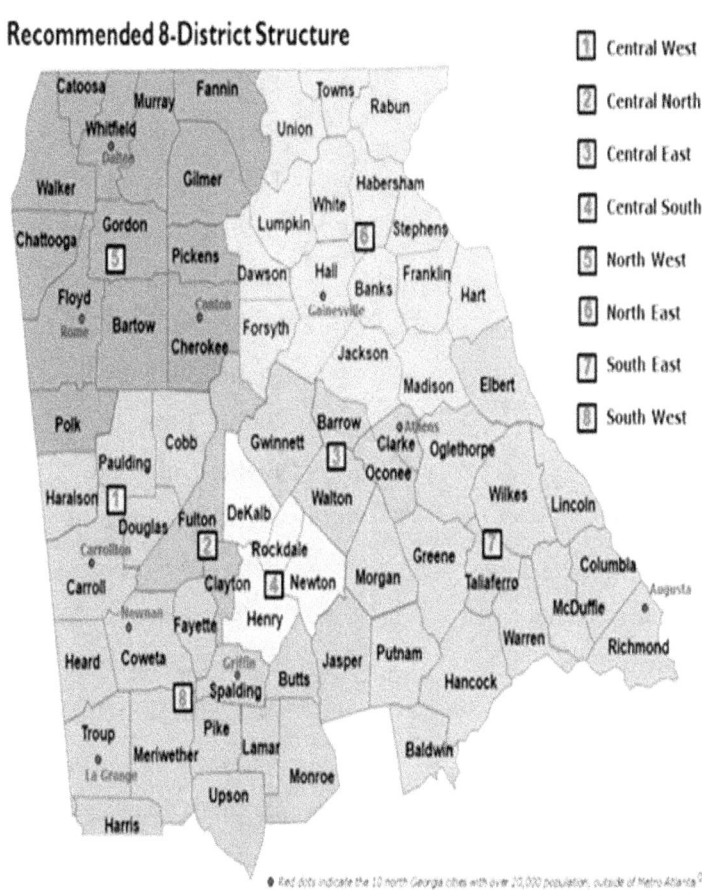

Appendix

The following is a list of the United Methodist Churches in the North Georgia Conference 2020:

A

- Acworth
- Adairsville
- Alcovy
- Aldersgate, Atlanta
- Aldersgate, Augusta
- Aldora
- Allen Lee Memorial
- Allen Memorial
- Allens
- Alleys Chapel
- Allgood Road

B

- Ball Ground 1 2
- Barnesville first
- Barton Chapel, Richmond Co.
- Bascomb
- Baxley First
- Beech Creek
- Bell Creek
- Belmont
- Belvedere
- Ben Hill
- Berlin
- Best Chapel
- Bethany, Atlanta
- Bethany, Fairburn
- Bethany, Jefferson
- Bethany, Lincolnton
- Bethel, Atlanta
- Bethel, Brookton
- Bethel, Dalton
- Bethel, Dawsonville
- Bethel, Milledgeville
- Bethel, Morganton
- Bethel, Mount Zion Charge
- Bethel, Paulding Co.
- Bethel, Stockbridge
- Bethel, Summerville
- Bethel, Turin
- Bethel, Union Co.
- Bethel, Washington
- Bethel, West Point
- Bethelview
- Bethesda, Hartwell
- Bethesda, Lawrenceville
- Bethesda, Lexington
- Bethesda, Manchester
- Bethesda, Woodbury

Appendix

- Bethlehem, Bethlehem
- Bethlehem, Elberton
- Bethlehem, Flowery Branch
- Bethlehem, Forsyth
- Bethlehem, Hoschton
- Bethlehem, Rome District
- Bethlehem, Stilesboro
- Big Springs, Atlanta
- Big Springs, Troup County
- Birmingham
- Bishop
- Blairsville
- Blair Village
- Blooming Grove
- Blue Ridge
- Blythe
- Bogart
- Boggs Chapel
- Bold Springs, Carnesville
- Bold Springs, Monroe
- Bolingbroke
- Boneville
- Bostwick
- Bowdon
- Bowdon Junction
- Bowen
- Bowersville
- Bowman
- Boyd's Chapel
- Boynton
- Braswell
- Bremen Circuit
- Bremen First
- Briarcliff
- Bright Star
- Brookhaven
- Brooks
- Broomtown
- Buchanan
- Buckhead
- Buford
- Burns Memorial
- Burnt Hickory
- Burts Chapel

C

- Calhoun First
- Calvary, Atlanta
- Calvary, Shady Dale
- Camak
- Campbellton 1 2
- Campground
- Campton
- Candler
- Caney Head
- Canon
- Canton First
- Capitol View

Appendix

- Carmel
- Carnesville
- Carrollton First
- Cartecay
- Cartersville Area
- Cascade
- Casey Springs
- Cave Springs
- Cedar Grove, Conley
- Cedar Grove, Kensington
- Cedartown First
- Celanese
- Center, Center
- Center, Crawford
- Center, Hoschton
- Center Hill
- Center Point
- Center Valley
- Central
- Chamblee First
- Charles F. Golden
- Chatsworth First
- Chattahoochee
- Cherokee Corner
- Chicopee
- Chipley
- Christ United
- Clapps Factory
- Clarkdale
- Clarkesville
- Clarkston
- Clayton First
- Clem
- Clemons Chapel, Lula
- Cleveland
- Clifton
- Cliftondale
- Clinton
- Cochran
- Cokesbury, Atlanta
- Cokesbury, Augusta
- Cokesbury, Elberton
- Coke's Chapel
- Colbert
- Coldwater
- College Park
- Collins Memorial
- Colonial Hills
- Columbia Drive
- Comer
- Commerce
- Concord, Concord
- Concord, Eatonton
- Concord, Elbert Co.
- Concord, Hickory
- Concord, Walker
- Confidence, Blairsville
- Confidence, Toccoa

Appendix

- Conyers First
- Cool Springs
- Coosa
- Corinth, Corinth
- Corinth, Winder
- Cornelia
- Corra Harris Chapel
- County Line, Paulding Co.
- County Line, Spalding Co.
- Cove, Chickamauga
- Cove, Dalton
- Covington First
- Covington Mills
- Crawford
- Crawfordville
- Culloden
- Culverton
- Cumming

D

- Dahlonega
- Dallas First
- Dalton First
- Danburg
- Danielsville
- Dawnville
- Dearing
- Decatur First
- Demorest
- Devereux
- Dillard
- Dillard's Chapel
- District Line
- Dixie
- Dodson
- Douglas Street
- Douglasville First
- Dover's Chapel
- Druid Hills
- Dry Pond
- Duluth First
- Dunagan
- Dunns Chapel
- Dunson
- Dunwoody

E

- East End
- East Lake
- East Newman
- East Point Avenue
- East Point First
- Eastland Road
- Eatonton First
- Ebenezer, Alpharetta
- Ebenezer, Ashland
- Ebenezer, Buchanan Charge

Appendix

- Ebenezer, Conyers
- Ebenezer, Fayetteville
- Ebenezer, Forsyth
- Ebenezer, Forsyth Co.
- Ebenezer, Habersham
- Ebenezer, Jefferson
- Ebenezer, Reynoldsville
- Ebenezer, Tallapoosa
- Ebenezer, Zebulon
- Elberton First
- Eliam
- Elizabeth
- Elizabeth Lee
- Ellenwood
- Embry Hills
- Emerson
- Emory Chapel
- England Chapel
- Epworth, Atlanta
- Epworth, Epworth
- Eton

F

- Fairburn
- Fairmount
- Fair Oaks
- Fairview, Forsyth
- Fairview, Lavonia
- Fairview, Waleska
- Faith, Clayton Co.
- Farmington
- Farmville
- Fayetteville
- Felton
- Field's Chapel
- Fincher
- Fishers Chapel
- Five Springs
- Flint Hill, Douglasville
- Flint Hill, Hiram
- Flippen
- Flovilla
- Flowery Branch
- Floyd Springs
- Forest park
- Forks Chapel
- Forsyth
- Franklin
- Friendship, Eatonton
- Friendship, Fayette
- Friendship, Hepzibah
- Fullers Chapel

APPENDIX

G

- Gaines Chapel
- Gainesville First
- Gainesville Mill
- Gaissert
- Gaither's
- Garrett's Chapel
- Gates Chapel
- Gay
- Glade
- Glen Haven
- Glencoe
- Glenn Memorial
- Godfrey
- Gordon Street
- Gordon's Chapel
- Grace, Albany
- Grace, Atlanta
- Gracewood
- Grant Park
- Gray
- Grayson
- Graysville
- Greensboro First
- Greenville
- Griffin Chapel
- Griffin First
- Grove Level
- Grove Park
- Grove Town

H

- Haddock
- Hamilton Street
- Hampton
- Hand Memorial
- Hanleiter
- Hapeville
- Harmony Grove, Lilburn
- Harmony Grove, Stilesboro
- Harris
- Harris Chapel
- Hartwell First
- Haygood Memorial
- Headland Heights
- Hephzibah
- Hiawasee
- Hickory Flat, Atlanta
- Hickory Flat, Lula
- High Shoals
- Highland
- Hightower
- Hillcrest
- Hillsboro
- Hinton, Hinton
- Hinton Memorial

Appendix

- Hipps Chapel
- Hiram
- Holly Springs, Cherokee Co.
- Holly Springs, Jackson Co.
- Holly Springs, Marietta
- Holonville
- Homer
- Hopewell, Baldwin Co.
- Hopewell, Hall Co.
- Hopewell, Paulding Co.
- Hopewell, Pine Mountain
- Hoschton
- Hyatt Memorial

I

- Imperial
- Independence
- Inman
- Inman Park

J

- Jackson
- Jackson's Chapel
- Jasper
- Jefferson
- Jefferson Street
- Jersey
- Jewell
- John Wesley
- Johnson, Warrenton
- Johnson, Watkinsville
- Johnson's Chapel, Armuchee Charge
- Jones Chapel, Coweta Co.
- Jones Chapel, Danielsville
- Jones Memorial First
- Jonesboro First
- Juliette

K

- Kelley's Chapel
- Kennesaw
- Kensington
- Kincaid
- Kirkwood
- Knowles Chapel
- Kresge Memorial
- Kynette

L

- Lafayette
- LaGrange First
- Lakewood Heights
- Lamar Johnson Memorial

Appendix

- Lavonia
- Lawrenceville
- Lawrenceville Road
- Lebanon
- Lebanon, Gainesville District
- Lee's Chapel
- Leland
- Level Creek
- Lewis Memorial
- Lexington
- Liberty, Augusta
- Liberty, Cedartown Circuit
- Liberty, Danielsville
- Liberty, Gracewood
- Liberty, Jasper Co.
- Liberty, White Plains
- Liberty Hill, Hartwell
- Liberty Hill, Elberton
- Liberty Hill, Hemp
- Liberty Hill, Morganton
- Lincolnton
- Lindale
- Lindsey Chapel
- Linton
- Lithia Springs
- Lithonia
- Little River
- Livingston
- Locust Grove
- Loganville
- Long Cane
- Loudsville
- Lovejoy, Covington
- Lovejoy, Lovejoy
- Lovejoy, Newton Co.
- Lovejoy Memorial
- Lowell
- Lula
- Luthersville
- Lyerly

M

- Macedonia, Chattooga Co.
- Macedonia, Cherokee Co.
- Macedonia, Hart Co.
- Macedonia, Thomson
- Madison First
- Manchester First
- Mann Memorial
- Mansfield
- Maple Avenue
- Marietta, Polk Co.
- Marietta Campground
- Marietta First
- Martha Brown 1 2
- Martinez
- Martin's Chapel
- Marvin, Barnesville

Appendix

- Marvin, Martinez
- Mary Branan Memorial
- Matilda Chapel
- Mayfield
- Mayson's
- Maysville
- McCaysville
- McDonough
- McEachern Memorial
- McGaugheys
- McKee's Chapel
- McKendree
- McKendree Memorial
- Meadow
- Menlo
- Merrill
- Mesena
- Metropolitan
- Middleton
- Midway, Alpharetta
- Midway, Auburn
- Midway, Bowdon Circuit
- Midway, Covington
- Midway, Douglas Co.
- Midway, Gillsville
- Midway, Glenn
- Midway, Lincolnton
- Midway, Spalding Co.
- Milledgeville First
- Milner
- Milstead
- Mineral Springs
- Mize Memorial
- Mizpah
- Molena
- Monroe First
- Monticello
- Montpelier
- Moore's Chapel
- Moreland
- Morris Street
- Morrow
- Mossy Creek
- Mount Bethel, Banks Co.
- Mount Bethel, Marietta
- Mount Bethel, McDonough
- Mount Carmel
- Mount Carmel, Bartow Co.
- Mount Carmel, Coweta Co.
- Mount Carmel, Norcross
- Mount Carmel, Senoia
- Mount Carmel, Walker Co.
- Mount Carmel, Walton Co.
- Mount Chapel
- Mount Gilead, Atlanta
- Mount Gilead, Holly Springs
- Mount Gilead, Turin
- Mount Gilead Campground

APPENDIX

- Mount Hope
- Mount Nebo
- Mount Olivet
- Mount Pisgah
- Mount Pleasant, Homer
- Mount Pleasant, Oglethorpe Co.
- Mount Pleasant, Rabun Co.
- Mount Pleasant, Rome Circuit
- Mount Pleasant, Social Circle
- Mount Pleasant, Whitfield Co.
- Mount Tabor, Floyd Co.
- Mount Tabor, Newton Co.
- Mount Tabor, Paulding Co.
- Mount Vernon, Douglasville Circuit
- Mount Vernon, Rocky Face
- Mount Vernon, Smyrna
- Mount Zion, Atlanta
- Mount Zion, Campground
- Mount Zion, Carroll Co.
- Mount Zion, Chatsworth
- Mount Zion, Dallas
- Mount Zion, Duluth
- Mount Zion, Ellenwood
- Mount Zion, Glenn
- Mount Zion, Lula
- Mount Zion, Marietta
- Mount Zion, Smarr
- Mount Zion, Spalding Co.
- Mount Zion, Washington
- Mountain City
- Mountain Park
- Mountain Springs
- Mountain View
- Mountville

N

- Nacoochee Valley
- Nazareth
- Nellie Dodd
- Nellie Peters
- Nelson First
- New Bethel
- New Echota
- New Gilead
- New Harmony
- New Holland, Gainesville
- New Holland, New Holland
- New Hope, Atlanta
- New Hope, Between
- New Hope, Carroll Co.
- New Hope, Clayton Co.
- New Hope, Fayette Co.
- New Hope, Forsyth Co.
- New Hope, Gwinnett Co.

Appendix

- New Hope, Jasper Co.
- New Hope, Locust Grove
- New Hope, Marietta
- New Hope, Meriwether Co.
- New Hope, Palmetto
- New Hope, Rabun Co.
- New Hope, Union Co.
- New Liberty, Hoschton
- New Liberty, Tallulah Falls
- New Pentecost
- New Prospect
- New Salem
- New Sugar Valley
- Newborn
- Newnan First
- Newnan Springs
- Newton Estates
- Nicholson
- Nine Mile
- Noah's Ark
- Norcross
- North Covington
- North Decatur
- North Rome
- Northside
- Northwoods
- Norwood

O

- Oak Grove, Decatur
- Oak Hill
- Oakland City
- Oakwood
- Ocee 1 2
- Oconee
- Odessadale
- Oglethorpe
- Old Camp
- Old Pentecost
- Old Sugar Valley
- Oostanaula
- Orange
- Ousley
- Owl Rock
- Oxford Old Church

P

- Paces Ferry
- Palmetto
- Palmyra Road
- Park Street
- Pattillo Memorial
- Peachtree Road
- Pecks Chapel
- Pendergrass
- Pennington
- Pennington Chapel

Appendix

- Pentecost
- Philadelphia, Columbia Co.
- Philadelphia, Conyers
- Philadelphia, Eatonton
- Philadelphia, Henry Co.
- Piedmont
- Pierce Memorial
- Pierce's Chapel
- Pine Grove
- Pine Log
- Piney Grove
- Pitts Chapel
- Plainville
- Pleasant Grove
- Pleasant Grove, Dahlonega
- Pleasant Grove, Dalton
- Pleasant Grove, Forsyth
- Pleasant Grove, Forsyth Co.
- Pleasant Grove, Habersham Co.
- Pleasant Grove, Milledgeville
- Pleasant Grove, Monroe Co.
- Pleasant Grove, Riverdale
- Pleasant Grove, Temple
- Pleasant Grove, Troup Co.
- Pleasant Grove, Walton Co.
- Pleasant Grove, Whitfield Co.
- Pleasant Hill, Lamar Co.
- Pleasant Hill, Rome
- Pleasant Hill, Towns Co.
- Pleasant Hill, Union Co.
- Pleasant Hill, Walker Co.
- Pleasant Valley
- Pomona
- Pope's Chapel
- Poplar Springs
- Poplar Springs, Atlanta
- Porterdale
- Poseyville
- Powder Springs
- Powell Chapel
- Powelton
- Powers Ferry
- Primrose
- Princeton
- Prospect, Athens
- Prospect, Augusta District
- Prospect, Covington
- Prospect, Elberton
- Prospect, Franklin
- Prospect, Jasper Co.
- Prospect, Lamar Co.
- Prospect, Lawrenceville
- Prospect, Rome
- Providence, Barrow Co.
- Providence, Hart Co.
- Providence, Toccoa
- Providence, Union Co.

R

- Raleigh
- Ramah
- Ranger/Old Shiloh
- Ray's Chapel
- Raytown
- Red Oak, Newton Co.
- Red Oak, Red Oak
- Red Oak, Williamson
- Redan
- Redstone
- Redwine, Hall Co.
- Redwine, Hart Co.
- Rex
- Reynolds
- Richland Charge
- Richmond Co.
- Rico
- Ridgeway
- Ringgold
- Riverview
- Rock
- Rock, The
- Rock Chapel, DeKalb Co.
- Rock Mills
- Rock Spring
- Rock Springs
- Rockland
- Rockmart First
- Rogers
- Rome District Parsonage
- Rome First
- Roopville
- Roswell 1 2
- Round Oak
- Royston Oak
- Ruckersville
- Rush Chapel
- Rutledge

S

- Saint Andrew, Augusta
- Saint Andrew, Carrollton
- Saint Andrew, College Park
- Saint Andrew, Marietta
- Saint James, Alpharetta
- Saint James, Athens
- Saint James, Atlanta
- Saint James, Augusta
- Saint James, Hogansville
- Saint James, Manchester
- Saint James, Toccoa
- Saint John, Atlanta
- Saint John, Augusta
- Saint John, LaGrange
- Saint Luke, Atlanta
- Saint Luke, Augusta

Appendix

- Saint Luke, Rome
- Saint Mark, Atlanta
- Saint Mark, Augusta
- Saint Mark, Washington Rd., Augusta
- Saint Marys
- Saint Matthew
- Saint Paul, Atlanta
- Saint Paul, Carroll Co.
- Saint Paul, Eatonton
- Saint Paul, Gainesville
- Saint Paul, Lincolnton
- Saint Paul, Lumpkin Co.
- Saint Paul, Marietta
- Saint Phillips, Gainesville
- Saint Phillips, Marietta
- Saint Stephen, Marietta
- Saint Stephen, Monroe
- Salem, Covington
- Salem, Franklin
- Salem, McDuffie Co.
- Salem, Oconee Co.
- Salem, Troup Co.
- Salem, Union Co.
- Salem Campground
- Sam Jones Memorial First
- Sandy Cross
- Sandy Springs
- Sardis, Atlanta
- Sardis, Buford
- Searcy Memorial
- Second Avenue
- Senoia
- Sewell
- Shady Grove, East Point
- Shady Grove, Union Co.
- Shannon
- Sharon, Dunwoody
- Sharon, Sharon
- Sharp Memorial
- Shiloh, Bowdon-Shiloh Charge
- Shiloh, Buford
- Shiloh Campground
- Shiloh, Carroll Co.
- Shiloh, Cherokee Co.
- Shiloh, Covington
- Shiloh, Forsyth Co.
- Shiloh, Sunnyside
- Shiloh, Thomson
- Shingleroof Campground
- Siloam
- Silver Creek
- Silver Hill
- Silvertown
- Simpsonwood
- Sixes
- Skyland

Appendix

- Smith Chapel
- Smyrna, Carroll Co.
- Smyrna, Hancock Co.
- Smyrna, Paulding Co.
- Smyrna, Smyrna
- Smyrna, Washington
- Snapping Shoals
- Snellville
- Social Circle
- Soules Chapel
- South Bend, Atlanta
- South Bend, Hall Co.
- South Broad
- South Carolina Campground
- Sparta
- Spring Hill
- Spring Place
- Standfordville
- Stark
- Starrsville
- Statham
- Stewart Avenue
- Stilesboro
- Stinchcomb
- Stockbridge
- Stone Mountain
- Stripling Chapel
- Sunshine II
- Swords

T

- Tabernacle
- Talbotton
- Tallapoosa
- Tallulah Falls
- Talmadge
- Tate
- Taylorsville
- Temperance
- Temple
- Temple, Carroll Co.
- Temple, Oglethorpe Co.
- Tenth Street
- Thomaston First
- Thomson First
- Tiger
- Tignall
- Tillman Memorial
- Tilton
- Toccoa
- Trinity, Atlanta
- Trinity, Austell
- Trinity, Dalton
- Trinity, Durand
- Trinity, Hall Co.
- Trinity, Rome
- Trinity, Royston

Appendix

- Trinity, Suwanee Charge
- Trinity, Walker Co.
- Trinity on the Hill
- Trion
- Tucker First
- Tuckston
- Tunnel Hill
- Turin
- Turners
- Turnerville

U

- Underwood Memorial
- Unidentified Church
- Union, Stockbridge
- Union, Waco
- Union Chapel, Fayette Co.
- Union Chapel, Putnam Co.
- Union Chapel, Walton Co.
- Union City
- Union Hill
- Union Hill, Alpharetta
- Union Hill, Hiawassee
- Union Point
- Union Point First
- Union Protestant
- Unity
- University Heights

V

- Vanna
- Van's Valley
- Van Wert
- Varnell
- Vaughn
- Victory
- Villa Rica

W

- Waco
- Waleska
- Walker's
- Wallaceville
- Walnut Grove
- Warm Springs
- Warrenton
- Warsaw
- Washington First
- Watkins
- Watkinsville
- Welcome
- Wesley
- Wesley Chapel, Atlanta
- Wesley Chapel, Cedartown
- Wesley Chapel, DeKalb Co.

- Wesley Chapel, Gordon Co.
- Wesley Chapel, Heard Co.
- Wesley Chapel, Lafayette
- Wesley Chapel, Madison Co.
- Wesley Chapel, Marietta
- Wesley Chapel, Oglethorpe Co.
- Wesley Chapel, Putnam Co.
- Wesley Chapel, Rome
- Wesley Chapel, Villa Rica
- Wesley Memorial
- Wesley's Chapel
- West Newnan
- West Point First
- West Rome
- White
- White Oak
- White Plains
- Whitesburg
- Whitesville Street
- Whiteville
- William's Chapel
- Williamstown
- Wilson's
- Winder First
- Winston
- Winters Chapel
- Winterville
- Wood Station
- Woodbury
- Woodlawn, Augusta
- Woodlawn, Elberton
- Woodstock
- Worthville
- Wrightsboro

Y

- Yatesville
- Yellow River
- Yorkville
- Young Harris
- Young Harris Memorial

Z

- Zebulon, Fincher
- Zebulon, Sparta
- Zebulon, Zebulon
- Zion
- Zion's Chapel
- Zoar

Appendix

2024 Map of the Five Districts of the North Georgia Conference of the United Methodist Church

Appendix

CATECHISMS

Bishop William Capers introduced catechisms similar to the one below after the Nat Turner Rebellion in Southampton, Virginia, on August 21–22, 1831. The catechism published by Bishop William Capers for Methodist missions among enslaved people was designed to teach the rudiments of Christian education to subdue slave revolts.

The catechism booklet is illustrated below.

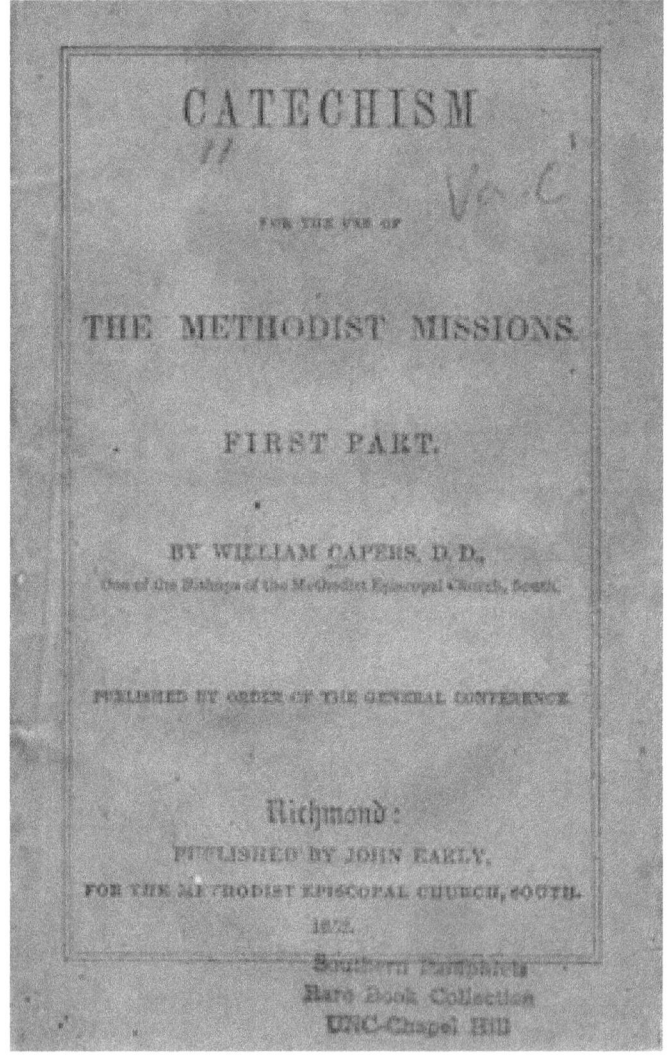

Appendix

CATECHISM
FOR THE USE OF
THE METHODIST MISSIONS

FIRST PART.

BY
WILLIAM CAPERS, D.D.,
One of the Bishops of the Methodist Episcopal Church, South.
PUBLISHED BY ORDER OF THE GENERAL CONFERENCE.

CHARLESTON:
PUBLISHED BY JOHN EARLY,
FOR THE METHODIST EPISCOPAL CHURCH, SOUTH.
1852.

PREFACE TO THE THIRD EDITION.

The author of this humble work begs leave to accompany it with a few brief remarks to those of his brethren who may think proper to use it.

1. It is believed that a Catechism for the mass of colored people, whether children or adults, had better be confined to the rudiments of Christian knowledge, simply, than diffused through a wide range of Scripture topics, doctrinal, historical, biographical, &c.; our object being not barely to communicate knowledge, but such as tends most to the glory of God—the knowledge of salvation.

2. The present little work has been composed under a persuasion that the persons to be instructed can more easily conceive the truth than comprehend the terms in which it is apt to be expressed. We have therefore discarded all hard words, and aimed to present truth in a guise so simple as to suit their capacities. This, however, is very difficult; we can only say, we have done what we could.

APPENDIX

3. It is not pretended that this Catechism contains all that ought to be taught; and yet, we fear, it will be found too full for many learners. It is designed as a *help* to the missionary in his truly Christian work of directing the untutored mind to the knowledge of God. The questions and answers may sometimes need explanation, and will often serve as a text for further instructions and exhortations. Other questions also will suggest themselves in the course of instruction.

4. For children, it may be well to follow the order of the chapters as they have been arranged, except the tenth chapter, which may be brought in at any place. If, however, in some cases, there appears no likelihood of children's getting through with the whole Catechism, the missionary will select particular questions, and arrange them into lessons, at his discretion.

For adults, particularly on the plantations, it is recommended to begin with those questions which are marked with an asterisk, (*,) and, perhaps, in the order in which they are numbered.

W. C.

Page 5

CATECHISM

CHAPTER I.
OF GOD.

Who made you?
God.
What did he make you for?
For his glory.
Who is God?
The Almighty, maker of heaven and earth.
What do you know of him?
God is holy, just and true.
What else do you know of him?
God is merciful, good and gracious.
How old is he?
God does not grow old; he always was, and always will be.
What is he able to do?
God can do all things.

What does he know?
God knows all things.
Where is he?
God is in heaven, and everywhere.
Does he always see us, and take notice of us?
Yes; nothing can hide us from God.
Does he care for us?
O yes; God is our Father in heaven.

Page 6

CHAPTER II.
THE CREATION OF MAN.

What did God make man out of?
The dust of the ground.
What does this teach you?
To be humble.
What else does it teach you?
To remember I must die, and my body turn to dust again.
But did God make man's soul out of the dust of the ground?
No; only man's body belongs to the dust.
How did God make man's soul?
With his own breath.
Will your soul turn to dust with your body when you die?
No: my soul cannot turn to dust.
When God first made man, was he good or bad?
God made man good, like himself.
Where did God put the first man and woman?
In the garden of paradise.
And was that a good place?
Yes; everything God made was good.
Was man happy in paradise?
Yes; everything was there to make man happy.

Page 7

Appendix

CHAPTER III.
THE FALL OF MAN.

What made man fall from paradise?
Sin.
What is sin?
Doing what God says we must not do.
What did God say the man and woman must not do in paradise?
He said they must not eat of the tree of the knowledge of good and evil.
And did they eat of it?
Yes; they did eat of it.
How did they come to eat of it?
The devil tempted the woman; and she did eat, and gave to her husband, and he did eat.
What happened to them then?
They were good no more, and God was angry with them.
And what did God do to them?
He turned them out of paradise.
What more did he do to them?
He sentenced them to labor and sorrow, pain and death.
Did they have any children before they sinned and lost that good nature that God made them in?
No; they sinned first, and their children were born in sin.
And are all men born sinners still?
None are born good; no, not one.

Page 8

CHAPTER IV.
THE PROMISE OF A SAVIOUR—CHRIST'S INCARNATION—THE CHILD JESUS.

Who is the Saviour of mankind?
Our Lord Jesus Christ.
What has he done to save mankind?
He came down out of heaven, and suffered and died on the cross.
Did he come, and steer, and die for men, as soon as the first man sinned?

APPENDIX

No: but he promised he would come, and he did come.
Who is our Lord Jesus Christ?
The Son of God.
Is he God, then?
Yes; he is very God.
But could the Son of God suffer and die?
He came to be man to suffer and die for us.
When he came down from heaven was he born a little child, and did he grow up to be a man, like all little children grow up?
Yes; he did.
Who was his mother?
A virgin, named Mary.
Where was he born?
In Bethlehem, a town among the Jews.
What sort of a place was he born in?
A manger, in a stable.
How did people know that he was born to be the Saviour?
The angels did tell it from heaven.

Page 9

What does the Scripture say about him when he was a child?
He was subject to his parents.

CHAPTER V.
THE MINISTRY OF CHRIST.

What happened when Jesus was baptized?
Heaven was opened, and the Holy Ghost came down like a dove, and lighted on him.
What else happened?
A voice came from heaven, and said, This is my beloved Son.
What did our Lord Jesus say about himself?
He said he came down from heaven.
What more did he say?
He said he was one with the Father.

What did he do to show the people that he was God and man, and was come to save them?
He did great wonders.
Tell me some of them.
He healed the sick, raised the dead, and cast out devils.
Did the people believe in him?
Some did; but many more did not.
Why did not all believe in him?
Because they loved sin more than God.
What did our Lord Jesus Christ do for them that believed in him?

Page 10

He pardoned their sins, and made them true Christians.
What did he say about them that would not believe in him?
He said they must die in their sins.
What did he say about little children?
He said they belonged to him.
What did he do to them?
He took them up in his arms and blessed them.
What did he preach to the people?
That they must repent and believe the gospel.

CHAPTER VI.
THE DEATH AND RESURRECTION OF CHRIST.

How did our Lord Jesus die?
Wicked men rose up and crucified him.
But why did he not save himself from them?
Because he came into the world to die for sinners.
Did he do nothing to those wicked men?
He prayed for them.
What happened when our Lord was crucified?
There was darkness over all the land.
What more happened?
The earth did quake, and the graves opened.
Where did they bury the body of Jesus?

Appendix

In a grave cut out of a rock.
What did his enemies do?
They fastened the grave, and set soldiers to watch it.

Page 11

How long did the body of Jesus lie in the grave?
Till the third day.
What happened when the Lord rose from the dead?
A mighty angel came from heaven, and there was a great earthquake.
What else happened?
The bodies of many of the saints came out of their graves.

CHAPTER VII.
CHRIST SEEN BY THE DISCIPLES—HIS ASCENSION AND INTERCESSION.

Did our Lord show himself after he rose from the dead?
Yes, very often.
Who saw him?
All the apostles, and many others, saw him.
Were they sure he was the very same Jesus that had been crucified, dead, and buried?
Yes; they knew him to be the very same.
How did they know it?
They talked with him, handled him, and saw the marks of the cross on his body.
What after this became of his body?
He went up in it into heaven.
Did the body of our Lord Jesus go up into heaven just as it was in the grave, without any change?
No; it was changed into a glorious body.

Page 12

APPENDIX

Did any one see him go up into heaven?
Yes; his disciples looked up after him.
How did he go up?
A cloud parted him from them, and he went up into heaven.
Does he now do anything for us in heaven?
He ever lives to pray for us.

CHAPTER VIII.
THE JUDGMENT.

Will the Lord Jesus come down again out of heaven?
Yes, at the last day.
What will he come for?
To judge all men.
How will he come?
In glory: with all the holy angels.
What will happen then?
The trumpet shall sound, and the dead shall be raised.
What will be done to them that are alive at that day?
They shall be changed in a moment.
What will happen to the world?
The heavens shall pass away with a great noise, and the earth shall be burned up.
What will become of mankind then?
The righteous shall be taken up into heaven, but the wicked shall be turned into hell.

Page 13

CHAPTER IX.
WHO ARE RIGHTEOUS—HOW WE BECOME, AND CONTINUE SO.

Who will be reckoned righteous in the day of judgment?
Such as believe the gospel and live by it.
What will become of little children, and them that know not right from wrong?
They will be reckoned righteous for Christ›s sake.

APPENDIX

How must we believe the gospel, so as for it to make us righteous?
We must take it to our heart for God's truth, and love it.
Can we turn our own heart to believe the gospel, and love it?
No: we must pray for grace to turn our heart.
Who works this grace in us to turn our heart?
The Holy Ghost.
Can our sins be forgiven us?
Yes, for Christ's sake.
What must we do for our sins to be forgiven?
God will forgive us, only for Christ's sake.
But will he forgive us if we take no pains about it?
No; we must confess our sins, and pray, believing in Jesus.
But must not our heart be sorry, and hate sin?
Yes; we must be sorry, and hate sin, and put it away from us.
How can we do all this?

Page 14

The Holy Ghost works it in us to feel right and do right.
If our sins are forgiven, and we get a new heart, can we fall away and lose it?
Yes; Adam fell away, and Judas fell away, and we can fall too.
How must we live so as not to fall from God's grace?
We must deny ourself, and take up our cross daily, and follow Jesus.

CHAPTER X.
PARTICULAR DUTIES.

What is your duty to God?
To love him with all my heart, and soul, and strength, and so to worship him, and serve him.
What is a child's duty to his father and mother?
To love them, honor them, comfort them, and mind what they say.
What is a servant's duty to his master and mistress?
To serve them with a good will heartily, and not with eye-service.
What is the duty of a husband to his wife?
To love her, and cherish her, as Christ loves the church.
What is the duty of a wife to her husband?

To honor and love him, as her head.
What is the duty of brothers and sisters?
To be patient, kind, and loving to one another.

Page 15

What is your duty to all men?
To do to them as I would have them do to me.
What is your duty to your enemies?
To love them, and pray for them.
What is your duty to them that do you any wrong?
To forgive them, as I pray God to forgive me.
What is the duty of parents to their children?
To be tender to them, and bring them up in the fear of God.

CHAPTER XI.
THE CREED.

*What is your belief?
    I believe in God the Father almighty, maker of heaven and earth; and in Jesus Christ his only begotten Son, our Lord; who was conceived by the Holy Ghost, born of the Virgin Mary, suffered under Pontius Pilate, was crucified, dead, and buried; the third day he rose from the dead; he ascended into heaven, and sitteth on the right hand of God the Father almighty; from thence he shall come to judge the quick and the dead.
    I believe in the Holy Ghost; the holy catholic church; the communion of saints; the forgiveness of sins; the resurrection of the body; and the life everlasting.
    *You believe in God the Father, and the Son, and the Holy Ghost; are these three Gods, or only one God?

Page 16

The Father, and the Son, and the Holy Ghost, are one God.
*Can you tell how these three are one God?

APPENDIX

No; we cannot find out God.
How, then, can you believe that it is so?
Because God says it is so.
You believe that the Son of God was conceived by the Holy Ghost, and born of the Virgin Mary: can you tell how that could be?
No; but God knows; nothing is hard for him.
Who was Pontius Pilate?
The governor that let the Jews crucify Jesus.
What do you mean by the catholic church?
It means the church of Christ.
Who belong to this church?
All true Christians.
What makes us call it the catholic church?
Because it is free for all people, if they repent and believe in our Lord Jesus Christ.

CHAPTER XII.
THE SACRAMENTS.

*1. *What is baptism?*
Baptism is a sign of the grace of God that makes us Christians.
*2. *Does baptism make us Christians?*
No; water cannot make us Christians; grace makes us Christians.
*3. *Who works that grace in us to make us Christians?*
The Holy Ghost.

Page 17

*4. *What do you promise when you come to be baptized?*
I promise to renounce the devil, and the world, and the flesh, so that I will not live in sin any longer.
What other promise do you make?
I promise to keep God's holy will and commandments.
How can you keep these promises?
I can keep them only by God›s grace.
Ought little children to be baptized?
Yes; they belong to Christ.

5. *What is the sacrament of the Lord's supper taken for?*
In remembrance of our Lord Jesus Christ, who died for us.
What does the bread of this holy sacrament show to us?
It shows Christ's body broken for us.
What does the cup show us?
The blood of Christ shed for us.
Who ought to take this sacrament?
All Christian people.
How often ought we to take it?
As often as we can.
How ought we to take it?
With an humble, loving heart, sorry for sin.
6. *Is it not very wicked for people to take the sacrament when they live in known sin; and, in particular, if they have any quarrel, or grudge against one another?*
Yes; if we take the sacrament so, we make it worse for us.

Page 18

THE LORD'S PRAYER.

Our Father which art in heaven, hallowed be thy name; thy kingdom come; thy will be done in earth as it is in heaven. Give us this day our daily bread; and forgive us our trespasses, as we forgive them that trespass against us; and lead us not into temptation, but deliver us from evil; for thine is the kingdom, and the power, and the glory, for ever and ever. Amen.

THE TEN COMMANDMENTS.

I.

Thou shalt have none other gods but me.

II.

Thou shalt not make to thyself any graven image, nor the likeness of anything that is in heaven above, or in the earth beneath, or in the waters

Appendix

under the earth. Thou shalt not bow down to them, nor worship them: for I, the Lord thy God, am a jealous God, and visit the sins of the fathers upon the children unto the third and fourth generation of them that hate me; and show mercy unto thousands of them that love me and keep my commandments.

III.

Thou shalt not take the name of the Lord thy God in vain: for the Lord will not hold him guiltless that taketh his name in vain.

Page 19

IV.

Remember that thou keep holy the sabbath day. Six days shalt thou labor, and do all that thou hast to do; but the seventh day is the sabbath of the Lord thy God. In it thou shalt do no manner of work; thou and thy son, and thy daughter, thy man-servant, and thy maid-servant, thy cattle, and the stranger that is within thy gates: for in six days the Lord made heaven and earth, the sea, and all that in them is, and rested the seventh day: wherefore the Lord blessed the seventh day, and hallowed it.

V.

Honor thy father and thy mother, that thy days may be long in the land which the Lord thy God giveth thee.

VI.

Thou shalt do no murder.

VII.

Thou shalt not commit adultery.

VIII.

Thou shalt not steal.

IX.

Thou shalt not bear false witness against thy neighbor.

X.

Thou shalt not covet thy neighbor's house, thou shalt not covet thy neighbor's wife, nor his man-servant, nor his maid-servant, nor his ox, nor his ass, nor anything that is his.

Page 20

SELECT PASSAGES OF SCRIPTURE

THE LORD'S SUPPER.

The Epistle to the Corinthians, chap. xi, verses 23 to 28.
    The Lord Jesus, the same night that he was betrayed, took bread, and when he had given thanks, he brake it, and said, Take, eat; this is my body, which is broken for you. This do in remembrance of me. After the same manner also he took the cup, when he had supped, saying, This cup is the new testament in my blood: this do ye, as oft as ye drink it, in remembrance of me: for as often as ye eat this bread, and drink this cup, ye do show the Lord's death till he come. Wherefore, whosoever shall eat this bread, and drink this cup of the Lord unworthily, shall be guilty of the body and blood of the Lord. But let a man examine himself, and so let him eat of that bread and drink of that cup.

DUTY TO A BROTHER OR SISTER IN THE CHURCH.

The Gospel by St. Matthew, chap. xviii, verses 15 to 17.
    Moreover, if thy brother trespass against thee, go and tell him his fault between thee and him alone. If he shall hear thee, thou hast gained thy

brother: but if he will not hear thee, then take with thee one or two more, that in the mouth of two or three witnesses every word may be established. And if he shall neglect to hear

---

Page 21

---

them, tell it unto the church; but if he neglect to hear the church, let him be unto thee as a heathen man and a publican.

DUTIES OF HUSBANDS AND WIVES.

Wives, submit yourselves unto your husbands, as unto the Lord: for the husband is the head of the wife, even as Christ is the head of the church. Therefore, as the church is subject unto Christ, so let the wives be to their own husbands in everything.

Husbands, love your wives, even as Christ also loved the church, and gave himself for it. * * * So ought men to love their wives as their own bodies. He that loveth his wife loveth himself. * * * Let every one of you, in particular, so love his wife even as himself; and the wife see that she reverence her husband. *Ephesians* v, 22–33.

DUTIES OF PARENTS AND CHILDREN.

Children, obey your parents, in the Lord, for this is right. Honor thy father and mother, that it may be well with thee, and thou mayest live long on the earth.

And ye fathers, provoke not your children to wrath; but bring them up in the nurture and admonition of the Lord. *Ephesians* vi, 1–14.

THE DUTY OF SERVANTS.

Servants, be obedient to them that are your masters according to the flesh, with fear and trembling, in singleness of your heart, as unto

---

Page 22

APPENDIX

Christ. Not with eye-service as men pleasers, but as the servants of Christ, doing the will of God from the heart. *Ephesians* vi, 5, 6.

Let as many servants as are under the yoke count their own masters worthy of all honor, that the name of God, and his doctrine, be not blasphemed. And they that have believing masters, let them not despise them because they are brethren, but rather do them service because they are faithful and beloved, partakers of the benefit. These things teach and exhort. 1 *Tim.* vi, 1, 2.

DUTY TO THOSE WHO INJURE US.

Ye have heard that it hath been said, An eye for an eye, and a tooth for a tooth; but I say unto you, That ye resist not evil, but whosoever shall smite thee on thy right cheek, turn to him the other also. * * * Love your enemies, bless them that curse you, do good to them that hate you, and pray for them which despitefully use you, and persecute you. *Matthew* v, 38–44.

OUR DUTY TO ALL MEN.

All things whatsoever ye would that men should do unto you, do ye even so to them; for this is the law and the prophets. *Matthew* vii, 12.

OF ADULTERY.

Ye have heard that it was said by them of old time, Thou shalt not commit adultery. But I say unto you, That whosoever looketh on a woman to lust after her, hath committed adultery

---

Page 23

with her already in his heart. *Matthew* v, 27, 28.

The Pharisees also came unto him, tempting him, and saying unto him, Is it lawful for a man to put away his wife for every cause? And he answered and said unto them, Have ye not read that he which made them at the beginning made them male and female; and said, For this cause shall a man leave father and mother, and shall cleave to his wife; and they twain shall be one flesh? What therefore God hath joined together let not man put asunder. And I say unto you, Whosoever shall put away his wife, except it be for fornication, and shall marry another, committeth adultery; and whoso marrieth her which is put away doth commit adultery. *Matthew* xix, 3–9.

AGAINST THEFT AND OTHER CRIMES.

Every one that stealeth shall be cut off. *Zechariah* v, 3.

Whoso is partner with a thief hateth his own soul. *Proverbs* xxix, 24.

By swearing, and lying, and killing, and stealing, and committing adultery, they break out, and blood toucheth blood. Therefore shall the land mourn, and every one that dwelleth therein shall languish. *Hosea* iv, 2, 3.

Know ye not that the unrighteous shall not inherit the kingdom of God? Be not deceived. Neither fornicators, nor idolaters, nor adulterers, nor effeminate, nor abusers of themselves with mankind, NOR THIEVES, nor covetous, nor drunkards,

nor revilers, nor extortioners, shall inherit the kingdom of God. 1 *Corinthians* vi, 9, 10.

AGAINST SWEARING.

But above all things, my brethren, swear not; neither by heaven, neither by the earth, neither by any other oath; but let your yea be yea, and your nay nay, lest ye fall into condemnation. *James* v, 12.

AGAINST SABBATH-BREAKING.

Ye bring more wrath upon Israel, by profaning the Sabbath. *Nehemiah* xiii, 18.

And while the children of Israel were in the wilderness, they found a man that gathered sticks upon the sabbath day. * * * And the Lord said unto Moses, The man shall be surely put to death; all the congregation shall stone him with stones, without the camp. And all the congregation brought him without the camp, and stoned him with stones, and he died; as the Lord commanded Moses. *Numbers* xv, 32–36.

AGAINST LYING.

All LIARS shall have their part in the lake that burneth with fire and brimstone, which is the second death. *Revelation* xxi, 8.

Blessed are they that do his commandments, that they may have a right to the tree of life, and may enter in through the gates into the city, (*heaven.*) For without are dogs, and sorcerers, and whoremongers, and murderers, and idolaters, AND WHOSOEVER LOVETH AND MAKETH A LIE. *Revelation* xxii, 14, 15.

Page 25

ORIGINAL HYMNS.

HYMN 1.

4 lines 7's

1 Children, join with one accord,
Join in praises to the Lord;
Join to sing the Saviour's name,
Sing hosanna to the Lamb.

2 Hail him Prophet, Priest, and King,
Louder, sweeter, children, sing;
Hail him by his fav'rite name,
Sing hosanna to the Lamb.

3 Men, and women, join to raise
Loud hosannas to his praise;
Praise the great Redeemer's name,
Sing hosanna to the Lamb.

APPENDIX

4 Praise him, all ye hosts above,
Praise him, praise him for his love;
Glory give to Jesus' name,
Hallelujah to the Lamb.

HYMN 2.

P. M.

1 Might a little child at prayer,
Hope to meet with Jesus there?
Tell me, Christians, can it be?
Can the Lord come down to me?
When, alas! I have been bad,
And my heart feels sore and sad,
And I know not what to say,
Will he bless me if I pray?

Page 26

2 Yes; he'll meet thee, little one;
Bid thy doubts and fears be gone:
Yes, he'll bless thee if thou pray,
Though thou know'st not what to say.
For the love he bears to thee,
By the cross on Calvary,
He will meet thee, he will bless,
He will bid thee go in peace.

HYMN 3.

C. M.

1 As Jesus his disciples taught
His Father's will to do,
Parents their little children brought,
That he might bless them too.

2 "Forbid them," the disciples cried,
"Nor make them any room:"
"Forbid them not," the Lord replied,
"But suffer them to come."

3 "Who, than the lambs, the Shepherd's care,
More fitly might receive?
And these my heavenly kingdom share:
I bless them, and they live."

4 Then in his arms he took them up,
And on them laid his hands:
Joy to the world for Israel's hope,
And Jesus' kind commands.

HYMN 4.

S. M.

1 There is a narrow way
That leads to heaven and God;
But sinners love to go astray,
And take a broader road.

Page 27

2 They will not seek the Lord,
And pray to be forgiven;
They will not mind his holy word,
And so they miss of heaven.

3 Lord, we are sinners too;
But O, our sins forgive!
And teach us what we ought to do,
And how we ought to live!

Appendix

HYMN 5.

L. M.

1 In every place
The God of grace
Is very near
To hear our prayer;
And all we say,
By night or day,
And all we do,
He knows it too.

2 Then let us try
From sin to fly,
And speak and do
What's right and true;
And since God hears
Our humble prayers,
Still let us pray,
Both night and day.

HYMN 6.

S. M.

1 Lord, teach me how to pray,
Teach me to love it too;
And grant thy Holy Spirit may
Make all my nature new.

Page 28

2 I want to be thy child,
I want my sins forgiven;
I want a spirit meek and mild,
I want to get to heaven.

3 Do show me, Lord, the way;
And guide me on the road;
And let me never go astray
Till I get home to God.

HYMN 7.

L. M.

1 Alas! how soon, and we must die!
We fear to think of death so nigh:
Our body dust, our life a breath,
Alas! how soon we sink in death!

2 But let us humbly trust the Lord,
And love his grace, and mind his word,
The dust shall rise, and death may be
The gate of heaven to you and me.

SELECTED.

HYMN 8.

4 lines 7's.

1 Poor and needy though I be,
God, my Maker, cares for me;
Gives me clothing, shelter, food;
Gives me all I have of good.

2 He will listen when I pray,
He is with me night and day,
When I sleep, and when I wake,
Keep me safe for Jesus' sake.

Page 29

3 He who reigns above the sky
Once became as poor as I;
He whose blood for me was shed
Had not where to lay his head.

4 Though I labor here awhile,
He will bless me with his smile;
And when this short life is past,
I shall rest with him at last.

HYMN 9.

C. M.

1 O that the Lord would guide my ways,
To keep his precepts still!
O that my God would grant me grace,
To know and do his will!

2 O send thy Spirit down, to write
Thy law upon my heart!
Nor let my tongue indulge deceit,
Nor act the liar's part!

3 Make me to walk in thy commands,
'Tis a delightful road;
Nor let my feet, or heart, or hands,
Offend against my God.

HYMN 10.

L. M.

1 This day belongs to God alone,
He chooses Sunday for his own;
And we should neither work nor play,
Because it is the Sabbath day.

2 'Tis good to have one day in seven,
That we may learn the way to heaven;

Page 30

Or else we never should have thought
About religion as we ought.

3 Then let us spend it as we should,
In serving God, and growing good;
And be the better every day,
For what we heard the preacher say.

4 And let this holy day be pass'd,
As if we knew it were our last;
For what would dying people give
To have one sabbath more to live!

HYMN 11.

P. M.

1 Come, ye sinners, poor and needy,
Weak and wounded, sick and sore,
Jesus ready stands to save you,
Full of pity, love, and power;
He is able,
He is willing, doubt no more.

2 Now, ye needy, come, and welcome,
God's free bounty glorify;
True belief, and true repentance,
Every grace that brings you nigh;
Without money,
Come to Jesus Christ and buy.

3 Come, ye weary, heavy laden,

Bruised and mangled by the fall,
If you tarry till you're better,
You will never come at all;
Not the righteous,
Sinners Jesus came to call.

Page 31

HYMN 12.

S. M.

1 Jesus, my strength, my hope,
On thee I cast my care;
With humble confidence look up,
And know thou hear'st my prayer.

2 Give me on thee to wait,
Till I can all things do;
On thee, almighty to create,
Almighty to renew.

3 I want a heart to pray,
To pray, and never cease;
Never to murmur at thy stay,
Or wish my suff'rings less.

4 This blessing, above all,
Always to pray, I want;
Out of the deep on thee to call,
And never, never faint.

5 I rest upon thy word,
Thy promise is for me,
My help and my salvation, Lord,
Shall surely come from thee.

APPENDIX

HYMN 13.

P. M.

1 Arise, my soul, arise,
Shake off thy guilty fears,
The bleeding Sacrifice
In thy behalf appears;
Before the throne my Surety stands,
My name is written on his hands.

Page 32

2 He ever lives above,
For me to intercede;
His all-redeeming love,
His precious blood to plead;
His blood atoned for all our race,
And sprinkles now the throne of grace.

3 Five bleeding wounds he bears,
Received on Calvary;
They pour effectual prayers,
They strongly speak for me:
Forgive him, O forgive, they cry,
Nor let that ransom'd sinner die.

4 The Father hears him pray,
His dear anointed One;
He cannot turn away
The presence of his Son:
The Spirit answers to the blood,
And tells me I am born of God.

APPENDIX

HYMN 14.

C. M.

1 Alas, and did my Saviour bleed,
And did my Sovereign die?
Would he devote that sacred head
For such a worm as I?

2 Was it for crimes that I have done
He groan'd upon the tree?
Amazing pity! grace unknown!
And love beyond degree!

Page 33

3 Well might the sun in darkness hide,
And shut his glories in,
When Christ, the mighty Maker, died,
For man, the creature's sin.

4 Thus might I hide my blushing face,
While his dear cross appears;
Dissolve my heart in thankfulness,
And melt my eyes to tears.

5 But drops of grief can ne'er repay
The debt of love I owe;
Here, Lord, I give myself away,
'Tis all that I can do.

HYMN 15.

4 lines 7's.

1 Loving Jesus, gentle Lamb,
In thy gracious hands I am;

Make me, Saviour, what thou art,
Live thyself within my heart.

2 I shall then show forth thy praise,
Serve thee all my happy days;
Then the world shall always see
Christ, the holy child, in me.

HYMN 16.

L. M.

1 Jesus, my all, to heaven is gone,
He whom I fix my hopes upon;
His track I see, and I'll pursue
The narrow way, till him I view.

2 The way the holy prophets went,
The road that leads from banishment;

Page 34

The King's highway of holiness,
I'll go, for all his paths are peace.

3 This is the way I long have sought,
And mourn'd because I found it not;
My grief a burden long has been,
Because I was not saved from sin.

4 The more I strove against its power,
I felt its weight and guilt the more;
Till late I heard my Saviour say,
Come hither, soul, I am the way.

5 Lo, glad I come, and thou, bless'd Lamb,
Shalt take me to thee, whose I am;
Nothing but sin have I to give,

APPENDIX

Nothing but love shall I receive.

6 Then will I tell to sinners round
What a dear Saviour I have found,
I'll point to thy redeeming blood,
And say, Behold the way to God!

HYMN 17.

C. M.

1 When I can read my title clear
To mansions in the skies,
I'll bid farewell to every fear,
And wipe my weeping eyes.

2 Should earth against my soul engage,
And fiery darts be hurl'd,
Then I can smile at Satan's rage,
And face a frowning world.

Page 35

3 Let cares like a wild deluge come,
Let storms of sorrow fall,
So I but safely reach my home,
My God, my heaven, my all.

4 There I shall bathe my weary soul
In seas of heavenly rest,
And not a wave of trouble roll
Across my peaceful breast.

APPENDIX

HYMN 18.

C. M.

1 Am I a soldier of the cross,
A follower of the Lamb?
And shall I fear to own his cause,
Or blush to speak his name?

2 Must I be carried to the skies
On flowery beds of ease,
While others fought to win the prize,
And sail'd through bloody seas?

3 Are there no foes for me to face?
Must I not stem the flood?
Is this vile world a friend to grace,
To help me on to God?

4 Sure I must fight if I would reign.
Increase my courage, Lord;
I'll bear the toil, endure the pain,
Supported by thy word.

5 Thy saints in all this glorious war
Shall conquer, though they die;
They see the triumph from afar,
By faith they bring it nigh.

Page 36

6 And when that glorious day shall rise,
And all thy people shine,
In robes of victory through the skies,
The glory shall be thine.

Appendix

HYMN 19.

S. M.

1 Hungry, and faint, and poor,
Behold us, Lord, again,
Assembled at thy mercy's door,
Thy bounty to obtain.

2 Thy word invites us nigh,
Or we should starve indeed;
For we no money have to buy,
No righteousness to plead.

3 The food our spirits want
Thy hand alone can give;
O hear the prayer of faith, and grant
That we may eat and live.

HYMN 20.

C. M.

1 Try us, O God, and search the ground
Of every sinful heart;
Whate'er of sin in us is found,
O bid it all depart!

2 When to the right or left we stray,
Leave us not comfortless;
But guide our feet into the way
Of everlasting peace.

3 Help us to help each other, Lord,
Each other's cross to bear;
Let each his friendly aid afford,
And feel his brother's care.

Page 37

APPENDIX

4 Help us to build each other up,
Our little stock improve;
Increase our faith, confirm our hope,
And perfect us in love.

5 Up into thee, our living Head,
Let us in all things grow;
Till thou hast made us pure indeed,
And spotless here below.

6 Then when the mighty work is wrought,
Receive thy ready bride;
Give us in heaven a happy lot,
With all the sanctified.

HYMN 21.

4 lines 7's.

1 Lord, we come before thee now,
At thy feet we humbly bow;
O do not our suit disdain!
Shall we seek thee, Lord, in vain?

2 Lord, on thee our souls depend!
In compassion now descend!
Fill our hearts with thy rich grace,
Tune our lips to sing thy praise.

3 In thine own appointed way,
Now we seek thee, here we stay;
Lord, we know not how to go,
Till a blessing thou bestow.

4 Comfort those who weep and mourn,
Let the time of joy return;

Them that are cast down lift up,
Make them strong in grace and hope.

Page 38

5 Grant that all may seek and find,
Thee a gracious God and kind;
Heal the sick, the captive free,
Let us all rejoice in thee.

HYMN 22.

S. M.

1 A charge to keep I have,
A God to glorify;
A never-dying soul to save,
And fit it for the sky.

2 To serve the present age,
My calling to fulfill;
O may it all my powers engage,
To do my Master's will!

3 Arm me with jealous care,
As in thy sight to live;
And O, thy servant, Lord, prepare,
A strict account to give!

4 Help me to watch and pray,
And on thyself rely;
Assured if I my trust betray,
I shall for ever die.

APPENDIX

HYMN 23.

P. M.

1 Come, thou Fount of every blessing,
Tune my heart to sing thy grace;
Streams of mercy, never ceasing,
Call for songs of loudest praise.
Teach me some melodious sonnet,
Sang by flaming tongues above;
Praise the mount; I'm fix'd upon it,
Mount of thy redeeming love.

Page 39

2 Here I'll raise my Ebenezer,
Hither by thy help I'm come;
And I hope, by thy good pleasure,
Safely to arrive at home.
Jesus sought me when a stranger,
Wand'ring from the fold of God;
He, to save my soul from danger,
Freely shed his precious blood.

3. O to grace how great a debtor
Daily I'm constrain'd to be!
Let thy goodness, like a fetter,
Bind my wand'ring heart to thee.
Prone to wander, Lord, I feel it,
Prone to leave the God I love;
Here's my heart; O take and seal it,
Seal it for thy courts above.

Praise God, from whom all blessings flow,
Praise him, all creatures here below;
Praise him above, ye heavenly host,
Praise Father, Son, and Holy Ghost.

Appendix

To God the Father, God the Son,
And God the Spirit, Three in One,
Be honor, praise, and glory given,
By all on earth, and all in heaven.

Now let the Father, and the Son,
And Spirit be adored,
Where there are works to make him known,
Or saints to love the Lord.

Page 40

To God the Father, Son,
And Spirit, One in Three,
Be glory as it was, is now,
And shall for ever be.
Lord, dismiss us with thy blessing,
Bid us now depart in peace;
Still on heavenly manna feeding,
Let our faith and love increase.

Fill each breast with consolation;
Up to thee our hearts we raise;
When we reach our blissful station,
Then we'll give thee nobler praise.

About the Author

DR. STEPHEN A. REDMOND, DMIN

STEPHEN REDMOND WAS BORN in Lexington, Mississippi, on May 9, 1970, and raised by a single mother and his grandparents (Rev. Warren G. Booker Sr. and Zeporah E. Gilley-Booker). At the age of five, Dr. Redmond was detained by police in his hometown of Lexington, Mississippi, for participating in a Civil Rights March led and organized by his grandfather, Rev. Warren G. Booker Sr.

Dr. Redmond grew up working on his great-grandfather's small farm twenty miles north of Lexington, Mississippi, in an area called Sweet Canaan and Black Hawk, home to Mississippi's Choctaw Indians. As a youth, he attended Epworth United Methodist Church in Lexington, Mississippi. Dr. Redmond graduated from Jacob J. McClain High School in Lexington, Mississippi, in 1989. After high school, Dr. Redmond enlisted in the US Marine Corps and enrolled in Rust College of Holly Springs, Mississippi, in 1989.

After completing his first year at Rust College, Dr. Redmond enlisted in the Marine Corps full-time, and from 1990 to 1991, he participated in the Desert Shield/Desert Storm ground-war campaign, earning a Combat Action Ribbon, Kuwait Liberation Medal, Southwest Asia Service Medal, and meritorious promotion.

In 1993, after receiving an honorable discharge from the Marine Corps, Dr. Redmond began working at Sears Roebuck and Company and re-enrolled in Rust College as a sophomore. While at Rust College, he majored in social work and minored in business administration with a management concentration. He also served as the Social Work Association vice president under the advisement of Dr. Gimma Beckley. The Social Work Association, a student-led organization, highlighted the social welfare

About the Author

needs of the college and the surrounding communities of Holly Springs, Mississippi.

After Dr. Redmond's junior year at Rust College, he relocated to Atlanta, Georgia, and completed his bachelor's degree in business administration in 1988 at Saint Leo University. Dr. Redmond then enrolled in Embry-Riddle Aeronautical University's master of business administration program, and in 2001, he interned with the Federal Aviation Administration Office of Performance Management and Cost in Washington, DC. His primary responsibilities were taking notes at congressional hearings on issues concerning aviation and transportation and reporting to the Office of Performance Management.

In January 2001, Dr. Redmond received his master's degree from Embry-Riddle. However, on September 11, 2001, a terrorist attack struck America, causing the aviation industry to go through a period of collapse. As a result, Dr. Redmond relocated to Atlanta, Georgia, where he taught algebra I at Fredrick Douglas High School from 2001 until 2003 in the Atlanta public schools.

From 2003 to 2005, Dr. Redmond served as the executive director of Metro Atlanta Respite and Developmental Center (MARDS), focusing on the educational and healthcare needs of children and young adults with physical and mental disabilities. In search of his family's religious origin, Dr. Redmond enrolled in the Candler School of Theology at Emory University in 2005. In 2009, Dr. Redmond earned a master of divinity degree and certification in "Black Church Studies" from Emory University.

After finishing his seminary training at Candler School of Theology, Emory University, he served as campus director of the Wesley Foundation at Alabama State University and as assistant pastor at Hoosier Memorial United Methodist Church in Atlanta, Georgia, from 2009 until 2012.

In 2012, Dr. Redmond served as the youth director at Union Hill United Methodist Church in Georgia and organized the church's first international mission journey in the church's 175-year history. The youth traveled to Eleuthera, Bahamas, and engaged in missions with the Bahamas Habitat for Humanity. During his tenure at Union Hill United Methodist Church, he was accepted into the doctor of ministry degree program at Perkins School of Theology, Southern Methodist University in Dallas, Texas. In 2015, Dr. Redmond wrote his dissertation ("Short-Term Missions as a Means of Engaging Youth in Cross-Cultural Intelligence") and was awarded a doctor of ministry degree from Perkins School of Theology, South Methodist University.

Upon completion of his doctoral degree, Dr. Redmond served five years as the Disaster Response Warehouse and logistic manager for the North Georgia Conference of the United Methodist Church and as the volunteer coordinator for the United Methodist Committee on Relief (UMCOR). As the warehouse and logistics manager, Dr. Redmond collected, housed, and distributed disaster response materials to areas across the Southeastern region of the United States that were impacted by hurricanes, floods, and tornadoes. In addition, he assisted with recruiting volunteers and helped to disburse volunteer teams to disaster areas.

In August of 2024, he served as campus chaplain and professor of religion at Rust College in Holly Springs, Mississippi. Dr. Redmond lives in Douglasville, Georgia and is married to Aliya Redmond, and they have four children (Brittany, Stephen, Aaron, and Elijah). Dr. Redmond is a member of Kappa Alpha Psi Fraternity Incorporated, Disabled Veterans of America, Veterans of Foreign Wars, and the Free and Accepted Prince Hall Masons. In addition, Dr. Redmond is a member of the Golden Key International Honour Society and is respectfully noted in Dr. Taharka Adé's (professor of African studies at San Diego State University) book, *W. E. B. Du Bois' Africa: Scrambling for a New Africa*. Dr. Redmond's hobbies are traveling, reading, journaling, listening to music, hiking, and engaging in cross-cultural immersions.

EXCLUSIVE THEOLOGY

The North Georgia Conference of the United Methodist Church reported an estimated membership of 340,000, with 57,045 of that population being African Americans. While the importance of ethnic and racial diversity has been a constant, the North Georgia Conference of the United Methodist Church's data illustrates that diverse ethnic and racial groups do not consider the North Georgia Conference to be wholly diverse and theologically inclusive.

The institutional and systemic racialized beliefs, values, and practices of exclusive theology within Methodism have historically inspired exploitation, subjugation, and physical violence against marginalized people, both domestically and internationally. Moreover, the North Georgia Conference of the United Methodist Church's behavior since the start of this in-depth research project regarding cultural inclusion and multiculturalism has been reflective of the church's racialized historical values, beliefs, and actions toward diverse groups, which stemmed from the earlier Methodist missional engagements to the Colony of Georgia.

The forefathers of the Georgia Methodist movements clearly practiced an exclusive theology motivated by White superiority, non-White inferiority, and Western imperialism. In 2024, while the church has made many important steps toward becoming more socially inclusive (ordaining LGBTQ+ persons and consecrating a greater number of non-White bishops), the reality of exclusive theology is still very much alive today within the United Methodist Church and can be witnessed with an in-depth look beneath the surface of the church's public persona.

Inclusive theology encourages cultural awareness, critical thought, and revolutionary action in challenging the status quo of institutional structures and socio-systems devoted to maintaining dehumanization and sectarianism. If ever the North Georgia Conference of the United Methodist Church honestly desires to eradicate human and theological exclusion within its boundaries, it will have to engage in radical institutional transformation whereby its historical White Southern beliefs, values, and practices will need to be fully exposed for everyone to bear witness to and reparations must then be rendered in accordance with the demands of those who have been historically exploited and marginalized.

Furthermore, the reparational scope should include a blank check with the financial amount to be written in by those racial and ethnic groups the church has historically oppressed, both stateside and globally. If these practical actions never become a reality and the church outwardly reinvents itself while covertly holding on to its aged, Southern, White conservative traditions, it will continue to perpetuate social injustice and violence against marginalized people in the future.

Bibliography

ABC News. "How Donald Trump Perpetuated the 'Birther' Movement for Years." Sept. 16, 2016. https://abcnews.go.com/Politics/donald-trump-perpetuated-birther-movement-years/story?id=42138176.

Adams, Henry. *Methodism in the West Indies*. London: Forgotten, 2018.

Adé, Taharka. *W. E. B. DuBois' Africa: Scrambling for a New Africa*. New York: Anthem, 2023.

Agence France-Presse. "Julian Assange Says Victorious Barack Obama's 'Wolf in Sheep's Clothing.'" NDTV World, Nov. 7, 2012. www.ndtv.com/world-news/julian-assange-says-victorious-barack-obama-wolf-in-sheeps-clothing-504019.

Anderson, Carol. *White Rage: The Unspoken Truth of Our Racial Divide*. New York: Bloomsbury, 2016.

Asbury, Francis. "The Journal and Letters of Francis Asbury—Volume 1." Wesley Center Online. https://wesley.nnu.edu/other-theologians/francis-asbury/the-journal-and-letters-of-francis-asbury-volume-i/.

Ashmore, Susan Y. "Thoughts on White Supremacy: Atticus Greene Haygood, White Southern Moderates, and the New South." Oxford College Founders' Week lecture, Emory University, Feb. 6, 2009, Atlanta, GA.

Associated Press. "Is Obama A Socialist?" CNBC. June 4, 2012. https://www.cnbc.com/2012/06/04/is-obama-a-socialist.html?msockid=0b9056a01a4a627f31e946b71b6663a1.

Bahamas Methodist Habitat. "Short Term Missions." https://www.methodisthabitat.org/short-term-missions.html.

Baker, Frank. "John Wesley's Last Visit to Charleston." *South Carolina Historical Magazine*, Oct. 1977.

Baker, Webster B. *History of Rust College*. Published by the author, 1924.

Bannon, Steve, dir. *Fire From the Heartland: The Awakening of the Conservative Woman*. Washington, DC: Citizens United, 2010.

Beckles, Hilary, and Verene Shepherd. *Caribbean Slave Society and Economy*. New York: New, 1991.

Bethabara. "The Stories of Bethabara's Enslaved." https://historicbethabara.org/the-stories-of-bethabaras-enslaved/.

Bevans, Stephen B., and Roger P. Schroeder. *Constants in Context: A Theology of Mission for Today*. Maryknoll, NY: Orbis, 2004.

Black Methodists for Church Renewal. "Our History." https://www.bmcrumc.org/about.

The Book of Discipline of the United Methodist Church. Nashville: United Methodist, 2016.

Bibliography

The Book of Discipline of the United Methodist Church. Nashville: United Methodist, 2012.

The Book of Resolutions of the United Methodist Church. Nashville: United Methodist, 2012.

Born, W. Michael. "Richard S. Rust, a Minister with a Mission." Worldwide Faith News, Oct. 3, 2000. https://archive.wfn.org/2000/10/msg00018.html.

Brawley, James P. *Two Centuries of Methodist Concern: Bondage, Freedom, and Education of Black People.* New York: Vantage, 1974.

Burke, Minyvonne, and Marianna Sotomayor. "James Alex Fields Found Guilty of Killing Heather Heyer During Violent Charlottesville White Nationalist Rally." NBC News, Dec. 7, 2018.

Candler School of Theology. "Mission, Vision, and Values." https://candler.emory.edu/about-candler/mission-vision-and-values/.

CBS News. "Full CBS South Carolina Republican Debate." Feb. 15, 2016. YouTube, 1:39:20. https://www.youtube.com/watch?v=Un3OhYs-tCE.

Central Jurisdiction Study Committee. "Central Jurisdiction Speaks." College of Bishops of the Central Jurisdiction and the Committee, 1962. Bridwell Library Special Collections, Southern Methodist University, Dallas, TX.

Champion, Lovelace, Sr. *Black Methodism Basic Beliefs: A Congress of Black Methodism* (C.O.B.M.). Nashville: AMEC Sunday School Union, 1995.

Chasmar, Jessica. "Rick Tyler, House Candidate, Wants To 'Make America White Again.'" *Washington Times*, June 22, 2016.

CNN Politics. "Full Text of Trump's Executive Order on 7-Nation Ban, Refugee Suspension." CNN, Jan. 28, 2017. www.cnn.com/2017/01/28/politics/text-of-trump-executive-order-nation-ban-refugees/index.html.

Coke, Thomas. *A History of the West Indies: Containing the Natural, Civil, and Ecclesiastical History of Each Island.* Vol. 3. New York: Routledge, 2006.

Cone, James H. *God of the Oppressed:* Minneapolis: Seabury, 1975.

———. "Sanctification and Liberation and Black Worship." *Theology Today* 35 (1978) 139–52.

Corbett, Steve, and Brian Fikkert. *When Helping Hurts: How To Alleviate Poverty Without Hurting the Poor and Yourself.* Chicago: Moody, 2009.

Crum, Mason. *The Negro in the Methodist Church.* New York: Division of Education and Cultivation Board of Missions and Church Extension, the United Methodist Church, 1951.

Culver, Dwight W. *Negro Segregation in the Methodist Church.* New Haven: Yale University Press, 1953.

Dash, Mike. "Antigua's Disputed Slave Conspiracy of 1736." *Smithsonian Magazine*, Jan. 2, 2013. https://www.smithsonianmag.com/history/antiguas-disputed-slave-conspiracy-of-1736-117569/.

Davis, Morris L. *The Methodist Unification: Christianity and the Politics of Race in the Jim Crow Era.* New York: New York University Press, 2008.

Digital Library of Georgia. "Kitty's Cottage Historical Marker." https://dlg.usg.edu/record/dlg_ghm_kittys-cottage.

"Disaffiliation Process and Information." The North Georgia Conference of the United Methodist. https://www.ngumc.org/disaffiliation-process-and-information.

Dixon, Thomas. *The Clansman.* Dunlop, New York: Grosset and AMP, 1905.

Donoghue, Eddie. *Black Breeding Machines: The Breeding of Negro Slaves in the Diaspora.* Bloomington, IN: AuthorHouse, 2008.

Bibliography

Dotson, Junius. "One Church Plan." *By Faith Magazine*, July/Aug. 2019.

Douglasville First United Methodist Church History Committee of 1980. *History of Douglasville First United Methodist Church*. Douglasville, GA: B & C, 1981.

Dunlap-Berg, Barbara. "Black Clergy, Laity Share Perspectives on Church's Future." UM News, Apr. 10, 2023. https://www.umnews.org/en/news/black-clergy-laity-share-perspectives-on-churchs-future.

Dunn, Adrienne. "Fact Check: Meme on Trump's 'Very Fine People' Quote Contains Inaccuracies. *USA Today*, Oct. 17, 2020. www.usatoday.com/story/news/factcheck/2020/10/17/fact-check-trump-quote-very-fine-people-charlottesville/5943239002/.

Dutton, Keith, "The Chapel Font. Wesley's Chapel and Leysian Mission." *Window on Wesley's*, Dec. 2018/Jan. 2019.

Dyde, Brian. *A History of Antigua: The Unsuspected Isle*. London: Macmillan Caribbean, 2000.

Erskine, Noel L. *Plantation Church: How African American Religion Was Born in Caribbean Slavery*. New York: Oxford University Press, 2014.

Evon, Dan. "Make American White Again." Snopes, June 22, 2016. https://www.snopes.com/fact-check/make-america-white-again-billboard/.

Farquhar, David U. *Missions and Society in the Leeward Islands, 1810–850: An Ecclesiastical and Social Analysis*. Boston: Mt. Prospect, 1999.

Felton, Ralph A. *The Ministry of the Central Jurisdiction of the Methodist Church*. New York: Division of National Missions of the Methodist Board of Missions, 1954.

Felton, Rebecca L. "Mrs. Rebecca Felton Speech Before the Georgia Agricultural Society." *The Weekly Star*, Aug. 11, 1897.

———. *My Memoirs of Georgia Politics*. Atlanta: Index Printing Company, 1911.

Ferree, Doris. "General BCMR Celebrated Its 50th Anniversary in Cincinnati, Ohio Where the First National Conference Was Held in 1968." *South Eastern Jurisdiction Informer* 5 (2017).

Fox News. "Trayvon Martin Attacked George Zimmerman, Report Says." Fox News, Mar. 26, 2012. www.foxnews.com/world/trayvon-martin-attacked-george-zimmerman-report-says.

Frank, Thomas E. *Polity, Practice, and the Mission of the United Methodist Church*. Nashville: Abingdon, 2006.

Frazier, E. Franklin. *The Negro Church in America*. New York: Random House, 1963.

Freire, Paulo. *Pedagogy of the Oppressed*. New York: Bloomsbury, 2018.

Friedman, Edwin H. *Generation to Generation: Family Process in Church and Synagogue*. New York: Guilford, 1985.

Friedman, Thomas. *The World Is Flat: A Brief History of the Twenty-First Century*. New York: Farrar, Straus, and Giroux, 2005.

Gerbner, Katharine. *Christian Slavery: Conversion and Race in the Protestant Atlantic World*. Philadelphia: University of Pennsylvania Press, 2018.

Georgia Historical Society. "First Methodist Church." https://www.georgiahistory.com/ghmi_marker_updated/first-methodist-church.

Goveia, Elsa V. *Slave Society in the British Leeward Islands at the End of the Eighteenth Century*. New Haven. Yale University Press, 1965.

Global Methodist Church. "Our Formation." https://www.globalmethodist.org/launch-information.

Graham, J. H. *Black United Methodists Retrospect and Prospect*. New Jersey: Vantage, 1979.

Bibliography

———. *Mississippi Circuit Riders, 1865–1965*. Nashville: Parthenon, 1967.

Green, Abigail, and Viaene Vincent. *Religious Internationals in the Modern World: Globalization and Faith Communities Since 1750*. London: Palgrave Macmillan, 2012.

Green, Emma, "Conservative Christians Just Retook the United Methodist Church." *Atlantic*, Feb. 26, 2019.

Gryboski, Michael. "The United Methodist Church Upholds Position Against Homosexuality, Same-Sex Marriage. *Christian Post*, Feb. 26, 2019. https://www.christianpost.com/news/united-methodist-church-upholds-position-against-homosexuality-same-sex-marriage.html.

Guder, Darrell L. *Missional Church: A Vision for the Sending of the Church in North America*. Grand Rapids: Eerdmans, 1998.

Gumbs, W. *Methodism in the MCCA: Its Past, Present, and Future*. St. Thomas, U.S. Virgin Islands: Supreme, 2007.

Hall, Edward, and M. R. Hall. *Understanding Cultural Differences: Germans, French, and Americans*. Yarmouth, ME: Intercultural, 1990.

Harrelson, Walter J. *The New Interpreter's Study Bible: New Revised Standard Version with the Apocrypha*. Nashville: Abingdon, 2003.

Hatfield, Jenn. "Partisan Divides over K–12 Education in 8 Charts." Pew Research Center, June 5, 2023. https://www.pewresearch.org/short-reads/2023/06/05/partisan-divides-over-k-12-education-in-8-charts/.

Haygood, A. G. *Our Brother in Black: His Freedom and His Future*. Nashville: Southern Methodist, 1881.

———. *Pleas for Progress*. Nashville: Southern Methodist, 1889.

Heitzenrater, Richard P. *Wesley and the People Called Methodists*. Nashville: Abingdon, 1995.

History.com Editors. "Nat Turner." History.com, May 28, 2025. https://www.history.com/articles/nat-turner.

———. "Trail of Tears." History.com, May 28, 2025. https://www.history.com/articles/trail-of-tears.

Huff, A. V., Jr. "Capers, Williams." South Carolina Encyclopedia, July 20, 2022. https://www.scencyclopedia.org/sce/entries/capers-william/.

Jackson, Edwin L. "James Oglethorpe, 1696–1785." New George Encyclopedia, July 21, 2020. https://www.georgiaencyclopedia.org/articles/government-politics/james-oglethorpe-1696-1785/.

Jaffe, Alexandra, and Corky Siemaszko. "Outrage as Trump Inspired Candidate Wants to 'Make America White Again.'" NBC News, Jun. 23, 2016. https://www.nbcnews.com/news/us-news/outrage-trump-inspired-congressional-candidate-wants-make-america-white-again-n597916?cid=sm_fb&fbclid=IwY2xjawM6kRZlehRuA2FlbQIxMQBicmlkETF0c1gzdk4ydUxvckJpTmQwAR6rgsMFVsCYUMGQT-PjA7n5PTe_9fkC2pHNfTx41oIjbOAvNGHK7PsdvJZClg_aem_-k8A0c9PYLBfSa9Cw8BGdw.

Johnson, Kevin. *Mission Trip Prep Kit Leader's Guide: Complete Preparation for Your Student's Cross-Cultural Experience*. Grand Rapids: Zondervan, 2003.

Jones, Rickey. "Trump, 'True' Americans Triumph." *Courier Journal*, Nov. 16, 2016. www.courier-journal.com/story/opinion/contributors/2016/11/16/rickyjones-trump-and-true-americans-triumph/93878136

Jones, Robert P. *The End of White Christian America*. New York: Simon and Schuster, 2016.

Bibliography

Levenson, Eric, et al. "What We Know About the 5 Deaths in the Pro-Trump Mob That Stormed the Capitol." CNN, Jan. 8, 2021. https://www.cnn.com/2021/01/07/us/capitol-mob-deaths/index.html.

Kendi, Ibram X. *Stamped from the Beginning: The Definitive History of Racist Ideas in America*. New York: Bold Type, 2016.

"Klan Is Established with Impressiveness." *Atlanta Constitution*, Nov. 28, 1915.

Lamothe, Dan. "Democracy Dies in Darkness." *Washington Post*, Oct. 5, 2019.

Lindsay, Nick. *And I'm Glad: An Oral History of Edisto Island*. Charleston, SC: Arcadia, 2000.

Livermore, David A. *Cultural Intelligence: Improving Your CQ to Engage Our Multicultural World*. Grand Rapids: Baker, 2009.

———. *Serving with Eyes Wide Open: Doing Short-Term Missions with Cultural Intelligence*. Grand Rapids: Baker, 2013.

Maddox, Randy L. *Responsible Grace: John Wesley's Practical Theology*. Nashville: Abingdon, 1994.

Malony, H. Newton, Jr. "John Wesley's Primitive Physick: An 18th–Century Health Psychology." *Journal of Health Psychology* 1 (1996) 147–59. https://journals.sagepub.com/doi/abs/10.1177/135910539600100201.

Manskar, Steve. "No Holiness but Social Holiness." Discipleship Ministries, Nov. 2015. https://www.umcdiscipleship.org/blog/no-holiness-but-social-holiness.

McClain, William B. *Black People in the Methodist Church: Whither Thou Goest?* Nashville: Abingdon, 1984.

McEllhenney, John. "Harry Hosier, c. 1750–1806." General Commission on Archives and History. https://gcah.org/biographies/harry-hosier/.

Methodist Church of Antigua & Barbuda. "Part 1: The Beginnings of Methodism in Antigua." https://methodistchurchantigua.org/our-history-1/.

Mills, Frederick V. "James Osgood Andrew, 1794–1871." New Georgia Encyclopedia, Sept. 15, 2014. https://www.georgiaencyclopedia.org/articles/arts-culture/james-osgood-andrew-1794-1871/.

Milman, Oliver. "Standing Rock Sioux Tribe Says Trump Is Breaking the Law with Dakota Access Order. *Guardian*, Jan. 26, 2017. www.theguardian.com/us-news/2017/jan/26/standing-rock-sioux-tribe-trump-breaking-law-dakota-access.

"Minutes of the Methodist Protestant Church, 1830–1839." Pitts Library Special Collections and Archives, Pitts Theology, Library, Candler School of Theology, Atlanta, GA.

Moran, Dan. "Annual Conference Sessions Weigh In on Possibility for 'A Way Forward.'" Juicy Ecumenism, Aug. 30, 2018. https://juicyecumenism.com/2018/08/30/annual-conference-weigh-in-on-way-forward/.

Mulberry Grove Foundation. "A Timeline of Mulberry Grove." https://www.mulberrygrove.org/timeline.html.

Murray, Peter C. *Methodists and the Crucible of Race*. Columbia: University of Missouri Press, 2004.

National Voluntary Organizations Active in Disaster. "Impact by the Numbers." https://www.nvoad.org.

Nicholson, Zoe. "Subsumed by Industry. How Do We Honor Its Conflicted History?" *Savannah Morning News*, Sept. 8, 2022.

The North Georgia Conference. "Disaffiliation Process and Information." Dec. 31, 2023. https://www.ngumc.org/disaffiliation-process-and-information.

Bibliography

The North Georgia Conference. "North Georgia Annual Conference Report 2022." Jun. 8, 2022. https://www.ngumc.org/newsdetail/north-georgia-annual-conference-report-16519407?fbclid=IwY2xjawM6mHVleHRuA2FlbQIxMABic mlkETFoc1gzdk4ydUxvckJpTmQwAR7tg62Nx9nA1w7AK1eoUhVeHoTAiVHD-VgcIeZ3viAqsXq63YMi5uYsks3Pa5Q_aem_XVXq06x-SqEupH5E9gvovg.

Obama, Barack. *Dreams from My Father: A Story of Race and Inheritance.* New York: Crown, 2004.

O'Neall, John B. *The Negro Law of South Carolina.* Columbia: John G. Bowan, 1848.

Ortiz, Erik. "Trump, Mexican President Pena Nieto Agree to End Public Tiff About Border Wall, Mexico Says. NBC News, Jan. 27, 2017. www.nbcnews.com/politics/2016-election/trump-mexican-president-pe-nieto-share-phone-call-amid-border-n713176.

Outtraveler Staff. "KKK to Protest Gay-Inclusive Methodist Conference." Advocate, Sept. 3, 2005. www.advocate.com/news/2005/09/03/kkk-protest-gay-inclusive-methodist-conference.

Oxford Historical Society. "Catherine ('Miss Kitty') Andrew Boyd." www.oxfordhistoricalsociety.org/catherine-miss-kitty-andrew-boyd.html.

Paris, Peter J. *The Social Teaching of the Black Churches.* Philadelphia: Fortress, 1985.

Pew Research Center. *America's Changing Religious Landscape: Christians Decline Sharply as Share of Population; Unaffiliated and Other Faiths Continue to Grow.* May 12, 2015. https://www.pewresearch.org/wp-content/uploads/sites/20/2015/05/RLS-08-26-full-report.pdf.

―――. *In U.S., Decline of Christianity Continues at Rapid Pace: An Update on America's Changing Religious Landscape.* Oct. 17, 2019. https://www.pewresearch.org/wp-content/uploads/sites/20/2019/10/Trends-in-Religious-Identity-and-Attendance-FOR-WEB-1.pdf.

Pollitzer, William S. *The Gullah People and Their African Heritage.* Athens: University of Georgia Press, 1999.

Preservation Society of Charleston. "Gadsden's Wharf." https://old.preservationsociety.org/locations/gadsdens-wharf/.

Pressly, Paul M. *A Southern Underground Railroad: Black Georgians and the Promise of Spanish Florida and Indian Country.* Athens. University of Georgia Press, 2024.

Raboteau, Albert J. *Slave Religion: The "Invisible Institution" in the Antebellum South.* New York: Oxford University Press, 1978.

Recinos, Harold J. *Good News from the Barrio: Prophetic Witness for the Church.* Louisville: Westminster John Knox, 2006.

Redmond, Stephen. "Short-Term Missions as a Means of Engaging Youth in Cultural Diversity in Small Churches." DMin diss., Perkins School of Theology, 2015.

Remillard, Arthur. *Southern Civil Religions: Imagining Good Society in the Post-Reconstruction Era.* Athens: University of Georgia Press, 2011.

Report of the Incorporated Society for the Conversion and Religious Instruction and Education of the Negro Slaves in the British West India Islands. London: R. Gilbert, 1825.

Richey, Russell E., et al. *American Methodism: A Compact History.* Nashville: Abingdon, 2010.

Robertson, Campbell, and Elizabeth Dias. "United Methodists Announce Plan to Split over Same-Sex Marriage." *New York Times,* Jan. 3, 2020.

Bibliography

Robinson, Morgan. "The American Colonization Society." The White House Historical Association, June 22, 2020. https://www.whitehousehistory.org/the-american-colonization-society.

Ryden, David B. *West Indian Slavery and British Abolition, 1783–1807*. Cambridge: Cambridge University Press, 2009.

Sanneh, Lamin, and Joel Carpenter. *The Changing Face of Christianity: Africa, the West, and the World*. New York: Oxford University Press, 2005.

Saunt, Claudio. "Creek Indians." New Georgia Encyclopedia, Aug. 25, 2020. https://www.georgiaencyclopedia.org/articles/history-archaeology/creek-indians/.

Schwartz, Marie J. *Birthing a Slave: Motherhood and Medicine in the Antebellum South*. Cambridge: Harvard University Press, 2006.

Setili, Amanda. "Redistricting in North Georgia for Mission and Stewardship—2020." The North Georgia Conference of the United Methodist Church. www.ngumc.org/district-restructure.

Sheets, Herchel H. *Methodism in North Georgia: A History of the North Georgia Conference*. Milledgeville, GA: Boyd, 2005.

Shepherd, Verene A. and Hilary Beckles. *Caribbean Slavery in the Atlantic World: A Student Reader*. Kingston, Jamaica: Ian Randle, 2000.

Sherlock, Hugh. *The Conference of the Methodist Church in the Caribbean and the Americas (M. C. C. A.)—Brochure*. Barbados, The B'dos Hardware Co. Dec. 8, 1968.

SlaveVoyages. "Voyages." https://www.slavevoyages.org/voyage/trans-atlantic#voyages.

Smith, David, and Ben Jacobs. "'Unfit to Be President': Obama Hammers Trump with Harshest Comments Yet." *Guardian*, Aug. 2, 2016. www.theguardian.com/us-news/2016/aug/02/barack-obama-donald-trump-president-republican-party.

Smith, Warren T. *John Wesley and Slavery*. Nashville: Abingdon, 1986.

Spencer, Charles. *Edisto Island, 1663 to 1860: Wild Eden to Cotton Aristocracy*. Charleston, SC: History, 2008.

St. James Community Church. "Our Story: Where Community Meets Spirituality." St. James Community Church. https://stjamescca.org/home/about-us/our-story/.

Sublette, Ned, and Constance Sublette. *The American Slave Coast: A History of the Slave-Breeding Industry*. Chicago: Lawrence Hill, 2016.

Sullivan, Andrew. "The First Gay President." *Newsweek*, May 14, 2012.

Thomas, James S. "Methodism's Splendid Mission: The Black Colleges." *Methodist History* 22 (1984) 139–57.

Thurmond, Michael L. *James Oglethorpe: Father of Georgia: A Founder's Journey from Slave Trader to Abolitionist*. Athens: University of Georgia Press, 2024.

UMVIM. "Trainings." https://umvim.org/trainings.

US Census Bureau. "Race and Ethnicity in the United States: 2010 Census and 2020 Census." Aug. 12, 2021. https://www.census.gov/library/visualizations/interactive/race-and-ethnicity-in-the-united-state-2010-and-2020-census.html.

Van Dyke, Michelle Broder. "This Miami Dolphins Player Got Emotional When Asked About Trump's 'Son of a Bitch' Comment." BuzzFeed News, Sept. 24, 2017. https://www.buzzfeednews.com/article/mbvd/real-men-cry.

Volle, Adam. "Gadsen Flag." *Britannica*. https://www.britannica.com/topic/Gadsden-flag.

Walker, Rob. "The Shifting Symbolism of the Gadsden Flag," *New Yorker*, Oct. 2, 2016. https://www.newyorker.com/news/news-desk/the-shifting-symbolism-of-the-gadsden-flag.

Bibliography

Walsh, Steve. "Marine Corps Aims to Tackle the Evolving Face of Racism." National Public Radio, Mar. 31, 2020. https://www.npr.org/2020/03/31/824370942/marine-corps-aims-to-tackle-evolving-face-of-white-supremacy.

Wason, Brandon. *Religion of the Heart: John Wesley and the Legacy of Methodism in America*. Pitts Theology Library, Candler School of Theology, Atlanta, Georgia, 2018. Published in conjunction with an exhibition of the same title, Dec. 11, 2017–Mar. 9, 2018. https://digital.pitts.emory.edu/files/exfiles/gallery/2017-WesleyanaCatalog.pdf.

Wells-Barnett, Ida B. *Southern Horrors: Lynch Law in All Its Phases*. New York: New York Age, 1892. https://encyclopediavirginia.org/primary-documents/southern-horrors-lynch-law-in-all-its-phases-by-ida-b-wells-1892/.

Wesley, John. *Journal from October 14, 1735, to November 29, 1745*. Vol. 1 of *The Works of John Wesley*. Grand Rapids: Zondervan, 1958. https://wesleyscholar.com/wp-content/uploads/2019/01/Volume-1-Journal-1735-1745.pdf.

———. *Primitive Physick: Or, an Easy and Natural Method of Curing Most Diseases*. 14th ed. Bristol: William Pine, 1770.

———. *Thoughts upon Slavery*. London: R. Hawes, 1774.

Wilder, Craig S. *Ebony and Ivy: Race, Slavery, and the Troubled History of America's Universities*. New York: Bloomsbury, 2013.

Willingham, Robert M., Jr. *History of the First United Church of Washington, Georgia*. Washington, GA: First United Methodist Church, 1984.

Wilson-Hartgrove, Jonathan. *Reconstructing the Gospel: Finding Freedom from Slaveholders' Religion*. Downers Grove, IL: InterVarsity, 2018.

Wise, Lindsay, and Andrew Duehren. "Mob Storms Capitol: Pro-Trump Rioters Break into Halls of Congress, Disrupt Electoral-Vote Ratification." *Wall Street Journal*, Jan. 7, 2021.

Wong, Edlie L. *Racial Reconstruction: Black Inclusion, Chinese Exclusion, and the Fictions of Citizenship*. New York: New York University Press, 2015.

Wood, Charles M., and Ellen Blue. *Attentive to God: Thinking Theologically in Ministry*. Nashville: Abingdon, 2008.

Woodson, Carter G. *African Myths: Together with Proverbs*. Washington DC: Association for the Study of Negro Life and History, 1928.

———. *The Education of the Negro*. Washington DC: Associated, 1919.

———. *Free Negro Heads of Families in the United States in 1830*. Washington DC: Association for the Study of Negro Life and History, 1925.

———. *The History of the Negro Church*. Washington DC: Associated, 1921.

———. *The Mind of the Negro: As Reflected in Letters During the Crisis 1800–1860*. Washington DC: Association for the Study of Negro Life and History, 1926.

———. *The Mis-Education of the Negro*. Washington DC: Associated, 1933.

———. *The Negro Professional Man and the Community*. Washington DC: Association for the Study of Negro Life and History, 1934.

———. *The Rural Negro*. Washington DC: Association for the Study of Negro Life and History, 1930.

Wuthnow, Robert. *Acts of Compassion: Caring for the Others and Helping Ourselves*. Princeton: Princeton University Press, 1991.

———. *After Heaven: Spirituality in America Since the 1950s*. Los Angeles: University of California Press, 1998.

———. *Sharing the Journey: Support Groups and America's New Quest for Community*. New York: Free Press, 1994.

Index

Adams, Henry, 53, 59
Alfonso V (King), 35
Allen, Beverly, 57
Allen, Richard, 43
Alley, Mary, 37
Anderson, Carol, 103
Andrew, James Osgood, 71, 75–79
Andrew-Shell, Kitty, 77–81
Aristotle, 29–30
Asbury, Francis, 42–43, 57, 59–60, 72
Ashmore, Susan Y., 99–100
Assange, Julian, 120
Aymar, James, 65

Baker, Frank, 57
Bangs, Nathan, 74
Bannon, Stephen, 125, 126
Bellah, Robert, 101, 102
Bellinger, William, 56
Berger, David, 15, 16
Bohler, Peter, 52
Booker, Warren G., 17–19, 94
Born, W. Michael, 85
Brawley, James P., 85
Breitbart, Andrew, 125
Brian, Hugh, 56
Brook, Robert N., xxiii
Bull, William, 56
Burke, Minyvonne, 87
Burton, John, 49

Callaway, Morgan, 23
Campbell, Sophia, 37
Candler, Warren A., 23

Capers, William, 23, 24, 58, 71–75
Coke, Thomas, 43, 57, 59–60
Cone, James H., 45, 108
Corbett, Steve, 111
Cotton, John, 31
Culver, Dwight W., 9
Cuthbert, Anne, 69
Cuthbert, John, 69

Dash, Mike, 60
Davies, Samuel, 58–59
Davis, Humphrey, 61
Davis, Jefferson, 102
Davis, Morris L., 90, 93
Dease, Robin, 135
Delamotta, Charles, 53
Dias, Elizabeth, 25
Dixon, Thomas, 27
Donoghue, Eddie, 10, 61–62
Dotson, Junius B., 21
Duehren, Andrew, 127
Dunlap-Berg, Barbara, 92
Dunn, Adrienne, 132
Dutton, Keith, 41, 60
Dyde, Brian, 62

Elizabeth (Queen), 45
Erskine, Noel Leo, 49, 107–8
Erwin, Richard, 93
Evans, James E., 23
Eveleigh, Samuel, 56–57
Evon, Dan, 125

Index

Felton, Rebecca L., 85–86
Ferree, Doris, 132
Fields, James Alex, 87
Fikkert, Brian, 111
Fisk, Wilbur, 74
Foss, Cyrus D., 91
Fresh, Fredrick, 25

Gammon, Elijah H., 91
Garden, Alexander, 55–56
Gasper, David, 60
Gerbner, Katharine, 13, 35, 47–48, 67
Gilbert, France, 60
Gilbert, Nathaniel, 37–40, 60–61, 64–65, 79, 98
Goveia, Elsa V., 50, 51
Graham, John H., 37, 43–44, 62, 89–93, 93, 95
Greenwood, Leonora, 77
Gryboski, Michael, 130
Gumbs, W., 43

Hall, Prince, 43
Hannity, Sean, 121
Harper, J. S., 23
Harry, Black, 43, 44
Hatfield, Jenn, 105
Haupert-Johnson, Sue, 25, 26
Hawkins, John, 45
Haygood, Atticus Green, 24, 82–85, 89, 96–101
Heitzenrater, Richard P., xxv, 9, 45–46, 49, 52
Hicks, John J., 93
Holsey, L. H., 23
Hoosier, Harry, 42–44
Horneck, Anthony, 45
Huff, A. V., Jr., 72

Ibn Khaldun, 30
Ingham, Benjamin, 53

Jackson, Andrew, 87, 102
Jackson, Thomas, 102
Jacobs, Ben, 118
Jaffe, Alexandra, 125
Jones, J. Scott, 13

Jones, Mary E., 92
Jones, Robert, 92–93, 118
Jordan, David, 18

Kendi, Ibram X., 29–32, 35–36, 68, 69, 79
King, James, 25
Kirk, W. Astor, 93

Lamothe, Dan, 15
LaPrade, W. H., 23
Lee, Robert E., 86, 102
Le Jau, Francis, 47–48
Levenson, Eric, 127
Lewis, Sharma, 92
Lindsay, Nick, 57
Loeffler, Kelly, 127
Lowery, Joseph E., 93–94, 106
Luther, Martin, King. Jr., 106

Malony, H. Newton, Jr., 62
Manskar, Steve, 22
Mather, Cotton, 31–32
Mather, Richard, 31
Maxey, R. A., 23
McClain, William B., 43
McCoy, Cameron, 15–16
McEllhenney, John, 42
McLeod Bethune-Cookman, Mary Jane, 86
McTyeire, Holland N., 75
Merunka (Sergeant), 14, 16
Mills, Frederick V., 78
Milman, Oliver, 124
Morris, Colonel Lewis, 73

Neau, Elias, 47
Nicholas V (Pope), 34–35
Nicholson, Zoe, 69

Obama, Barack, 4, 27, 102–4, 117–34
Oglethorpe, James, 10, 53
Oldendorp, Christian Georg Andreas, 10
O'Neall, John B., 56
O'Reilly, Bill, 121
Orr, Gustavus John, 98, 101
Ortiz, Erik, 124
Ossoff, Jon, 127

Index

Paine, Robert, 24
Paris, Peter J., 108
Pattillo, W. P., 23
Pelosi, Nancy, 127
Pence, Mike, 127
Penn, Irvine Garland, 93
Perdue, David, 127
Perkins, William, 31
Pierce, George F., 23, 89
Pierce, Lovick, 82–83
Pinckney, Charles Cotesworth, 73
Plummer, Troy, 88
Pollitzer, William S., 53
Porteus, Beilby, 50–51
Pretty, William, 32

Raboteau, Albert J., xxv, 31, 54, 70
Recinos, Harold J., 41, 107–9
Remillard, Arthur, 96, 101–2
Richey, Russell E., 71, 73–75
Rivers, Richard H., 75
Robertson, Campbell, 25
Robinson, Morgan, 74
Rust, Elizabeth, 85
Rust, Richard S., 82, 85, 98, 100

Schwartz, Marie J., 63
Sheets, Herchel H., 23–24, 65, 67–68, 78–79, 83, 85–86, 89, 97
Siddiqui, Raheel, 15
Siemaszko, Corky, 125
Simmons, William J., 86–87
Singeltary, John, 71
Skene, Alexander, 56
Slater Fund, John F., 97
Smith, David, 118
Smith, Warren Thomas, 10, 29, 33–34, 42, 46, 50, 53–56, 58, 59, 61, 65, 70
Smith, William A., 75
Spencer, Charles, 57–58

Sublette, Constance, 10, 45, 74, 81
Sublette, Ned, 10, 45, 74, 81
Sullivan, Andrew, 117

Thomas, James S., 93
Trump, Donald, 103, 114, 117–18, 122–28
Turner, Nat, 74
Tyler, Rick, 125

Van Dyke, Michelle Broder, 132
Volle, Adam, 15, 115

Walker, Rob, 114
Walsh, Steve, 15–16
Warnock, Raphael, 127
Wason, Brandon C., 42, 53
Wells-Burnett, Ida B., 86
Wesley, Charles, 10, 32, 46, 52, 54, 57
Wesley, John, xxv, 9, 10, 13, 22, 33–34, 37, 38, 41–42, 45–66, 67–68, 70, 72, 98, 134
Wesley, Matthew, 92
Wesley, Samuel, 46
Whitefield, George, 42, 52–53, 57–58, 64–65, 67–68, 72, 98
Wicke, Lloyd C., 95
Wilberforce, William, 42, 51
Williams, Avis, 76, 79
Williams, Gregory S., 129
Williams, Peter. Sr., 65
Willingham, Robert M., Jr., 71, 76
Wilson-Hartgrove, Jonathan, 133
Wimberly, Anne, 8–9
Wise, Lindsay, 127
Woodson, Carter G., 9, 97
Wright, Anderson, 14, 84

Zurara, Gomes Eanes de, 35

www.ingramcontent.com/pod-product-compliance
Lightning Source LLC
Chambersburg PA
CBHW070250230426
43664CB00014B/2476